PRAISE FOR
BUILDING AN INCLUSIVE ORGANIZATION

'Understanding and building inclusive organizations and workplaces is at last being seen as a critical business agenda, but we still have a long way to go. This book, by two real thought leaders in the field, provides a comprehensive, well-researched, and highly accessible guide for leaders and managers, as well as HR practitioners, on how to create genuine inclusion from top to bottom. The lessons everyone can learn will help drive more sustainable and responsible business, but also opportunity and fairer access to work for all, which is good for wider society.'
Peter Cheese, Chief Executive, CIPD

'Frost and Alidina have set out a holistic, step-by-step guide on how to build an inclusive organization. It is a must-read for diversity and inclusion practitioners, leaders and future leaders who want to understand how they can ensure that they can make a difference.'
Simon Fillery, former Head of Inclusion, Bank of England

'This is the go-to book for inclusion 3.0 and how to truly have a culture of respecting and embracing difference in a positive way. This book will get you one step closer to organizational change and improve the three Cs: our companies, cultures and colleagues.'
John Athanasiou, Director of People, HarperCollins Publishers

'This book is more than just an account of the authors' experiences or a compendium of case studies. It gives clear tangibles on how to take action, and how to deliver in a way that is effective and, most importantly, sustainable. It provides multiple pathways to an inclusive organization and a solid framework for getting there. I highly recommend this book to anyone looking to take a confident step in developing a more inclusive organization and culture.'
Claire Camara, HR Director, Co-op

'Frost and Alidina know the research and they understand how organizations work, from the boardroom and c-suite to mid-level management to frontline employees. This book will help organizational leaders think about what they can do personally and strategically to seize the opportunities and overcome the challenges of inclusion in today's diverse workplaces.'
Hannah Riley Bowles, Roy E Larsen Senior Lecturer in Public Policy and Management, and Co-Director of the Women and Public Policy Program, Harvard Kennedy School

'Diversity and inclusion are not simply aspirational goals for organizations, they are the underappreciated yet essential mechanisms for organizational success in this rapidly changing world. While inclusion's significance is imperative, its implementation is not always obvious. Frost and Alidina provide the skills to accomplish this and, much more importantly, the practical, financial and humanitarian reasons why it should be embraced. *Building an Inclusive Organization* is far less an instructional tool, though it certainly is that, than it is a call to action and a veritable survival guide for organizations and businesses seeking to remain relevant in the decades to come. This book is a master class for diversity and inclusion.'
Brooke Ellison, Assistant Professor of Health and Rehabilitation Sciences, Stony Brook University, New York

'Working with Stephen on some of the ideas that he articulates in this fascinating and important book has genuinely changed the way I think. But, more importantly, it has changed what I do. It's the most compelling thing that I've experienced about inclusion and diversity, both as an employer and a television producer.'
Diederick Santer, CEO, Kudos

'Frost and Alidina have written a book that not only makes a powerful case for why we need to build inclusive organizations, but tells us how to do so in very practical ways. Running Fulbright founded on the premise of fostering mutual cultural understanding between peoples worldwide, it is essential we embrace these ideas and this gives me and my board a clear roadmap to a more inclusive future.'
Penny Egan, Executive Director (2006–2018), US–UK Fulbright Commission

'Stephen Frost has been a wise companion and guide on Wellcome's still-unfinished journey towards becoming a more inclusive organization. His low-key but practical approach has helped to make diversity and inclusion a natural part of the decision-making process. My leadership team colleagues and I have learnt volumes about the impact of our behaviour and the benefits of thinking differently. We still have a long way to go, and I hope that our steps and missteps featured in this book will help others to make progress more swiftly.'
Mark Henderson, Director of Communications, Wellcome Trust

'The authors of this terrific book are kind enough to say that the senior people in Wellcome "get it" – that we get the importance of diversity and inclusion both in achieving our mission and in how we achieve it. Before I met them, I barely realized there was so much I did have to understand, but working with them over the last 18 months has transformed the way Wellcome thinks, and the way I think. This book sets out the authors' message persuasively and clearly and will be essential reading for the largest funder or university as well as for the newly-fledged lab head.'
Jim Smith, Director of Science, Wellcome Trust

'This book provides a step-by-step approach for leaders, HR professionals and diversity and inclusion (D&I) officers on how to understand and lead organizational change in this area. There is plenty of practical advice, grounded in good theory, both on inclusive leadership behaviours, as well as on systems and structures. This makes the book a must-read for any CEO, business owner or HR professional working with this agenda.'
Kristian Villumsen, CEO, Coloplast A/S

'This book is a must-have guide for HR professionals working with inclusion and diversity. It gives you concrete advice on how you work with behavioural change, as well as all the HR systems. Altogether an inspiring book that helps you drive the D&I agenda and create sustainable change.'
Stine Fehmerling, Head of D&I, Coloplast

'What I like most about *Building an Inclusive Organization* is that it goes beyond their case studies and translates lessons from those into action. I definitely recommend this book to anyone looking to make their organization more inclusive.'
Rebekah Martin, Head of Reward and Diversity, AstraZeneca

'This book is excellent. It is a roadmap for the next iteration of what D&I should look like. It is clear, concise, practical and full of useful takeaways at the end of each chapter. If you work in an organization, at any level, and you care about what you do, you should read this book.'
Linzi McDonald, Pro Bono and Responsible Business Manager, Kingsley Napley

'This book describes D&I the way it should be and is an unexpectedly gripping read, from the first case study to the last. It contains valuable guidance around how to be creative and brave, yet ultimately practical.'
Cindy Godwin, Global Leader: Diversity, Inclusion and Social Responsibility, AlixPartners

STEPHEN FROST
RAAFI-KARIM ALIDINA

BUILDING
AN INCLUSIVE
ORGANIZATION

Leveraging the power
of a diverse workforce

KoganPage

Publisher's note

Every possible effort has been made to ensure that the information contained in this book is accurate at the time of going to press, and the publishers and authors cannot accept responsibility for any errors or omissions, however caused. No responsibility for loss or damage occasioned to any person acting, or refraining from action, as a result of the material in this publication can be accepted by the editor, the publisher or the authors.

First published in Great Britain and the United States in 2019 by Kogan Page Limited

2nd Floor, 45 Gee Street	c/o Martin P Hill Consulting	4737/23 Ansari Road
London	122 W 27th St, 10th Floor	Daryaganj
EC1V 3RS	New York, NY 10001	New Delhi 110002
United Kingdom	USA	India
www.koganpage.com		

© Stephen Frost and Raafi-Karim Alidina, 2019

ISBNs

Hardback	978 0 7494 9777 4
Paperback	978 0 7494 8428 6
Ebook	978 0 7494 8429 3

British Library Cataloguing-in-Publication Data

A CIP record for this book is available from the British Library.

Library of Congress Cataloging-in-Publication Data

Names: Frost, Stephen, 1977- author. | Alidina, Raafi-Karim, author.
Title: Building an inclusive organization : leveraging the power of a diverse
    workforce / Stephen Frost and Raafi-Karim Alidina.
Description: London ; New York : Kogan Page Limited, [2019] | Includes
    bibliographical references.
Identifiers: LCCN 2018051190 (print) | LCCN 2018053912 (ebook) | ISBN
    9780749484293 (ebook) | ISBN 9780749484286 (alk. paper)
Subjects: LCSH: Diversity in the workplace–Management. | Organizational
    behavior–Management. | Multiculturalism.
Classification: LCC HF5549.5.M5 (ebook) | LCC HF5549.5.M5 F764 2019 (print) |
    DDC 658.3008–dc23
LC record available at https://lccn.loc.gov_2018051190

Typeset by Hong Kong FIVE Workshop
Print production managed by Jellyfish
Printed and bound by CPI Group (UK) Ltd, Croydon CR0 4YY

To our grandfathers, Donald Rex Simpson and Ismail Vasanji Alibhai

CONTENTS

13 To all organizations: make inclusion part of your purpose 211

ABOUT THE AUTHORS

STEPHEN FROST MA (HONS) MPP/UP FRSA FCIPD

Stephen is the CEO of leadership consultancy Frost Included, specializing in diversity and inclusion. He works with boards and executive teams to facilitate more inclusive, effective decision making to benefit individuals, organizations and the world at large.

He was Head of Diversity and Inclusion for KPMG, Chief of Staff and Head of Diversity and Inclusion for the London 2012 Olympic and Paralympic Games, and established the workplace team at Stonewall, developing the Workplace Equality Index, LGBT+ Leadership programme and Diversity Champions programme.

He is a Visiting Fellow in the Women and Public Policy Program at Harvard University and Adjunct Lecturer at Sciences Po in Paris, where he teaches inclusive leadership. He gives talks and presentations at conferences and universities around the world.

He was a Hertford College Scholar at Oxford University, a Fulbright Scholar at Harvard and is a Fellow of the Royal Society of Arts. He was Vice President of the Chartered Institute for Personnel and Development and a World Economic Forum Young Global Leader.

Stephen's previous books include *The Inclusion Imperative* (Kogan Page, 2014) and *Inclusive Talent Management* (Kogan Page, 2016). He was born in North Yorkshire, England, went to his local comprehensive school and is a keen cyclist.

RAAFI-KARIM ALIDINA MPP

Raafi is a consultant with Frost Included, working with clients to help create more inclusive workplace cultures. His expertise is particularly in data analysis and measurement of inclusion and using behavioural economics to create more diverse and inclusive environments.

He was a Research Fellow at the Center for Public Leadership at the Harvard Kennedy School, where, under the guidance of Dr Hannah Riley Bowles, he did research on implicit gender bias in negotiations. He was also previously an International Development and Management Fellow with the Aga Khan Foundation and a Research Analyst with the Mass Movements Project working under Dr Stephen Kosack.

He completed his undergraduate degree at Harvard University in 2012 and was a Lara Warner Scholar at the Harvard Kennedy School where he earned a Master's in Public Policy in 2017. His research on using behavioural economics for inclusion in organizations and the development of a behavioural measure for inclusion was awarded the Jane Mansbridge Research Award for outstanding research on women and gender, and the Susan C Eaton Memorial Prize for the top HKS Masters Thesis in Social Policy.

Originally from Sherwood Park, Canada, Raafi is a die-hard ice hockey fan, and loves cooking, baking, playing music and woodworking.

ACKNOWLEDGEMENTS

STEVE

First, I'd like to thank my wonderful co-author Raafi. About 90 per cent of the way through the writing process he casually mentioned to me he had written parts of the book using thumbs on his mobile phone on the train. I wrote in a closed room in silence. We are living proof of the generational, cognitive and other differences we celebrate in this book.

I'd also like to thank the whole f(i) team, especially Charlie and Carly for keeping the show on the road while we were distracted with literary pursuits.

This book is only possible thanks to the courageous, principled and inspiring clients we get to work with on a daily basis, and our colleagues in the D&I world that continue to work towards more inclusive workplaces. Thank you for inviting us into your organizations, and thank you for working with us on this book. Rob Adediran, Eliot Buchanan, Julie Chakravarty, Yasmine Chinwala, Sue Coffey, Lauren Couch, Ben Delk, Simon Fillery, Shruti Kannan, Anne Kirtley, Lucille Legiewicz, Amy Moore, Birgit Neu, Anjani Patel, Alex Pedley, Mike Peters, Melanie Richards, Diederick Santer, Roger Wilcock and many others.

Also thanks to Mum, Em and the many friends and colleagues that read draft after draft, including the Frost Included Advisory Board: Sue Hunt, Jayne Vaughan and Melissa Andrada.

And finally, many thanks to Lucy, Stephen and the Kogan Page team for their advice, support and wisdom during the whole process.

RAAFI

I'd like to begin by thanking my incredible co-author Steve. His support and mentorship are what gave me the opportunity to write this book, and our different styles and backgrounds have really helped me find new perspectives and learn more and more about working on diversity and inclusion.

I wouldn't even be writing about this topic, though, if it weren't for the support and guidance of my teachers over the years. In particular, I want to thank Dr Hannah Riley Bowles – she found a way to take a topic I was becoming increasingly passionate about and channel that energy into a career path. Her guidance has become the basis of my entire career, and I am eternally grateful to her.

Finally, I'd like to thank my family and friends for their constant love and support throughout this process. I am especially thankful to my partner Zuzanna Wojcieszak for reading drafts, pushing me to do better, and inspiring me and keeping me smiling every day.

PROLOGUE

ONE SUNDAY AFTERNOON IN MARCH

On 27 March 1977, KLM flight 4805 departs Amsterdam for the sunny island of Gran Canaria in the Canary Islands with a total of 235 passengers and 14 crew on board. In command is Captain Jacob Veldhuyzen van Zanten, aged 50. He is something of a 'celebrity' in the Dutch airline KLM, and the company's chief flying instructor with 11,700 hours of recorded flying time. His confident, square-jawed face is widely known as the face of KLM advertising.

Van Zanten's co-pilot (but subordinate) is 42-year-old First Officer Klaas Meurs. Meurs has 9,200 hours of flying time. The third flight deck member is 48-year-old Flight Engineer and Second Officer Willem Schreuder, who has 15,210 hours of flying time under his belt.

The same day, Pan Am flight 1736 is arriving in the Canary Islands from Los Angeles, after a stopover in New York. It has 396 passengers and crew on board.

At 13:15 local time, a bomb explodes at La Palma airport on Gran Canaria. Both KLM flight 4805 and Pan Am flight 1736 are diverted to Los Rodeos airport, now known as Tenerife North. Los Rodeos is a small regional airport with only one runway, one taxiway and several small taxiways connecting the two. It is not designed for large aircraft, such as the two jumbos now arriving.

After landing on Tenerife at 14:00, the two jumbos are parked one behind the other at the end of the taxiway, the Dutch in front, the Americans behind.

The Dutch crew is concerned that they are about to exceed their allowed flying time limit. Should that occur, their flight to their original destination would be cancelled pending a new set of pilots arriving from Amsterdam. If they exceed their flying time limit they could also lose their licences. They decide to refuel in order to save time refuelling once they get to Gran Canaria.

An hour later, it starts to rain.

About 16:00, Gran Canaria airport reopens. Eager to get going, Pan Am 1736 asks KLM 4805 how long it will take them to refuel. They are told, 'half an hour'. The Dutch pilots, already concerned about their flying time restriction, now realize they have only two hours remaining before the flight is grounded. They are tired, frustrated, and eager to get going. Captain Van Zanten's irritability has been noted by other pilots and Air Traffic Control (ATC).[1]

The rain has turned to fog. Visibility is now limited to a few hundred metres.

ATC instructs KLM 4805 to begin taxiing down the runway in preparation for take-off. Pan Am 1736 is ordered to follow KLM 4805, but to exit the runway onto another taxiway, the third exit to the left, leaving the runway clear for KLM to take off. The crew are unfamiliar with this airport and check an airfield map. Pan Am doesn't exit at the third turning, as the angle is too sharp for a large 747, and proceeds to the fourth exit instead.

Captain van Zanten lines up KLM 4805 for take-off and immediately advances the throttles, before clearance is given. First Officer Meurs cautions, 'wait a minute, we don't have ATC clearance'. Captain Van Zanten replies, 'no I know that, go ahead, ask'. ATC clears their route to Gran Canaria but not their clearance for take-off. Van Zanten says, 'We're going, check thrust'. The Dutch captain leads take-off, on a foggy runway, completely without permission.[2]

The ATC tower says, 'stand by for take-off. I will call you'. Pan Am 1736, still taxiing to exit four on the same runway, says, 'And we're still taxiing down the runway'.

Being focused on his take-off, Van Zanten and his first officer appear to miss the fact that Pan Am 1736 is still on the runway. The Dutch Second Officer, sitting behind them, does not. He questions the Captain and First Officer, his bosses, by saying, 'Is he not clear? That Pan American?' 'Oh, yes', Van Zanten answers, keen to get going.

Pan Am 1736 is still taxiing down the runway, approaching the fourth exit. In the cockpit, the flight crew see KLM 4805 hurtling down the runway towards them, head on. Captain Grubbs exclaims, 'There he is. Look at him … (he) is coming!' They immediately turn left to try to exit the runway, but it is too late.

As the KLM flight takes off, its undercarriage smashes into the centre of the Pan Am plane fuselage as the American plane is exiting the runway. The Dutch plane crashes back on to the runway and explodes, igniting its full belly of fuel and killing everyone on board. The majority of people on board the American plane are also killed.

With 583 fatalities, this remains the worst aircraft disaster of all time.

TECHNICAL AND LEADERSHIP LESSONS FOR US ALL

Investigators from the United States, the Netherlands as well as Spain investigated the crash and analysed what happened. KLM initially requested Van Zanten to lead their investigation, before realizing he was actually the Captain in charge of one of the doomed aircraft.

The investigators' preliminary conclusions were in many ways technical. They included the rationale for Pan Am 1736's decision to exit at the fourth junction instead of the third because it would have been impossible for a jumbo to manage the earlier exits, as the angles were too sharp. There were also problems with the radio communication and some messages not being fully received, especially that Pan Am 1736 was still on the runway.

However, the conclusions weren't only technical. KLM 4805 'informed' air traffic control, but they never actually received clear permission to take off – they assumed it. KLM 4805 confused permission to take off with permission for the route to Gran Canaria. ATC were only giving instruction on what to do *after* take-off but KLM took it as permission to take off.

Crucially, investigators believe that no one effectively challenged the Dutch captain owing to his 'superstar' status in the company. It was also Van Zanten's first flight in three months. He was usually based in the Netherlands, leading training for new pilots in the flight simulator. There, he never had to answer to ATC. He may have conducted take-off without being properly cleared because he was usually the one giving the clearance and the orders in the flight simulator.[3,4]

Van Zanten had privilege. He operated within a set of norms. He could have listened more, and he wasn't effectively challenged.

The worst aircraft disaster of all time teaches us many things. Among them is that strong, square-jawed, respected, famous, experienced, skilled men are not infallible. Especially when they exclude other perspectives from other people whose expertise is crucial.

NORMS

We are all governed by norms, just like KLM 4805 and Pan Am 1736 were. Some of those norms are helpful, such as customer service. Some of those norms were deadly, such as assuming, rather than seeking, permission to take off.

Norms are linked to our in-groups. It is easier to disregard views we disagree with than ones that appeal to our instinctive prejudices and proclivities. We like norms we agree with, or that we already subscribe to. They are comforting and reassuring. We dislike norms that challenge our current world view or *modus operandi*.

Norms are intermixed with power and privilege. Van Zanten was used to being in charge, used to teaching junior pilots in a flight simulator. His colleagues, peers, subordinates and few superiors were male, Dutch and technically excellent. And probably a lot of them had square jaws to boot.

He probably wasn't exposed to much difference, he probably didn't seek it out, and he wasn't effectively challenged. In the end, it contributed to his death and those of 582 other people.

But norms can be changed. One legacy of the disaster is that many airlines implemented Crew Resource management that trained captains at how to better interact with their crew, especially interaction with subordinates.

The airline industry is one of the best at learning lessons, tweaking systems and processes and constantly improving. Technically, at least. But other industries have also adapted.

The UK National Health Service (NHS) has adopted new processes in Accident and Emergency rooms. Before every operation, every member of the surgical team is consulted, including the most junior, and asked for their viewpoint.[5] This stops the surgeon amputating the wrong leg. It challenges the innate hierarchy in the situation and any 'rock star' status that is confounded on the surgeon. It allows the less powerful to challenge the powerful. It results in safer, less risky, better operations.[6]

You might be thinking, this is all well and good in small groups like a surgical team or in a cockpit on board an aircraft, but what about larger organizations? The US State Department came up with a solution to this problem: Dissent Channels.

The Dissent Channel system was created during the Vietnam War by Secretary of State William Rogers. It permitted 'any State Department employee who is a United States citizen, anywhere in the world, to voice criticism and have it addressed by the State Department's elite policy planning staff'. The dissenter is protected from reprisal, and there are even yearly awards for employees who dissent in the most effective way.[7,8]

There are multiple examples, but one notable one is from 1992, when several members of the State Department voiced concerns about US inaction during the Bosnian genocide. They protested that the government's inaction and lack of condemnation of what was going on there amounted to complicity in the violence. Their documentation of the extent of violence and reframing of it as tacit complicity pushed policy makers to consider taking action as an act of respecting peace instead of disrespecting sovereignty.[9]

However, the NHS example and the State Department's dissent resulting in the Dayton peace accords are still rare examples. More common are the stories of Lehman Brothers, Nokia, Kodak and Swissair. All male-dominated companies, with strong norms, that have also faced difficulties or collapse. Even in the realm of aviation which, more than most sectors, has adopted a policy of constant improvement, things are far from perfect. Watch the reaction of some of your fellow passengers next time the captain addresses your flight and it's a female voice.

INCLUSION MATTERS

To build an inclusive organization is not only a worthwhile endeavour in and of itself. It's also an increasingly essential way to adapt. Whilst we can never conflate a sudden tragedy and the loss of 583 lives with organizational design that is rarely sudden and rarely results in obvious and immediate loss of life, the analogy is important if only to stress the importance of what we are about to discuss.

According to a recent study, only 12 per cent of organizations believe they are inclusive.[10] And even those place too much emphasis on extrinsic factors such as the recruitment pipeline, rather than intrinsic factors such as leadership behaviour and culture.

In other words, they focus on diversity and representation – getting the right mix of people, with the right skills and competencies. They don't focus enough on inclusion – making sure the mix we have works. It's about people feeling a sense of belonging, feeling respected, and valued for who they are.

Inclusion is about adapting to new circumstances and new people. It's about you adapting rather than assuming 'they' will. Ask any minority person in a majority culture and they have been adapting their whole life. Unconsciously and consciously, adaptation is essential to fit in, to be accepted, to belong. The issue we are facing today, however, is that it's the dominant group that needs to adapt – that's the issue. The modern-day Van Zantens are still expecting others to adapt to them instead of appreciating that if they could adapt to others, it could benefit all of us.

Some of us choose to adapt. Some of us have to adapt. But all of us need to adapt. As such, those who are most experienced with adaptation – minorities – might be the most likely people to understand its importance, and so might find it easier to lead inclusively. Inclusive leadership is a way forward for organizations that wish to thrive. How ironic that minorities might be best placed for the future. The question before us is whether people more powerful but potentially less qualified will allow them to take pole position.

INCLUSION SAVES THE FUTURE OF SPACE FLIGHT

The United States in 1961 was a volatile time – the height of the cold war, the fight for racial equality, the start of the Space Race. At NASA these tensions coalesced around a particular problem: how to launch astronaut John Glenn aboard the Mercury 5 spacecraft into space, have him orbit the

Earth, and return safely. NASA had some of the smartest minds in the world, but this spaceflight required mathematical skills and physics that had never been done before. And getting it wrong was literally a matter of life and death.

The Space Task Group – originally formed in 1958 – was tasked with inventing the new mathematics and solving the physics dilemmas necessary for John Glenn's upcoming flight. The biggest issue wasn't getting Glenn up into orbit, it was how to get him out of orbit and back down to Earth without his spacecraft burning up in the atmosphere or exploding upon landing.

Led by Robert Gilruth, the team pored over potential solutions. In the end it was Katherine Johnson, a Black woman who was originally part of the Flight Research Division, who was a major part of finding the solution. By going back to Euler's Method, developed in the mid-18th century, she formed the basis of the mathematics used to bring John Glenn back.

While she had to be persistent to be let into meetings and recognized by name in reports, Gilruth's trust in her and willingness to ignore the societal norm of disregarding Black women and subordinates inspired the rest of the team to do the same. This gave her the space to approach the problem from a different angle. Famously, John Glenn himself specifically requested that Johnson check the formulae at the last minute to confirm that he would be safe.

The mathematical solutions Johnson developed with her colleagues became the basis not only for the Mercury missions, but also for the successive Gemini and Apollo missions as well. If we stand on the shoulders of giants, surely Johnson is one of them. And if not for Gilruth being inclusive, we may never have realized Johnson's intelligence, and it may have been much longer before NASA was able to find a solution to their problem.[11]

Inclusion matters. For many people, it matters because it's simply the right thing to do. But, in the final analysis, it matters because it is a prerequisite for survival.

ENDNOTES

1 Smith, P (2013) *Cockpit Confidential: Questions, answers, and reflections on air travel*, Sourcebooks Inc, Naperville, Ill

2 Ibid

3 Smith, P (2017) The true story behind the deadliest air disaster of all time, *Daily Telegraph*, 27 March

4 http://www.askthepilot.com/essaysandstories/tenerife-we-gaan/

5 Royal College of Surgeons (2014) *The High Performing Surgical Team: A guide to best practice*, RCS Publications

6 Gawande, A (2010) *The Checklist Manifesto*, Penguin Books India

7 Christopher, W (1995) Secretary of State Christopher's Message on the Dissent Channel, US Department of State Archive, Information Released January 20, 2001 to January 20, 2009, United States Department of State

8 Wolfowitz, P D (2017) A diplomat's proper channel of dissent, *New York Times*, 31 January

9 Katyal, N K (2016) Washington needs more dissent channels, *New York Times*, 1 July

10 Bersin by Deloitte impact study 2017

11 Shetterly, M L (2016) Katherine Johnson Biography, NASA; Shetterly, M L (2016) Hidden Figures, William Morrow; Katherine Coleman Goble Johnson biography (nd), School of Mathematics & Statistics University of St Andrews; Smith, Y (2015) Katherine Johnson: The girl who loved to count, NASA; Oral History Archive: Katherine Johnson, National Visionary Leadership Project, 2005

PART ONE

UNDERSTAND

1

DIVERSITY IS A REALITY, INCLUSION IS A CHOICE

Whether you are continuously attached to your phone's news feed, or you have consciously placed yourself on a current affairs digital detox, we can all see that the world is in an interesting place right now in terms of diversity and inclusion. In this introductory chapter, we will analyse global D&I in the world at large, followed in Chapter 2 within organizations and then in Chapter 3 at the personal level. This is the essential context for the organizational work that follows.

WHAT THE WORLD NEEDS NOW

The US Presidential election of November 2016 was a defining moment. Norms were challenged as never before. A person best known as a television celebrity became the leader of the Free World. People were shocked. Many of his supporters didn't expect him to win. His opponents were horrified he did. People who did not vote for Donald Trump, or indeed who opposed him, were visibly shaken. Their norms were completely upturned. For many, the result seemed to defy logic, merit or ethics. What they had previously assumed to be established protocol was suddenly just a point of view.

NORMS ARE NOT INFALLIBLE

A norm is a usual or typical convention or standard we use to govern our actions.

When we have particular behaviours or actions we desire as a society, but feel that we can't or shouldn't create a law to enforce them, norms are often what drives those behaviours. For example, we may decide that theft is something we so strongly want to deter that we create a law punishing those who commit that particular crime. However, while a society may also not want people to be scantily clad in public, they may also want to maintain citizens' freedom of choice as to whether or not to do so. Thus, as a society we can try to create norms around what we wear to deter others from wearing lingerie in public. In this way, we often assume norms to be limiting.

In our example here, limiting how people dress could limit a clothing designer's creativity or an individual's form of expression through clothes, but perhaps we've decided that this is a necessary cost of encouraging our desired behaviour. Other norms that limit us, though, can be much more damaging, such as the norm that surgeons are male and nurses are female. This limits the free flow of labour and stymies a true meritocracy because talented potential female surgeons and talented potential male nurses are needlessly limited due to invalid criteria.

We must be careful, though, of unintentionally changing norms that we like through our actions. Some norms such as politeness, respect, and the rule of law are important norms. The norm before November 2016 was that sexist behaviour would disqualify any candidate from election. The norm after was that even if people view a candidate's statements about women as derogatory, supporters might be willing to explain them away. Making those types of statements appears no longer to be a definite barrier to election. This example shows how radical Trump has been in overturning (temporarily or permanently) deeply embedded norms. Norms are vital in governing the way we experience the world. As such, it is important to be aware of challenges to them, as Trump has shown.

We are governed by norms, and any organizational change programme has to calmly assess:

which norms are enabling and we want to preserve;

which norms are limiting and we want to challenge;

which norms are in the 'too difficult' box and we leave for another day.

For example, we might want to maintain our values such as rule of law, freedom of speech and desired gender equality. We might want to limit the norm of women as the sole provider for children. Many Scandinavian countries have introduced shared parental leave so that it is increasingly normal for men to also care for children, levelling the career playing field for both sexes. However, many countries have considered transgender rights too complicated or lacking sufficient public support and so it has not been a priority to date, although that is starting to change.

Generally speaking, is there enough moral, conscious thought being applied in terms of the three types of norms detailed above? Which ones do we as a society deliberately want to safeguard? And which ones, as a society, do we deliberately want to challenge? If we don't think about these questions deeply and pre-emptively, radical forces and unpredictable events may change them for us without our consent or understanding.

This is often why it is difficult for many to go along with progress and instead fight against, say, marriage equality. In the United States, a majority of people once believed not too long ago that same-sex marriage should not be allowed. In fact, according to the Pew Research Center, as recently as 2001, 65 per cent of Americans did not support same-sex marriage.[1] They might have felt that it was part of American identity to adhere to that norm. Thus, when the tide turned over the last 20 years and the majority now believed in marriage equality (62 per cent support in 2017)[2] and the courts made it legal, it makes sense that those who still thought it was morally wrong felt hurt.

It wasn't just that they disagreed with the decision, it was that they now felt the United States didn't represent them anymore, or at least not in that way. To some degree, a part of their identity was being stripped away from them. Whether we believe they are right or wrong, we can empathize with their pain and difficulty.

Most of us rely on the supposed permanence of norms and live our lives with that understanding. However, norms can change. The question is whether we are changing them consciously in a positive sense or allowing them to be changed for us unconsciously, without even being fully aware.

BIAS RUNS RAMPANT

If you are human, you are biased. Bias, when speaking about people, is a preference or prejudice for certain groups over others. We will discuss bias, both conscious and unconscious, in more depth later in the book, especially Chapter 5. But for now, it's important to acknowledge the increasing importance of how bias is impacting our daily lives and our societal norms.

The more we are able to personalize services through technology, the more we are able to indulge our points of view, however ill-informed they may be. This bias is exhibited most clearly in social media. There, expressing opinions can be taken as fact. Your likes or dislikes can be used by commercial and political entities to feed you similar opinions or products that speak to your point of view, indulging the natural human desire to have your ideas affirmed.

Social media, however, is simply one example of how new technology has narrowed the range of opinions we consume. Consider television – the number of channels available, not to mention the number of ways to watch television programmes, has grown exponentially in the last 20 years. As a result, we now have the ability to choose to only watch content that caters to our point of view. This is precisely what many of us do, even though we may not do it consciously. And it's understandable that we do this, because why would we want to spend our time watching things that will simply make us angry or annoyed at the way a topic is presented? The same is true of radio, news, and film.

In this hyper-personalized, hyper-indulged situation we find ourselves in, our biases, rather than being checked and countered, can actually be inflamed and exacerbated.

This is even more so when we feel we have permission. When authority figures exhibit bias, we may feel a sense of validation, or even a sense of entitlement. This mimicry enables and empowers points of view but may in turn shut down others.

We tend to copy those in power, like Van Zanten, and not those with less power, like Schreuder. In this sense, in the guise of individual emancipation, we may in fact simply be entrenching questionable power bases and thwarting diverse voices. Similarly, if leaders in your organization are exhibiting inclusive behaviour, since they have power and authority they will be mimicked by others in the organization and the culture will become more inclusive. If they act non-inclusively, then so will others and so will the organization as a whole.

Take for example the election of Rodrigo Duterte, who became the 16th President of the Philippines in 2016. Duterte, who ranked on the Forbes list of the world's most powerful people, has advocated the extrajudicial killing of drug pushers. This challenged the widely positively regarded norms of law and order previously in place. At the same time he, perhaps surprisingly, supported the push for gay marriage, arguably challenging a restricting norm. In both cases his authority has been used to challenge norms and to empower others who would seek to challenge them also.

Consider Malala Yousafzai, the youngest ever winner of the Nobel Peace Prize. She was shot by the Taliban in response to her activism challenging the Taliban-instigated norm of denying girls education equivalent to boys. Previously just another teenager, she achieved global significance and recognition in view of her challenging of norms. That global significance empowered other schoolgirls to also fight for the right to education.

POLARIZATION, 'IN' AND 'OUT' GROUPS

The United States' political situation also represents acute polarization. It has solidified 'in' and 'out' groups, which is important for anyone wanting to build an inclusive organization. In-groups are our relatively small inner circles of friends and colleagues with whom we share identities, interests or perspectives. Out-groups are the opposite – they're the people who are different from us, with whom we may not share aspects core to our identities and have had different life experiences. We will discuss them more in subsequent chapters.

However, the response of Trump's opponents has perhaps unintentionally solidified his support base. Similarly, the rhetoric from Trump's base has solidified the left's opinion of them. Attacking, rather than empathizing, initiates a race to the bottom. For his opponents, delisting Trump supporters on a Twitter feed or Facebook profile doesn't mean they don't exist, and vice versa. It just means they are not challenged any more, and neither are his opponents. Polarization begets polarization.

Research in social psychology suggests that, at a very primal level, our default position is to congregate into groups that afford us safety. Our natural reaction is also to reject the unfamiliar, in a 'flight or fight' unconscious response.

Furthermore, the academic literature explains that humans identify with groups of their own kind, and will make attempts to fit into these groups to secure their social status.[3] This effect can explain why we have segregated communities in the first place, and also why we curate the information we see online the way we do.

However, discrimination, marginalization, stereotyping and bias (both conscious and unconscious) can create additional fear that triggers the basic need for safety, similarity and familiarity. Our increasing self-segregation, both physical and in our online communities, gives us more space to indulge our opinions. We increasingly see our own views as correct, and we also dismiss other opposing ideas, even when they might be valid.

If we aren't surrounded by difference, our ideas become increasingly reinforced by similar people around us. We might not be willing to even entertain the idea that those with different opinions might have a point or that their point of view could be valid. What's worse, we begin to attribute our hatred for those ideas to the people who espouse them, and so we don't just dismiss the ideas, but the people themselves. And we don't even know we're doing this to ourselves. So whilst segregation may be a natural phenomenon, it can be compounded and accelerated by unchecked human actions.

For example, whatever your view on Britain's decision to leave the European Union, the vote itself was polarizing, turning a complex set of issues and perspectives into a binary decision. The resultant political change, rather than being a steadying measure and counterweight to polarization, has actually exacerbated it.

It's fairly evident that when UK Prime Minister Theresa May triggered Article 50 she unleashed a wave of behaviour detrimental to inclusion efforts. Practically, companies and workers are struggling with labour mobility – in 2017 the British government had to launch an investigation into reports that EU nationals in the UK were being illegally blocked from applying for jobs and renting properties.[4] Socially, a 2017 report revealed higher levels of hate crimes since the Brexit vote.[5] Politically, an event meant to unite the Conservative party has ended up dividing the country.

THE DAMAGE TO DIVERSITY

Less diversity in the UK workforce could result in even lower productivity, lower resilience to shocks and higher exposure to risk. Exchange rate changes have made foreign travel (and cultural experiences) more expensive. There are dangers for Britain's research community with European partners dropping collaborative projects, fearful the UK won't be able to access EU funding.

The Chartered Institute of Personnel and Development (CIPD) found 57 per cent of employers have concerns that Brexit will significantly weaken their ability to acquire and retain skilled employees.[6] The argument of the leavers is that British workers can now take these jobs. But this like-for-like substitution is simplistic, ignoring different skill sets, geographical locations and desire or aptitude to actually undertake the work. In this sense the vote has not only damaged Britain's reputation as a good home to overseas workers, it could also signal regression in former progress towards more multicultured workplaces.

Our natural tendency is to recruit people like us because they are the ones that 'get it'. In this sense, Brexit simply indulges pre-existing unconscious biases. It allows us a false sense of security, comfort in being around people like us. If we don't create and nurture a culture where an inclusive and diverse workforce is viewed in a positive light then the business benefits of diversity simply won't follow. The way the campaign was run, and the way it is still being conducted, is perhaps most harmful of all.

Once-fringe views are now acquiring mainstream status. To be clear, the threat to diversity comes not just from the leavers – social harm is also being inflicted by remainers too. Extreme remainers query the intelligence of the 'leavers' and whether they should have even had the right to vote on such an important topic. This goes back to the point above, about how we begin to attribute our feelings about an opinion to the person espousing that opinion, and it can have dangerous consequences.

In fact, we've been here before. In the United States, when African-Americans gained the right to vote, many states instituted intelligence tests requiring that Black citizens pass them if they wanted to vote.[7] While these rules were certainly driven by animus against a racial group, intelligence was used as a scapegoat for their more sinister points of view. It seems a bit ironic, then, that some extreme remainers who might self-identify as 'liberals' are considering the merits of trying to limit the voting rights of those they disagree with based on a similar argument.

ARE THERE ANY POSITIVES?

The 'shock' result has refocused attention on diversity, including widening rates of inequality in Britain. We are reminded that segregation is the default position and multiculturalism actually has to be built, it doesn't just happen.

The vote realigned party and social allegiances. Both bankers and teachers voted to remain. Both elderly rich rural dwellers and young poor urban citizens voted to leave. In that sense it redefined party politics and reawakened civic interest. Therein lies new space to find common ground among previously fractured groups, new opportunities for inclusion.

Diversity and inclusion has now moved up the agenda. What were once fringe topics seen as a subset of HR, are now acquiring front-page status in global newspapers and becoming a standing agenda item in many boardrooms and executive committees.

This new prominence is largely a result of a now burning platform for action. Whatever your views on Brexit, or the US election, or the European refugee crisis, it is clear that inclusive policies are now required if we are not to implode.

EMPATHY FACILITATES INCLUSION

Empathy is required on all sides of the debate. It may be a bitter pill to swallow for *Guardian, Le Monde* or *New York Times* readers to contemplate empathy for Trump supporters, and for some Brexiters to fully empathize with immigrants, but that is, now, what is sorely needed. Inclusive leaders need to lead the empathy revolution. Illiberal liberalism can be just as problematic as some forms of xenophobia and jingoism.

Empathy is seen as soft, yet we are in desperate need. That does not mean we need to accept the other point of view as right, just that it may not be completely irrational. In this way, empathy is the antidote to polarization. By being able to see a situation from someone else's perspective, we might be able to find common ground.

Empathy is related to gender inequality. Various studies have shown that, overall, there is a statistically significant gender difference in the human mirror neuron system, with female participants tending to exhibit stronger motor resonance than male participants. This is related to women having higher Empathy Quotient (EQ) scores than men.[8] This could be directly related to evolution, with women more often taking the primary caregiver role. Moreover, studies have shown that whereas women can empathize more with non-verbal cues and facial expressions, men tend only to respond better to threatening or aggressive behaviour.[9] We refer you to the above sections detailing the behaviour of the Presidents of the United States and the Philippines.

Therefore, since women have been taught the importance of empathy for generations, it makes sense in a male-dominated world that empathy has traditionally been something society does not find to be valuable in the workplace or in leaders. This leads us to devalue important and useful skills that many women have learned from a young age that men may not have, and so devalue women. This does not mean that men cannot learn empathy, or that there aren't empathetic men. It simply means that if we want to solve the problems that currently exist in the world that we've described above, we need to consciously teach empathy to men and boys and ensure that it becomes ingrained as a new social norm.

This isn't just about gender. The success of the Paralympic Games in recent years, for example, has contributed to placing disability on the global agenda. Since 1960 the event has grown into the world's third-biggest sporting event in terms of ticket sales; only the Olympics and the FIFA World Cup now sell more. The mission is 'to enable Para athletes to achieve sporting excellence and inspire and excite the world'. It's aspiration – its *raison d'être* – is to make for a more inclusive society for people with a disability through Para sport. In fact, today the Paralympic Games are regarded as the world's number one sporting event for driving social inclusion.

ZERO-SUM GAMES

Current polarization and its associated challenging of norms can best be described as a zero-sum game. This lack of empathy means that we not only want to win, but the other side winning means that we lose. We get stuck in a zero-sum game mentality. In an age of plenty we are still fighting over a fixed pie.

Steve teaches the Harvard MBAs a class on inclusive leadership. We ask the students to have an arm wrestle, the goal being to score as many points as possible in one minute and, if at all possible, avoid litigation. After one minute the room of future CEOs splits into two camps. In one, 80–90 per cent of the room, predominantly men, have scored zero points, or possibly one or two. In the other, 10–20 per cent of the room, predominantly women, have scored 30–40 points. They simply let each other win, and through cooperation as opposed to confrontation, enlarge the pie for all parties.

The classic application of zero-sum theory is to trade. When the Trump administration decided to impose tariffs on imported goods in June 2018, it provoked a response from key trading partners such as Canada, Mexico and the European Union. This is the global equivalent of a traditional arm wrestle whereas the route to increased trade would be to simply cooperate. It is worth noting the gender differences in the arm-wrestling exercise as well as in the empathy quotient findings – more gender diversity among global trade negotiators might contribute to better outcomes.

It is also worth pointing out that only 38 per cent of 146 nations studied by the World Economic Forum have ever had a female leader. With the exception of one four-month stint in Canada, the United States, Canada and Mexico have never had a female leader. Two-fifths of female global leaders have been from Europe.[10]

ARE WE THERE YET?

To be positive, things are in many ways becoming more inclusive. Gay marriage is increasingly normal in Western countries. Gender equality tops the boardroom agenda. Millions of people of all genders are marching for women's rights. Many of our elected officials are more diverse (and therefore representative) than ever.

However, progress is not linear. And it doesn't just happen.

Following their first Black president ever, the United States elected someone who has put in place some of the least progressive measures in recent history. He has banned Syrian refugees from entering the country and trans people from serving in the military, withdrawn the United States from UNESCO and the Paris Climate Accords, and acted as a fulcrum for other populist figures worldwide. Breaking of positive norms gives permission to others to mimic it.

Many people thought Obama heralded the end of racism in the United States. Many of Trump's comments and policies suggest that this is not the case.

To give another example, when Grenfell tower burnt to its core in London in 2017, needlessly killing 70 innocent people in the middle of one of the wealthiest parts of the UK, profound questions were posed about social mobility in modern Britain. How could a building burn like a roman candle in London in 2017? The tentative answers pointed to a council detached from its voiceless poorer residents, cladding put up for decorative purposes for those living outside (rather than inside) and the establishment guilty of ignoring citizens in the false belief it was being inclusive.

This all seems a far cry from the British Prime Minister's July 2016 inaugural address on the steps of Number 10 Downing Street when she promised to place D&I at the top of her agenda, 'fighting against the burning injustice that, if you're born poor, you will die on average nine years earlier than others'.[11]

Education isn't inclusive either. Cardiff University research has found that students from state schools gain better degrees than privately educated students with the same A-level grades. However, levels of diversity at Oxford and Cambridge universities are decreasing. Nationwide, 7 per cent of students are educated at private schools, yet Oxford and Cambridge colleges recruit 40 per cent from the private sector.[12]

It gets no better in the workplace, as made evident by the reporting of Harvey Weinstein's sexual assaults. Here was a progressive, Jewish, Democrat who had been accused by multiple women of being a misogynist abuser of power. As more and more women came forward to out not only Weinstein's behaviour but also that of other powerful men, the #MeToo campaign went viral. In an era of discussing gender pay it seemed we were back to the most basic of rights, women's safety.

The lack of inclusion seems to be a problem all over the world, across all sectors, and in all industries. So tackling this problem may seem like a daunting task. But the answer may lie in narrowing the problem down.

Whilst norms can be changed for the worse, they can also be adapted for the better. Good people want to live in a community and work in an organization full of positive reinforcement. For example, we don't want to live in a community subject to crime and we can reinforce the norms necessary to build community cohesion. In the same way, we increasingly view gender equality and LGBT+ inclusion as positive norms and so we introduce legislation highlighting the gender pay gap and cheer on the Pride parade with more organizations taking part than ever before.

Whilst bias runs rampant, we are more aware of it than ever before, we are learning how to tackle it, and good people genuinely seek objectivity in their decision making. For example, tech companies are now starting to take fake news seriously. Parliaments all over the world are considering legislation they can introduce to penalize misinformation. Behavioural economics is helping us deploy insights for social good, whether that's placing healthy food at the front of the counter and sweets and chocolate further back to help us eat more healthy meals, or whether that's de-biasing a recruitment process by using gender-neutral language and blind CVs.

Whilst in and out groups are subject to polarization, people are still curious about diversity, whether it be in food, travel or people. Next time people stigmatize others, it's worth reflecting on the food they eat and where it's come from, or where they go on holiday. In organizations, people are increasingly aware of the need to reach out to people different from them in order to inform their perspective. The more society seems to pull apart, the more this organizational need becomes apparent. Empathy can help us overcome division.

Whilst there is much to be disheartened about, and whilst the challenges before us can appear overwhelming, progress is possible. Over the pages that follow, we will try to demonstrate this, one workplace at a time.

TAKEAWAYS

1 Norms are changing more than we might at first appreciate. We need to actively take part in creating them and benefitting from them, or risk having unforeseen norms affect us and society in potentially harmful ways.

2 Advances in technology have indulged our biases by curating content to expose us to similarity at the expense of challenge. This can lead to complacency and polarization.

3 Increased polarization is exacerbating the barriers between our in- and out-groups, making diversity even more difficult to deal with in the workplace and elsewhere.

4 Our siloed existence, exacerbated polarization, begets a lack of empathy for those different from us and a focus on everything as zero-sum.

5 Progress is not linear, it is a constant back and forth. But with conscious, constant and consistent effort, we can improve societal outcomes.

ENDNOTES

1 http://www.pewforum.org/fact-sheet/changing-attitudes-on-gay-marriage/

2 Ibid

3 Tajfel, H (ed) (2010) *Social Identity and Intergroup Relations*, Cambridge University Press

4 https://www.theguardian.com/politics/2017/sep/11/no-europeans-need-apply-growing-evidence-discrimination-uk-brexit

5 https://www.independent.co.uk/news/uk/home-news/racist-hate-crimes-surge-to-record-high-after-brexit-vote-new-figures-reveal-a7829551.html

6 https://www.cipd.co.uk/news-views/brexit-hub/workforce-trends

7 http://www.slate.com/blogs/the_vault/2013/06/28/voting_rights_and_the_supreme_court_the_impossible_literacy_test_louisiana.html

8 Schulte-Rüther, M et al (2008) Gender differences in brain networks supporting empathy, *Neuroimage*, **42** (1), pp 393–4031

9 Kret, M E and De Gelder, B (2012) A review on sex differences in processing emotional signals, *Neuropsychologia*, **50** (7), pp 1211–21, doi:10.1016/j.neuropsychologia.2011.12.022

10 http://www.pewresearch.org/fact-tank/2017/03/08/women-leaders-around-the-world/

11 https://www.gov.uk/government/speeches/statement-from-the-new-prime-minister-theresa-may

12 https://www.theguardian.com/education/2013/jun/16/accesstouniversity-private-schools

2

ORGANIZATIONS TO THE RESCUE

If we want to make society more inclusive, the organization[1] might be a great place to start. We spend much of our lives at work, we often interact with diverse groups of people at work, and this is becoming increasingly true as the workplace becomes more diverse. It certainly feels a bit more achievable to change our workplaces than our societies writ large. But also, it's easy to make the case to businesses that inclusion is in their own best interest.

Businesses are the new centre ground. They have the commercial incentive to build inclusive cultures that will help them protect their talent and therefore their brand. It's now almost inconceivable that a major, serious business would ignore diversity and inclusion. In the UK FTSE 100, every company has women on their board (just about), every annual report mentions the 'diversity' word and many have signed up to the various charters, such as the Women in Finance Charter.

However, is this enough? Moreover, is this about what business is 'doing' for D&I or what D&I could be doing for business?

Diversity is a reality, inclusion is a choice. Whether business is sufficiently harnessing diversity is something we will discuss in a moment, but diversity clearly offers benefits to business, right here, right now. Different people, with different perspectives, different ideas and different skill sets contribute more than the sum of their parts. Organizations that reject diversity are, quite simply, missing a trick.

The business case is widely documented and whilst we can't prove causation, we can confidently demonstrate the correlation between diversity and performance. For example, McKinsey and Company found that companies in the top quartile of gender diversity are 15 per cent more likely to have financial returns that were above their national industry median. For ethnic diversity that number was 30 per cent.[2] Gender is perhaps the most obvious one but this process is infinite and includes not only the other protected characteristics like race, disability and so on, but also the way they intersect. So a group of diverse women is even more valuable.

Business on the whole is harnessing diversity more than in the past. For example, the proportion of women on FTSE 100 boards has increased from 12.5 per cent to 29 per cent in seven years.[3] The proportion of companies taking part in the annual Pride March in London has increased exponentially in the last five years. The number of participants and the overall score in the Stonewall Workplace Equality Index has increased substantially since Steve's team launched it in 2005.

However, is this embracing deep and profound, or still relatively superficial? How many of the increased number of women in FTSE board positions were from ethnic minorities? How many were disabled? How many are truly empowered to challenge the still male-dominated discussion and decision-making process? The intersectionality debate is still to play out. Moreover, while the composition of the board certainly matters, does that mean anything for the executive pipeline, people near the bottom of the pyramid or for the gender pay gap?

WHERE BUSINESS IS STILL MISSING OUT

Based on quantitative evidence and anecdotal facts garnered throughout our combined three decades in business, we feel that organizations are still missing out. That's primarily because business has not truly grasped the exam question in the first place. The goal here is not representation per se (although that's crucial). The real goal is surely business performance. That's what business is concerned with: its performance, value creation, and success.

By continuing to see diversity as a separate work stream and an issue of representation only, we would argue that business is actually dodging the exam question, which is really how can we correct business under-performance? How much better could business be doing if we corrected the market failure of homogeneity and groupthink?

Doing nothing is not an option, unless we are willing to sit passively as segregation strengthens before us. What's required now is leadership: a better articulation of the benefits of difference, a rediscovery of the differ-ence that lies all around us, and then the gumption to take advantage of it.

YOUR EMPLOYEES ARE YOUR CONSTITUENTS

In corporate life, think of your employees as voters. If they had a ballot paper, and your election was today, would they vote for the status quo – for you – or for change?

You can develop early warning signs, such as employee engagement sur-veys. But misdirected, or ignored, they can be of limited value. Aggregate results don't give you the full picture. Break down the results by diversity and by identity and take a closer look. That's how Macron, and Trump, won their elections – they recognized trends in rhetoric and expression that were cutting along different identity groups, and leveraged that knowledge to accomplish their goals.

If the 'white backlash' is happening when white people still control most of the decision making in the Western world, and if the 'male backlash' is happening when men still control most of the decision making in organiza-tions, we need to re-examine how people understand 'diversity' in the first place. If your people think diversity is about 'other' groups then you have failed to communicate it effectively. Diversity is personal, as we will explore in more detail in later chapters. Diversity includes Trump voters, Le Pen supporters and all those white and male employees (falsely) fearing their seat at the table is threatened.

People are increasingly venting on glassdoor.com rather than via 'official channels'. What we learn is that people want to be treated as human, rather than a factor of production. People want to feel that diversity includes them rather than being about some other group. And if they feel they cannot express themselves publicly, then they will privately, at the ballot box.

THE GOLDEN AND PLATINUM RULES

Steve was brought up in rural North Yorkshire, England, and Raafi was brought up in suburban Alberta, Canada. We were taught to treat others as you would wish to be treated. This was incredibly well intentioned, and came from a place of kindness, politeness and respect for the other person. We can call it the Golden Rule. Treat others as you wish to be treated.

It's nice, polite and kind, but there's no adaptation going on.

In London Steve learnt the Platinum Rule – treat others as they want to be treated. This is more about you adapting to them, because they might not want to be treated like you. Or they don't experience being treated like you in the same way or can't relate to being treated like you. It's a basic rule of better customer service to adapt to them if you really want to include them.

We often hear clients and colleagues talk of the need to be fair to people. Absolutely. But if being fair means treating people 'the same' then people who start with disadvantage will never be fully included. If we treat different people the same, we end up with unequal results.

WHY ORGANIZATIONS NEED TO ADAPT

In a time not so long ago, we tended to think of the political right as the party of business and the political left as the party of the worker. HR often felt torn, between doing what was right for the business and doing what was right for people.

It's really been the seismic events of technological, social and political change that have made us once again reappraise pre-existing conventions. Can HR still do what is right for business but intersect this (almost perfectly?) with what is right for people?

Brexit showed us that voters of lower socio-economic status, of both left and right, voted to leave. Similarly, the opposite was true of both left- and right-leaning more privileged people. Trump has become a symbol of a divided nation with almost daily culture wars occurring over abortion, healthcare, LGBT+ rights and immigration. As a result, in the workplace we are increasingly divided, and those divisions are being brought to the fore.

As politics becomes more polarized, who now speaks for the centre? Who now gains value from bringing people together rather than benefitting from further polarization?

When we ask executives to name their closest friends and closest colleagues, nine times out of ten, the colleagues are more diverse than their friends. This means it is the workplace, not our personal lives, that is the catalyst for D&I. In our personal lives we are free to exclude. In our professional lives we have a responsibility to include in order to get work done.

In the UK, all parties are officially on board with LGBT+ rights, gender pay reviews and race equality impact assessments. But in practice, it is the organizations that have to make this real. It is companies that are the cauldrons of contention. Whilst politicians proclaim, it is professionals in organizations who deal with the fallout on a daily basis.

HR's dependencies include the state of society, the state of skilled labour and their ability to work well together to create value. All of these things are currently up in the air.

OUR MATURITY MODEL FOR DIVERSITY

After the London Olympics in 2012, Steve reviewed D&I efforts to date, worldwide, and developed the diversity maturity model detailed in Figure 2.1.[4]

In the not too distant past, the corporate approach to diversity was a very basic 101, like an introductory course in university. This was about attaining a minimum, not a maximum. It was compliance driven with legislation being the impetus for change. Recent, essential legislative changes have ensured better checks and balances against racial discrimination and gender pay gaps, for example. Some legislative changes, though, aren't that effective, such as disability quotas in China where the fine is so small that companies rarely follow the law.[5]

The China example shows how doing something just because you have to doesn't drive discretionary effort, and that people will try to find a way

Table 2.1 Diversity maturity model

Paradigm	Diversity 101 'diversity for diversity's sake'	Diversity 2.0 'diversity for social responsibility'	Inclusion 3.0 'diversity as business strategy'
Definition	Programmes designed to raise awareness of difference	Programmes designed to draw out the benefits of difference	Integrated systems designed to embed the benefits of difference
Origins	Colonialism, nature versus culture, civil rights movement	Shareholder pressure, HR and marketing functions and corporate social responsibility	Recognition of unconscious bias, egocentricity and leadership deficit
Education method	Diversity training, compliance-based business case	Diversity workshops, up-to-date business case	Structured conversations, original interventions, evidenced-business case
Leadership approach	Top down, authority led, compliance driven	Top down, authority led, auditing approach	Bottom up, top-level support, creative group leadership, peer review
Delivery mechanisms	Equalities team, equality impact assessments	Diversity team, needs assessments	Whole organization, benchmarking and information sharing
Measurement	Quotas, legal reporting	Voluntary targets, corporate social responsibility reporting/PR	Target zones, high-frequency real-time reporting and individual accountability

around it. People resent being told to 'get' more women or 'promote' more minorities. It's a technical fix to a cultural problem, and it's not personally meaningful. To include diversity there has to be discretionary goodwill. This will never originate from compliance.

But many businesses today have exceeded the Diversity 101 model and the extent to which they were obliged to comply with the law. To derive more benefit they are venturing into the world of 'taking a stand'. In Texas,

CEOs from 14 companies including American Airlines, Texas Instruments and AT&T wrote an open letter to the Governor Greg Abbot against a bill banning Trans-friendly bathrooms that would 'seriously hurt the state's ability to attract new businesses, investment and jobs'.[6] IBM took out full-page ads in opposition to the bill. This marketing-led approach can be labelled Diversity 2.0.

While these efforts are certainly laudable, they are also insufficient. This is because when these campaigns are not backed up by concrete action, consumers often feel that it isn't authentic. This can make the dominant group feel good about themselves but make the minority group you are trying to attract even more cynical and less likely to join in. It causes a credibility gap that can actually make things worse in the eyes of the public.

Business in the future will need to go further. Neutrality or silence won't be an option. Crass corporate mandates of 'we value all our people' will ring hollow in an age of Glassdoor when savvy employees and contractors will be looking for evidence of them walking the talk. Meaningless mantras will fall short when people of fundamentally different world views are unable or unwilling to work together.

In this sense, businesses need to evolve to an Inclusion 3.0 level where inclusive thinking is embedded in all the decisions they take. Not driven by compliance, lobbying or marketing but by a desire to create the conditions where intelligent people can actually work together productively.[7]

If we understood that lack of meritocracy was just as much a critical business issue as sales, we would give D&I the same attention as sales. So include the statistics on your dashboard. Empower all the people in your organization to speak up. Make all people decisions transparent and have the humility to admit when you've got it wrong and show tangible commitments to improvement.

We need to realize and then act on the fact that we are part of the problem, but also part of the solution. It's about us, not 'them'. Look in the mirror at your own inclusion efforts and how you can adapt, rather than expect 'them' to fit in. That's a more productive and successful approach to gaining the benefits of diversity for your organization.

The more society pulls apart, the harder businesses will have to work to pull their workers back together.

It means challenging discrimination in the workplace and in so doing being a role model for the kind of behaviour we would expect outside the workplace too. It means pushing forward acceptance of minorities as business as usual and in so doing pushing society forward too. It means bringing different people together to solve problems and in so doing being the only place they might meet, in a world of echo chambers and social segregation.

It means standing up to the backlash – and there will be backlash – to seemingly radical programmes and efforts that will actually help marginalized groups of people at work. We'll discuss how to actually do this in an effective way in Chapter 8, with examples from different industries throughout Part Three.

If society is not at ease with itself, then business is going to have to work harder to build workforces that are. That is not simply a laudable aim and a question of social responsibility. It is actually a performance and existential issue for businesses themselves.

WHEN DIVERSITY IS INCLUDED IT'S GOOD FOR BUSINESS

If you want to better address market needs, innovate and engage customers, diversity is essential. But it is insufficient by itself. There are three things you have to consider:

1 **Diversity – and inclusion.** Many companies now focus on diversity, and are disappointed that nothing seems to change. There are a plethora of inadequate diversity articles that claim diversity will cause greater performance. It won't – on its own. The key difference is inclusion. Many workplaces are actually quite diverse, they are just siloed and so much of that diversity is not leveraged. If it were, we would find that diversity actually has quite a strong correlation with performance.

2 **Internal factors as well as external fixes.** Companies will often try to 'fix' the pipeline or other external factors to increase the supply of diversity into the organization. Often a focus on extrinsic factors such as recruitment simply leads to more attrition as organizations have failed to address the intrinsic factors (such as management capability or culture). You have to want diversity, as well as increase its supply.

3 **Play the long game**. In the short term, homogeneous teams can often outperform diverse teams. They have pre-established norms such as trust and language. Trying to 'fix' diversity and hope for immediate results will result in disappointment. However, diversity plus inclusion can yield superior results over the medium to long term, as the more varied skill set is actually utilized efficiently.

We will see these three insights play out in the rest of the book. However, most organizations, even in HR, prioritize diversity and downplay inclusion, rely on recruitment and other external factors to 'solve' the problem and are set short-term targets by executives who don't understand the above. Where do we go from here?

INCLUSIVE TALENT MANAGEMENT (ITM)

In many organizations today, we see the consequences of largely homogeneous, mostly male teams insufficiently checked by different people with different points of view. If they better included diversity, thought more about internal culture as well as external factors and saw the medium- to long-term danger, would many extinct companies still be here today? The consequences of their actions were not as immediate as those of Captain van Zanten, but the parallel remains.

Inclusive Talent Management (ITM) is about managing people accounting for, and benefitting from, difference. Compare this with the standard homogeneous talent management (HTM), where we fail to include difference, by reference to the table below:

Table 2.2 Talent management approaches

Talent management approach	Risk	Resilience	Productivity
HTM	Increases	Lowers	Can increase short run Can lower medium – long run
ITM	Lowers	Increases	Can increase medium – long run, dependent on inclusive leadership

A more concentrated pool of specialists could actually increase organizational exposure to systemic risk. Diversity can mitigate risk and also increase the resilience of teams in the face of change and unpredictable events. We'll discuss this more in Chapter 5. Whilst a homogeneous team may work better than a more diverse team, benefitting from shared norms and trust for example, this effect is often short-lived. Over time, if a diverse team is inclusively led, they can produce superior returns as they benefit from a more diverse skill base.

By inculcating true diversity in all its aspects into our day-to-day thinking on the job, we can reap benefits for free. Why would we persist with 'recruiters' and 'diversity recruiters' when diversity can aid recruitment for all? Yet most Fortune 500 and FTSE 100 companies have 'diversity recruiters'. Why do we persist with seeing 'diverse' people as though some of us were not part of that diversity? Yet most executive teams we facilitate (comprising largely straight white men) think that they are the norm and diversity is about other people (usually women and ethnic minorities) and does not include them.

Diversity, inclusively managed and led, can yield four significant benefits:

Figure 2.1 Benefits of diversity

Benefits of diversity, when led inclusively:
Increased customer growth and retention
Greater employee engagement
Improved productivity and innovation
Better decision making

CUSTOMER GROWTH AND RETENTION

Conventional wisdom for many years around organizational diversity was that as long as your company had roughly the same demographic distribution as your customer base, then you would thrive. If you more accurately represent your customers, you are more likely to be able to understand their needs and so develop products that will keep them coming to your business. Again, diversity is important.

António Simões, formerly Chief Executive of HSBC in the UK, articulates his organizational challenge as having to deal with 'being behind society'.[8] As a retail bank, with the widest possible range of customers and the most diverse marketing campaign of any major financial institution, Antonio has identified that his customers are still outpacing him in terms of diversity. The external factors within which HSBC are operating are dynamic – the challenge is to instil them in the internal dynamics too; to add value to HSBC by embedding some of that external, infinite diversity in the internal infrastructure where decisions relating to customers are actually made.

However, research by Marc Bendick Jr and colleagues across the US advertising industry and a large US retailer published in 2010 showed that simply trying to increase diversity to match employees and customers often led to tokenistic silos, where, for example, Black employees were placed in the 'urban' department.[9] As a result, nobody's diversity was leveraged and stereotypes thrived, actually decreasing customer satisfaction.

What they concluded was that companies needed not just diversity, but also inclusion, or what they called diversity *climate*. Their findings were confirmed by a much larger study published in 2011 by Patrick McKay and colleagues. They analysed longitudinal data from nearly 60,000 employees and 1.2 million customers across 769 units of a large retail organization and found that more inclusive workplaces had higher customer satisfaction.[10] What's more, they found that workplaces that became more inclusive over time also showed an increase in customer satisfaction. Thus, while diversity may be necessary, you also need inclusion in order to drive customer growth and retention.

A great example of this is the Olympic movement. The Baby Boomers who watched Seb Coe win Gold in the 1980 and 1984 Games were still watching him and the Olympics in Beijing in 2008 – but the new generation was not. The Olympics fan base was ageing. The younger, more diverse, more global generation, empowered by technology, was not engaged. The most recognized brand in the world was slowly dying. It was in this context that London offered to reconnect the Olympic movement with a new, diverse customer base. That's why, 'in a world of many distractions', London offered to inspire young people to choose sport.[11] The movement chose diversity and inclusion, perhaps without even realizing it. However, it was only by sowing an inclusive feeling around the Games, 'Everyone's 2012', that the benefits were reaped.

EMPLOYEE ENGAGEMENT

Maslow's hierarchy of needs is a well-known tool for assessing employee needs (and human needs generally). If you don't get the basics right (food, water, shelter) then the additional stuff (company car) is a rather moot point. However, new research shows that what we might have perceived as a lower-priority need (belonging) is actually a basic need. We neglect this at our peril.

To engage employees is to try to reap discretionary effort. To try to gain this marginal value through an 'engagement programme' is problematic. It sounds additional. By practising real inclusion, embedding it in an organization's policies and leaders' practices, engagement will come. When leaders explicitly express their desire for employees to feel comfortable being themselves at work, and follow that with actions that attempt to actually make it part of the organization's ethos, employees are more likely to see that desire as authentic. It's that authenticity around inclusion that drives engagement.

As evidence of this effect, analysis by the US Department of Veterans Affairs showed that only 27 per cent of government employees are engaged in their jobs.[12] But it was shown that with increased inclusive practices, engagement increases, and so does productivity. Bringing that engagement level up, they say, could save taxpayers as much as $18 billion each year.[13]

This has been shown in many other sectors as well. Recent research in the health sector has shown that more inclusive practices lead to more engagement of health practitioners, leading to better patient outcomes.[14]

PRODUCTIVITY AND INNOVATION

Barriers to enhanced quality economic growth and productivity are not just inflexible labour markets and taxes; they are also unconscious bias, implicit associations and sexist and homophobic attitudes that are deeply inefficient, as well as distasteful. In order to compete, an organization needs everyone working to his or her individual optimum.

Gay people kept in the closet, women suffering from glass ceilings and disabled people facing inaccessible environments are all barriers to more productive employees. In fact, the combined effect of these microinequities is estimated to cost $64 billion per year in the United States alone.[15] That amount represents the annual estimated cost of losing and replacing more than 2 million American workers who leave their jobs each year due to unfairness and discrimination.

However, Meghna Sabharwal's research in 2016 found that once you control for demographics, availability of resources, and employee expectations for opportunities the diversity productivity effect disappears.[16] What she did find is that organizations combining diversity programmes with an inclusion programme that focuses on taking employee backgrounds and views into account are what leads to increased productivity, performance, and innovation. Thus, again, while diversity definitely matters, it is leveraging that diversity through an inclusive workplace culture that allows an organization to reap the benefits.

People perform better when they can be themselves. This is something Steve solidified in 2004 as the tagline for Stonewall's Diversity Champions employer programme. Of course, for many HR professionals, this is a big shift in approach from trying to integrate people into an established culture. This approach is not easy, and there is a tension between assimilation and allowing unique spirits to blossom. The art is to find the middle ground so that neither is lost.

In many ways, diversity is already present in the organization – it is simply being inefficiently utilized. The discretionary effort each (diverse) person is capable of, capturing individual marginal productivity, is not being tapped into. By removing barriers such as tolerance of sexist language in meetings, fixed working schedules, alcohol-only Friday drinks, and steps instead of ramps, and then by marketing that fact to the entire talent pool, stakeholder community and customer base, a great return is possible. We will explore further ideas and initiatives of this nature in later chapters.

It is a simple, yet important, insight that rather than constructing a whole host of new initiatives to 'build' a D&I programme, we should focus on what barriers we can remove to the potential already present.

DECISION MAKING

When it comes to decision making, the most commonly cited bias that arises from high levels of homogeneity is groupthink. This idea – that when too many minds that think similarly simply egg each other on instead of presenting different points of view – has been famously demonstrated in a number of major decisions with disastrous results. This includes NASA's decision to launch the space shuttle Challenger, which exploded killing multiple people, John F Kennedy's famously botched Bay of Pigs invasion, and the multiple decisions in the financial sector that led to an overinvestment in a small sector and an eventual global market crash.

There is ample evidence from many sectors showing how diversity – and, importantly, allowing for the leveraging of that diversity – leads to better decision making. For example, Scott Page at the University of Michigan has shown that a diversity of viewpoints in a group is often more important than the intelligence of the group in decision making and task performance, even if the group is made of experts and the task has to do with the field they are experts in.[17] In his book, *The Wisdom of Crowds*, James Surowiecki came to a similar conclusion, showing that the collective ideas and decisions reached by diverse groups are often better, more likely correct, and more accurate than those reached by non-diverse groups.[18]

Similar results have been found in workplace studies as well. A 2013 study found that diversity in social category[19] increases the extent to which individuals consider their own and others' perspectives before an interaction, which leads to better performance in decision-making tasks than groups with social category homogeneity, and this effect is even more pronounced in more complex tasks.[20] It is clear, therefore, that diverse groups that leverage their diversity are more likely to make better decisions overall.

In an environment of real inclusion there is greater potential for internal crowd sourcing of ideas, challenging of ideas, and refining ideas in real time. Procter & Gamble's 'Connect and develop' tool increased Research and Development productivity by 60 per cent.[21] In 2012, the London Organizing Committee of the Olympic and Paralympic Games' (LOCOG) internal, online communication tool 'the Knowledge' saved Steve hours of research time by finding people with answers in real time. As we learned from *The*

Wisdom of Crowds,[22] it is logical that individual life experience to date and bias will limit the ideas any one individual can come up with alone, but diversity improves collective intelligence.

And we know from recent academic research that it's collective intelligence that matters. Indeed, collective intelligence has been linked to increased performance in brainstorming tasks, negotiations, problem solving, making moral judgments, and other types of tasks. This research also found that ensuring women are on the team (this study specifically tested gender as an aspect of diversity), and increasing the share of women on the team so that it was more balanced, also improved task performance.[23]

So having diverse teams can improve the quality of decision making at all organizational levels, reduce groupthink and allow assumptions to be challenged more effectively. Heterogeneous teams are, on average, better than homogeneous teams on creative and complex problems.[24] They increase the number of perspectives, provide better understanding of customer needs and flex management approaches.[25] However, diversity needs to be managed in order to avert its negatives, especially unproductive group conflict. Inclusive leadership is required.

To make organizations more inclusive and actually encourage people to bring their whole selves to work, we can't just institute organizational policies. People have to follow those policies and be equipped with the skills to do so. If that happens, they will be better equipped to adapt and realize the incredible benefits a diverse workforce has to offer, from improved customer service to increased productivity and innovation to increased engagement to better decisions and performance. But for that to happen, the leaders and employees themselves need to have the skills and the desire to be more inclusive. After all, organizations are made up of individuals and they are the ones that need to create inclusive workplaces.

Organizational leaders, then, need to be the exemplars of inclusive skills and behaviours. Inclusive leadership is critical for inclusive organizations, and so narrowing our analysis even further to the individual is a key factor for success.

TAKEAWAYS

1 Appreciate the need for organizations to adapt in order to survive and thrive. Doing this pre-emptively, and keeping up with a changing marketplace, is preferable to reacting late, which could be fatal.

2 Use the Diversity Maturity Model: Diversity 101 (compliance-based), Diversity 2.0 (marketing-led), Inclusion 3.0 (embedded inclusion) as a guide to where your organization currently is, and might desire to be.

3 Focus on inclusion (rather than just diversity), on internal work (rather than just extrinsic factors), and long-run outcomes (not just immediate results).

4 Diversity, when included, is better for customers, engagement, productivity, and decision making.

5 Inclusive Talent Management can help your organization perform better than standard homogeneous talent management.

ENDNOTES

1 We recognize some organizations are for profit and others are not. We have tried to be sensitive to the different and collective drivers for organizational performance. In general, though, we use the terms 'organization' and 'business' interchangeably.

2 Hunt, V, Layton, D and Prince, S (2015) *Diversity Matters*, McKinsey & Company

3 https://www.gov.uk/government/news/record-number-of-women-on-ftse-100-boards

4 Frost, S and Kalman, D (2016) *Inclusive Talent Management: How business can thrive in an age of diversity*, Kogan Page Publishers

5 https://aeon.co/essays/what-is-life-like-for-disabled-people-in-china

6 https://www.theverge.com/2017/5/29/15708558/texas-bathroom-bill-apple-google-facebook-letter

7 For more on the maturity model see Frost and Kalman (2016) *Inclusive Talent Management*, Kogan Page

8 Conversation with author, Cambridge, MA, April 2013

9 Bendick Jr, M, Lou Egan, M and Lanier, L (2010) The business case for diversity and the perverse practice of matching employees to customers, *Personnel Review*, **39** (4), pp 468–86

10 McKay, P F et al (2011) Does diversity climate lead to customer satisfaction? It depends on the service climate and business unit demography, *Organization Science*, **22** (3), pp 788–803

11 Seb Coe speech, Singapore, 6 July 2005

12 Presentation by Georgia Coffey, US Department of Veterans Affairs. Described in Clark, P (2015) Diversity and inclusion is an agency imperative, *Public Manager*, **44** (2), pp 42–45

13 Ibid

14 Downey, S et al (2015) The role of diversity practices and inclusion in promoting trust and employee engagement, *Journal of Applied Social Psychology*, **45** (1), pp 35–44

15 Burns, C (March 2012) *The Costly Business of Discrimination*, Centre for American Progress

16 Sabharwal, M (2014) Is diversity management sufficient? Organizational inclusion to further performance, *Public Personnel Management*, **43** (2) pp 197–217

17 Page, S (2007) *The Difference: How the power of diversity creates better groups, firms, schools, and societies*, Princeton University Press

18 Surowiecki, J (2004) *The Wisdom of Crowds*, Anchor Books

19 Loyd, D L et al (2013) Social category diversity promotes premeeting elaboration: the role of relationship focus, *Organization Science*, **24** (3), pp 757–72. The study defines social category as important differences that people use to separate themselves into different categories, which defines their in-groups and out-groups

20 Ibid

21 Mary Martinez, London Vanguard seminar, 16 March 2012

22 Surowiecki, J (2004) *The Wisdom of Crowds*, Anchor Books

23 Woolley, A W et al (2010) Evidence for a collective intelligence factor in the performance of human groups, *Science*, **330** (6004), pp 686–88

24 Hoffman, L R (1965) Group problem solving1, in *Advances in Experimental Social Psychology* (Vol 2, pp 99–132), ed L Berkowitz, Academic Press;

Triandis, H C, Hall, E R and Ewen, R B (1965) Member heterogeneity and dyadic creativity, *Human Relations*, **18** (1), pp 33–55

25 Singh, V (2008) Diversity management practices in leading edge firms, in *Building More Effective Organizations*, ed R Burke and C Cooper, Cambridge University Press

3

IT STARTS WITH YOU

Having reviewed diversity and inclusion from a global perspective in Chapter 1 and at the organization level in Chapter 2, let us now turn to the individual level. A great deal of progress could be made if we simply incorporated inclusion in our understanding of leadership overall. Good leadership is by default inclusive leadership – taking a wide range of perspectives on board in order to inform and calibrate our decision making. However, just as with homogeneous talent management (failing to account for difference), much 'leadership' work remains segregated from thinking preemptively about inclusion or even empathy. Furthermore, there remains a confusion between management and leadership in the first place.

MANAGEMENT AND LEADERSHIP

Management is technical work. It's often essential, and without it things wouldn't happen. But management is operating within pre-determined norms and parameters, and executing accordingly. Leadership is adaptive work. It's also essential, and without it things certainly don't improve. Leadership is about pushing the parameters, challenging norms and moving a group from A to B. As with our discussion about norms in Chapter 1, there is an ethical or even moral element to it. However, as we have seen, leadership and challenging discriminatory or inefficient norms don't always go hand in hand.

Management is trying to figure out how to get things done within the current constructs of the business and current norms of society and industry. Leadership is trying to find ways to change the current constructs of the business and push the boundaries of societal and industrial norms in order to create new possibilities for the organization.

It's understandable, then, that it is difficult for one individual to be both an effective manager and a good leader. But inclusive leadership is a good bridge between the two. As we'll see in later chapters, inclusive leadership practices tend to also be just good management practices. They allow you to bring in the voices of people who might have been previously marginalized and so improve the workplace culture and practices for all employees.

YOUR PERSONAL BUSINESS CASE

There are a plethora of business cases for diversity available. But most miss the point. To succeed, we need to answer the WIIFM question. What's in it for me? Only by making this personal will you really care.

We don't mean to say here that caring about inclusion isn't deeply personal. Indeed, for many of us equality in this sense is something we do truly care about. But when we say 'make it personal', we mean it can't just be some abstract concept that matters to you. It needs to feel like it will significantly impact your life, your happiness, your ability to do your work, or even your own identity. It needs to mean something deep within you.

The reason we say D&I needs to be so deeply personally meaningful is that if you lead a team, you already have a tough job. If you are an executive with objectives, you already have a tough job. Having a team made up of people with many differences can cause friction among those team members, and managing that friction takes active effort. Given that a diverse team could create more conflict, why on earth would you want to recruit diversity?

The answer lies in our own enlightened self-interest.

The amount of information we have to process in our daily lives is doubling roughly every two years.[1] Whilst the technological world increases exponentially, our mere human minds are expanding in a linear fashion at best.

So we have two choices. We can persevere in our own bubble, our own way of doing things and train our own brain to see blind spots, consider different perspectives and identify risks. This is theoretically possible, but hard.

Or we can surround ourselves with as much diversity as possible and get others to do that for us. If you have a team of brilliant, but different, people they will see blind spots you miss, they will offer perspectives you have never thought of and they will identify risks that could have taken you down.

But of course for this diversity to work, it has to be given permission to live, to thrive – and it has to be led inclusively. Properly led, diversity is one of the best free resources available. It can help us shift from System 1 thinking (our instinctual, gut reactions) to System 2 thinking (more thought out, reasoned ideas), which we will explore in more depth in Chapter 5. It can mitigate our risks, increase our perspectives and offer us enhanced innovative and creative problem-solving resources.

Determining how inclusion features in your daily decision making is directly related to your personal 'why'. If it features in your daily decisions, it significantly impacts your life and your ability to do your work. Thus, determining where inclusion fits in your day-to-day life will help you answer the all-important question: why do you care about inclusion? Only by answering this question will it become embedded in daily leadership practice.

SELF AND ROLE

Inclusion doesn't just happen. People leading make it happen. A useful concept is differentiating between self and role.

We all have a self – who we love, our political and religious views, what kind of cake we like – which is sacrosanct. In other words, your self is your identity and values. But we also have a role – our job, for example – which is a choice. You can flex your role without compromising your self. And when your self is uncompromised, you can flex your role to perform actions that reflect that identity and those values. And the more you can do that and empower others to do the same, the more you will include.[2] Moreover, the more you feel able to do that yourself, the more you will feel included as well.

For example, Raafi often talks about how, when he was an undergraduate at Harvard, he sometimes felt excluded because he didn't have as much money as others around him, and so couldn't constantly go out for dinners or to shows with his friends. He would often make excuses so that they wouldn't know lest they feel awkward or just decide to stop inviting him out. He wasn't the only student who had to deal with this problem, but what he didn't consider was that there were staff and administrators at Harvard who had had similar experiences in university.

Some of those administrators got together to figure out what they could do. They came from low-income backgrounds and cared deeply about ensuring that current students from similar backgrounds were able to participate fully in the Harvard undergraduate experience, including being able to attend concerts and plays on campus.

Harvard – like any organization – tries to keep its costs low, so the administrators had to find a way to help these low-income students while making it a win for the university. These administrators had the power to come up with ideas, but if they were to default to their System 1 thinking they would likely see these two forces as diametrically opposed. How could they keep costs low, and yet simultaneously pay for tickets so that low-income students could attend campus events?

In the end, they created the Student Events Fund, where students who were on a certain level of financial aid were able to request tickets to shows for free, and then pick them up at the box office just like any other paying student. This did cost the university some money, but because they had made the campus more hospitable to students from low-income backgrounds, the students felt more included and it became an incentive for more of those students to apply.

These administrators were able to empathize with the problems faced by students like Raafi, but then were able to flex their role when it came down to arguing the case with the university, showing how it could be a win-win. In this way, the administrators were able to enlarge the pie. However, had Harvard not been conscious about making sure those administrators felt like they could bring their entire selves to work – even in an atmosphere where they may not be like everyone else – they likely wouldn't have come up with the idea at all. They might have just stuck to their System 1 thoughts and seen the issue as unsolvable. The diversity of the administrators, and active inclusion by their employer, were what allowed for this more creative solution.

For some, diversity is still a half-baked idea. The Harvard classroom arm wrestle as well as the Student Events Fund show it can actually enlarge the pie for all of us. Our default seems to be to think of the world as a competition, to think of every interaction as a zero-sum game unless proven otherwise. But if we could simply shift our thinking so that the default is to find solutions that enlarge the pie we might see the benefits of diversity more clearly. It's time for a real discussion on inclusion and to swiftly follow up the talk with concrete actions. There will never be enough time, there will never be enough resources. But diversity is free, in infinite supply and largely within our own control.

INCLUSION IS NECESSARY FOR DIVERSITY TO SUCCEED

What does inclusive leadership look like? Often people focus on extrinsic factors such as recruitment or additional initiatives that they can undertake. But these miss the point somewhat. It's not about extracurricular activities done off the side of your desk. That's rather like relying on foreign aid instead of changing the terms of trade. It's about giving due consideration to applying an inclusive lens to your day job.

When you have a diverse workforce, it can be difficult for those different people to find common ground and work together. Often, diversity can cause friction in a team, and when that friction isn't managed the team isn't able to work well together. In these cases, diversity likely will not lead to the incredible benefits it could bring because it will make people feel more guarded and instead stifle their ability to bring their whole selves to work.

Inclusive leadership helps manage that friction. When people bring their whole selves to work, they are able to leverage every aspect of their perspectives as they approach problems, leading to more creativity and innovation. If we use the analogy of trying to cross a river, one side of the riverbank is diversity, the other side is positive work outcomes, and the river itself is the friction that difference can bring. The bridge then that you as a leader must build is inclusion.

Let's take an example: men and gender pay parity. The gender pay gap is predominantly seen as a female issue. In many cases, women are only paid 80 per cent of what men are paid.[3] However, how could a man lead on this issue and frame it as a problem for men too? Men seeing a gain for women as a loss for men is the zero-sum arm wrestle example playing out in real life.

In 2017, 45 female stars, led by Jane Garvey, wrote to the BBC Director General, Tony Hall, to complain about pay inequity.[4] But where were the men? Where were the male signatories? This principle is about all of us, the men and the women, for all staff, not just the 'stars'. The principle is not a female principle. It is a human principle. It is one of fairness and merit assured through transparency. Inefficient and unfair markets hurt us all. This pay injustice is morally repugnant for many of us, but it is inefficient for all of us.

All of us, whether directly or indirectly, are dependent on women being paid fairly. All of us suffer when a labour market becomes distorted and paid not on the basis of merit but on the basis of bias and favour. All of us suffer from market failure when we don't ensure checks and balances on the best succeeding. Diversity is the enemy of mediocrity. And transparency is its facilitator.

The UK changed the law on equal pay in 1970 but the cultural work hasn't been done yet. In some cases, it hasn't even started. With gender pay reporting, the British government changed the law in 2017 to demand transparency. This is now the opportunity to work with leaders on that cultural shift.

We have done this in the past with military leaders working to include their LGBT+ personnel for the overall good of the mission. Steve vividly recalls working with senior officers in the Royal Navy on helping them articulate their own business case for gay personnel on ships, and a decade later for women on submarines. Only when they could rationalize it in their own minds did we stand a chance of success. In the same way, the new laws around gender pay transparency gives us the opportunity to work with business leaders on why transparency and inclusion is a business good, not a cost.

This can be done. One, we need leadership training for executives, especially men, on why transparency and inclusion is a business asset, not a cost. Two, we need simple systems that allow for checks and balances and to act as a nudge against discriminatory behaviour. In Norway, they have been doing this since 2001 through measures like an obligation to report pay gaps, creating special discrimination tribunal courts (which creates increased incentives for organizations to be more careful), and requiring reports from all companies on how they are ensuring gender equality.[5] It's not just about pay parity, it guards against tax evasion, protects meritocracy and encourages responsible behaviour.

We now need business leaders, especially male business leaders, to become visible and vocal in the name of transparency, and properly functioning free labour markets.

At a time of Brexit, when all UK legislation is supposedly being copy-pasted across the statute books, when gender pay reporting is compulsory, and at a time when the UK is facing some segregating forces as a society, this is the time when men need to show solidarity with women for the sake of all of us.

PROTECT YOURSELF FROM COSTLY ERRORS

In order to be a valuable contributor to your organization, or your family, or to society generally you have to be able to function well. High cognitive load, stress and work can all detract from well-being. Ironically, rather than seeing D&I as additive to well-being, many still view it as a threat. It is important to address this if we are to co-opt former cynics to the cause. The System 1 and 2 example above is instructive here. If we can frame diversity as de-risking personal decision making, or adding to the richness of one's life, we might be able to challenge the defensiveness.

That framing is often the key for making D&I personal with some of our clients. Yes, they want to be ethical. Yes, they want the better business outcomes that diversity brings. But what gets many truly, deeply, personally invested is the idea that it can help them make better decisions themselves. When we discuss the idea that people are more prone to errors and stereotypes when they don't have time to stop, when they're stressed, tired, hungry, under time pressure, preoccupied with other things, it really resonates with them.

We've all had the experience of making more typos or inputting the data wrong when we're tired. But what also seems to resonate is that someone else's stereotypes or errors may be different than the ones you would make. So even if your whole team is under high cognitive load, if that team is diverse you will still be able to cover each other's blind spots because you all have different ones.

In this way, we de-risk personal decision making. And thinking about D&I this way allows us to make it personally meaningful. It gives us skin in the game.

COGNITIVE DIVERSITY

Another idea that helps make D&I personal for many people is the relatively more recent idea of cognitive diversity. By this, we mean ensuring not just that the traditionally protected characteristics like race and gender are represented, but really focusing on making sure different ways of thinking are represented.

In truth, this is what really creates the positive benefits of diversity – that different people approach problems in different ways. These differences, then, that we are trying to include shouldn't be just limited to visible differences, but to more subtle ones too that certainly influence our approaches to situations. These include levels of introversion and extraversion, socioeconomic background, educational background both in terms of level and in terms of field of study, and other areas. Framing the diversity we desire on a team in this way tends to make people feel like they're a part of diversity, and so fighting for increased inclusion becomes a personal mission.

Lately, though, we have seen many people and organizations use cognitive diversity as a way to justify their lack of visible diversity. They say, 'We may be all white and mostly male, but we have cognitive diversity so it's not a problem.' It may be true that they have non-visible differences in that team, but to say that the lack of visible diversity isn't a problem is false. Growing up with a disability, or as part of an ethnic minority, or as a woman, or as a gay person means that you will have had different life experiences than a straight, able-bodied, white man. Those different life experiences mean you will have learned to approach problems differently than others.

A person's race does matter in informing their cognition. Critical race theory explains how aspects of our identity inform how we see ourselves. Additionally, people of different races have systematically different experiences in the world.[6] So while Raafi as an ethnically Indian person approaches problems in a particular way, the theoretical white version of Raafi – even if every other aspect of him stayed the same – would likely approach those same problems differently. This is because white Raafi would have, for example, had different experiences after 9/11 than Indian Raafi for whom it was a formative time that led him to approach people with much more empathy than he might have had he not had those experiences.

Not having that racial diversity in a team, then, means you are missing those different approaches and perspectives. The same goes for all the traditionally protected characteristics. They are aspects of cognitive diversity, and not including them will still mean you are not covering your blind spots. Therefore, we must be careful not to replace traditional diversity with cognitive diversity, but simply *supplement* traditional diversity with other aspects of cognitive diversity.

DEFINING YOUR OWN PERSONAL 'WHY?'

If we reflected on our closest friends, our closest colleagues, our partner(s) and neighbours, would we find that we liked diversity as much as we profess? What would this 'In-group' tell us about our instinctive feelings about diversity?

The world over, in varied cultures, environments and countries we tend to prefer sameness to difference. This phenomenon is called *homophily* and is natural and normal to human beings. If you have a relatively homogeneous in-group, you are like 90 per cent of the population – your in-group looks pretty much like you. Not just in terms of the demographics such as race, but in terms of political leanings, alcohol preference and sense of humour. That's great and should be celebrated. We need space to be ourselves, to relax, to have commonalities with people, norms and protocols that require no deep understanding or effort.

But too much homogeneity, especially in a professional context, can be dangerous.

Be aware of the in-group and out-group lens in your interactions and include others in your in-group to make the lens wider and more accurate. Not doing so allows bias free rein and doesn't challenge our decision making sufficiently. Instead, surround yourself with those who are different from you and make a point to consult them as much as possible.

Examples of this might include speaking with someone who doesn't drink when planning a staff social event, checking with carers to make sure the time of the event doesn't conflict with school runs, or asking someone with access requirements when choosing a venue. But it would also be assigning someone to the differing protagonist perspective in a board meeting. How can you consciously step into someone else's shoes to see the decision from their perspective and so better calibrate the decision you are about to make?

Additionally, take the extra step to combat systemic biases that contribute to inequality. Clients often speak to us about how they want more women and ethnic minorities at the top but they just don't apply or push for the promotion. This is a big contributor to pay gaps and other workplace inequality issues. What we often then ask is if they personally have sought out qualified women or minorities and encouraged them to apply. To pull, rather than expect them to push.

Furthermore, when minorities do 'push', often they are perceived as acting outside their stereotype and are penalized for it, akin to the double bind women face. We mentioned that white men and extroverts are more likely to be self-promoters. However, they may not be the best candidates overall. Instead, go for competence, even if this means having to dig a little deeper and encourage women, minorities and introverted men to put themselves forward. Make a point to find out both the credentials and aspirations of these people on your team, and give them your support.

IMPROVING SOCIETY

This work of including our out-groups is in more than just our professional interest, though. It's in our societal interest as well. When we interact with people who are different from us, we begin to empathize more and break down the polarization we described in Chapter 1.

Studies testing this in microcosms like university dormitories have further shown that this effect can perpetuate through to our close friends and family as well. In fact, a review of 515 studies shows that out-group contact and regular engagement with out-groups reduces intergroup prejudice and bias. This is true not just for visible out-groups (eg race/ethnicity, gender, sex, disability, etc) but other groups as well such as LGBT+ individuals or people from lower socio-economic backgrounds.[7]

This concept, called intergroup contact theory, has the potential to change the way we engage with one another. This could even begin to reduce bias in society by changing the way we portray different groups in the media. But it requires active efforts on our parts to consciously and consistently include our out-groups.

Examples could be something as simple as talking to the neighbours, joining a different social group, celebrating a different festival. But if we don't proactively and consciously include, we will unconsciously exclude to our own detriment.

Surrounding ourselves with difference is not only good professionally in terms of decision making, it is also great for the common good and living in a more peaceful society.

You can appreciate the urgency of this endeavour and the importance of these insights. As leaders, we have a greater responsibility than most to use our expertise, to use our insights for benefitting not only ourselves and our organizations but also the wider world around us.

TO ADAPT, OR NOT TO ADAPT, THAT IS THE QUESTION

It's understandable many people use cognitive diversity as an excuse to exclude traditional diversity. It makes it easier for them to avoid having to adapt. But in the world today, the majority not adapting to changing times can be perilous.

Let us go back to politics as an example. In 2016, Hillary Clinton lost despite the polls indicating that she was going to win in a landslide. In the 2017 French Presidential election, Macron didn't want to be in such a situation. He beat Le Pen by 32 percentage points.

In the United States, voters didn't so much desert Obama's legacy – rather, they rejected the two-party system that they felt was not representing them. In France, voters also rejected the system, but they also rejected Le Pen because Macron learned from what happened in the United States and adapted to the situation. He decisively co-opted and embodied a change to the system (even if for selfish reasons).

In creating a new party, he understood that people wanted an alternative to nationalism and isolation. The divide has shifted from left/right to globalist/nationalist but people want to be rooted in locality, to be listened to and engaged with. They wanted to feel a personal connection, that they were heard and that whomever they elected would act in their best interest. They wanted to feel like they belonged in their system. Macron adapted to their need and gave them an option that would give them a sense of belonging.

THE NEED TO BELONG

In 2012, the London Olympics and Paralympics triumphed in no small part because we succeeded in making everyone in the UK feel like they belonged. In the seven years since, we have wobbled.

One narrative is that diversity has 'gone too far' and people wanted Trump after a Black president, Brexit after immigration and felt that all the rights won for minorities had been at the expense of the majority. But as inclusive leaders, we can offer an alternative framing, that people haven't necessarily rejected diversity – they have rejected one interpretation of it.

That's why we undertake leadership work that is intensely personal. By reframing diversity as a leadership competency, we offer people a stake in the diversity conversation, allow them to determine their own skin in the game, allow them to reconcile their own self-interest with the greater good.

It is a basic human need to feel like you belong. Feeling lonely has now been cited as a greater contributor to death than smoking and heart disease in many places including the United States.[8] We need to feel like we are not being rejected by the society around us. Many people who are not in the majority have thus created their own communities where they can be totally themselves so that they can feel this sense of belonging.

But what if work could be one of those communities too? We spend almost a third of our lives at work, so why shouldn't that also be a place where we feel like we belong? Shouldn't such a significant place in our lives be one where we contribute, where we grow, and where we can feel comfortable rather than only feeling that way when we go home?

Inclusion facilitates belonging. It is the actions you take as an inclusive leader that will help people feel like they belong. Everyone needs a reason to believe, whatever your colour, creed or background. Will we be able to create the cultures that allow everyone to have a stake?

Diversity is a reality. Globally we have leaders from Trump to Macron, Xi to Merkel. Organizations are more diverse than we often give them credit for. And people are infinitely diverse. No two people are the same. The question before us is more about inclusion. Diversity may be a reality, but including this difference remains a choice.

Many people make choices to avoid having to adapt. As we discussed in Chapter 1, it's understandable that this is the case, but it remains problematic nonetheless. This approach may suffice in the short term, but ultimately, as history has shown us, adaption is necessary for survival. As Bob Dylan said, the times they are a changin'. Will you pre-empt change – or be subsumed by it?

TAKEAWAYS

1 Define your personal 'why'. Only when inclusion really matters to you personally will you integrate it in your daily work.

2 Understand the difference between your Self and your Role, and play with them to better include others, adapt to different situations and lead inclusively.

3   Decide how much of an Inclusive Leader you want to be. What is your level of self-awareness and how much development are you willing to engage in?

4   Think about cognitive diversity in addition to traditional diversity and how this can enlarge the pie for all parties, whilst not acting as a convenient excuse to exclude minorities.

5   Empathize with everyone's need to belong. This is an inclusive concept that can bring us together.

ENDNOTES

1   https://qz.com/472292/data-is-expected-to-double-every-two-years-for-the-next-decade/

2   For more on Self and Role see Frost, S and Kalman, D, (2016) *Inclusive Talent Management*, Kogan Page

3   https://www.aauw.org/research/the-simple-truth-about-the-gender-pay-gap/

4   https://www.telegraph.co.uk/women/work/bbc-gender-pay-gap-women-won/

5   http://kifinfo.no/en/2017/09/new-anti-discrimination-act-twist

6   https://www.psychologytoday.com/us/basics/race-and-ethnicity

7   Pettigrew, T and Tropp, L (2006) A meta-analytic test of intergroup contact theory, *Journal of Personality and Social Psychology*, 90 (5), pp 751–83

8   http://www.apa.org/convention/2017/loneliness.aspx

4

DEFINING THE CHALLENGE

MISDIAGNOSING THE PROBLEM

In 2018, Microsoft joined the long list of tech companies accused of sexism. An investigation by the *Seattle Times* revealed that Microsoft allegedly failed to hire or retain more women and that its male-dominated hierarchy may have nurtured a culture of casual sexism and poor resolution of grievances.[1]

There is an emerging pattern here of organizations that thought they were 'doing' diversity but turned out to be left wanting. This is primarily because they misdiagnosed the problem, and then applied the wrong solution.

The misdiagnosis revolves around the fact that men and/or those running organizations tend to think diversity is about somebody else: 'women', 'minorities'. We regularly get comments in boards and executive committees from men who say, 'I'm not diverse'.

Yet diversity is actually infinite and means all of us, as we have explored in Chapter 3 and will continue to explore throughout this book. And when you consider that majority groups often have more control over power, hierarchy, culture and privilege, it is easy to make the case that the problem is really about the majority group. This means the men and the people in charge not adapting to new circumstances and contexts rather than 'minorities' not assimilating. This is not what most of those people currently believe. Let's start with a clear example of how companies are tackling the wrong challenge.

GENDER PAY GAPS AND HOW TO REALLY CLOSE THEM

For a long time now, we have suspected that there has been more 'noise' around gender equality than actual action. Not only is this unhelpful, it may be lulling us into a false sense of security that we are actually doing something, when we are simply masking the problem. So now that gender pay gaps (GPG) are public knowledge in the UK, we did some research to test our hypothesis:

We correlated gender awards won with actual gender pay gaps in those same organizations. We took the *Times* Top 50 Employers for Women 2017, the Catalyst Group Award Winners (awards for organizations making the most progress towards creating more inclusive cultures given by Catalyst, a non-profit organization that works towards making more inclusive workplaces for women) for the last 10 years, and the Glassdoor Top 50 in the UK (the PR) against the same companies' actual gender pay gaps (the reality). Here's what we found.

THE RESULTS

Our hypothesis was correct. Take a look at the next two graphs and you'll see that many of the companies have huge GPGs despite being highly regarded/awarded.

Across all three award-winning categories, most of these celebrated companies were actually *worse* than the UK average. Of Catalyst Award recipients, in the last 10 years, only four of the 22 UK companies that have won (18 per cent) have had a GPG that was better than the national average. Of the *Times* Top 50, only three (6 per cent) had a GPG better than the national average. Of the Glassdoor Top 50, only 13 (26 per cent) had a GPG better than the national average.

Figure 4.1 Gender pay gaps of Catalyst Award winners

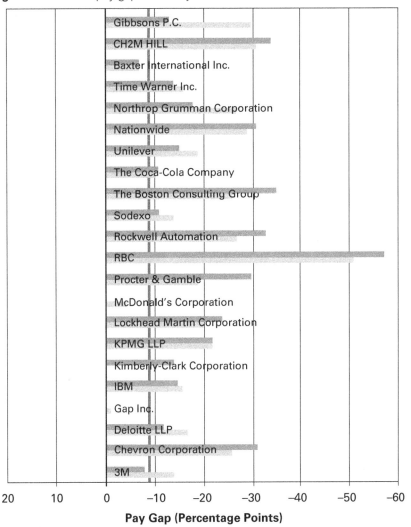

Pay Gap (Percentage Points)

Women's mean hourly earnings vs men
Women's median hourly earnings vs men
UK Average GPG

Figure 4.2 Gender pay gaps of *Times* Top 50 Employers for Women

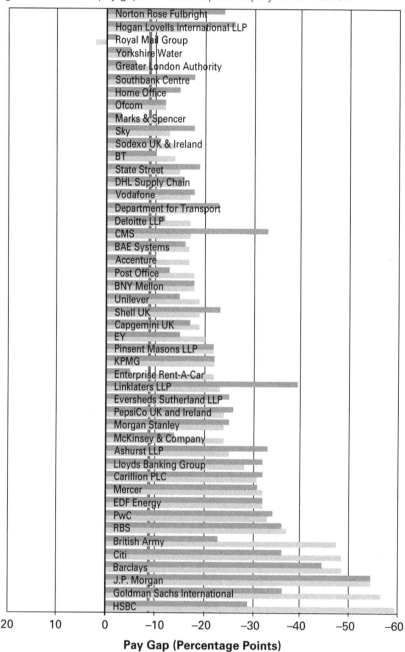

Pay Gap (Percentage Points)

Women's mean hourly earnings vs men

Women's median hourly earnings vs men

UK Average GPG

THE REASONS

Undoubtedly, many of these award winners are doing good work. But it is not resulting in smaller gender pay gaps. As we found, a majority of these award winners were actually worse than the average.

It's highly likely that these organizations are focusing time and effort on Diversity 101 compliance activities such as training, and Diversity 2.0 activities such as events and awards, but insufficient time and effort on Inclusion 3.0 work such as leadership programmes and embedding nudges into how decisions get made to reduce the effects of unconscious bias. We'll say more about nudges in Chapter 8.

The reason why they are still getting these awards, though, is likely in part due to the fact that the awards only measure 1.0 and 2.0 activities. They look at the organizational policies of the business and how those might affect different groups. They look at what gets publicized and at the stories put forward by the organization.

But how do you measure Inclusion 3.0? How do you measure the embedding of inclusion in the day-to-day work of the organization? This is the challenge of these awards – they're not measuring the culture broadly, they're measuring single instances of good work. It's the equivalent of trying to make a generalization based on an anecdote instead of the full data. We'll talk more about what it means to measure this later on in this chapter, as well as the specifics of how to do it and how to leverage those measurements in Chapter 8.

These results show we have been misdiagnosing the problem. When we reward organizations and policies that help 'the other' assimilate, we're not really rewarding inclusion. We're not recognizing what would actually help organizations thrive and employees to flourish. Organizations need to adapt to people. The majority needs to adapt to the marginalized groups. The extent to which that adaptation occurs in an organization is what we should be measuring and awarding. Perhaps then we'll start to see different, more positive, results.

Q&A with Steve and Raafi

Are you surprised by recent gender pay gap results?

Not at all. It has been well established for many years in both the academic literature and in the experience of other countries similar to the UK like the United States, Australia, and Canada that the gender pay gap is still quite big, and that it is in part driven by a gender pyramid in seniority in many organizations and industries. Banking is often cited as one of the worst offenders on this front, so we're not surprised that the gap is so large for them.

In gender pay gap reports some finance companies make the point that the GPG is driven by higher numbers of men in senior roles earning more and higher numbers of women in junior role earning less, arguing that, on balance, men and women earn the same for the jobs they're paid for. One bank goes so far as to provide an adjusted mean pay gap that reveals a 2 per cent gap. What do you make of this as a justified assessment?

There is a lot to unpack here. First of all, definitions and distinctions – the equal pay gap should be zero, and a gender pay gap is evident but hopefully reducing. Second, even if this bank's assessment of their adjusted mean pay gap is accurate and comparable across their competitors, a 2 per cent pay gap for equal work is not 0 per cent. While it's great that it's low, it's still not enough – in fact, we should be pushing even more, asking why there is still a 2 per cent pay gap for equal work.

On what is driving their GPG, there is definitely merit to that point that a large portion of the gender pay gap is driven by the gender seniority pyramid. That is well established in the literature and is consistent with what we're seeing in other countries. However, there are other aspects of gender disparity that play into this gap as well.

For example, in many of these jobs an employee's chance of getting a raise, prospects in pay negotiations, and bonus size are tied to a combination of results and perceived dedication to the company or job (as measured by performance reviews). However, since women are culturally more likely to spend time as the main caregiver for children, the home and older family members, that limits their ability to spend more time at work. As a result, this gender-imbalanced distribution of household labour directly affects many women's ability to be on the same playing field as men at work. This is pronounced even more at places like banks where jobs can often be highly stressful, demanding and time-consuming. The issue is part of a much larger system.

Additionally, those reports don't even tell the whole pay gap story. The gap in bonus payments is significantly larger than the gap in base pay. It's upwards of 70 per cent or even 80 per cent at some banks.[2] This may well reflect male and female differences in negotiation style as well as bias and networks effects at play. Men tend to demand more from their employer; for example they tend to ask more than women for salary increases and bonuses. There is rarely sufficient compensatory behaviour on the part of the employer.

However, it's important to note that even though it's a systemic issue, that doesn't mean organizations like these banks can't do anything to help solve the problem. Allowing for more flexible ways of working, having more anonymized reviews, internally publishing salaries to level the negotiation playing field... all of these techniques and so many others could help to reduce the gender pay gap, and that's not even including the work to increase promotion and retention rates of women.

What impact do you think the government's gender pay reporting legislation is having so far, based on your experience?

We actually think it's having quite a big impact, in that it's forcing people to pay attention to the issue. Gender equality has been gaining in prominence as a global issue in many ways, but this type of legislation helps to ensure it stays at the forefront and doesn't just fall away like a fad. Whether it will have more effect than just causing moral outrage in the public remains to be seen, but given the grassroots motivation to solve these problems we're hopeful for a more equal future.

APPLYING THE WRONG SOLUTION

Once men/management realize it's about 'us' rather than 'them' we need to apply different solutions. It's less about 'schemes' or 'programmes' for women, helpful though they can be. It's more about leadership training for the men on increasing self-awareness, adopting more inclusive behaviours, and learning to adapt.

That's why we focus on male leadership and why we work on reframing diversity as a leadership issue.

If we tackle the culture, the diversity will follow. If we keep trying to 'fix' diversity, the culture won't change. If we try to solve culture with a 'technical fix', we will technically hire and then simply increase attrition.

WE ALWAYS ASK MINORITIES TO ADAPT

We teach our children to be cautious, to be wary of strangers and to mitigate risk. As adults, we too use this learned behaviour. We use stereotypes, as a cognitive short-cut to minimize potential danger. Those of us for whom the stereotype is that we are dangerous know this, and often take steps to signal to others that there is no need to worry. For example, Raafi is a Muslim of Indian descent, and he knows that there are stereotypes of people who look like him being terrorists. As such, when he is at airports, he takes particular care to smile, not question any authority figures, and dresses smartly to counter those stereotypes.

As another example, take Brent Staples, a columnist for the *New York Times*. He is brilliantly intelligent, holds multiple degrees, and is very kind to strangers. But when he walks down the street at night, people tend to cross over the road to avoid him.

Brent is Black. He would say this is merely one aspect of his identity; however, it's one that people see before they see the rest of him.[3] When walking down a street at night the stereotype can be Black = danger. Black = to be avoided. And so many people (of all races, but especially white people) cross the road.

Many Black colleagues could tell you that in spite of being just as smart and just as capable they regularly experience subtler forms of 'crossing the road'. At a restaurant, the waiter might have an unchecked bias that Black diners know less about wine and consistently fail to ask their opinion. At work, Black colleagues might tell you about meetings where people seemed to avoid eye contact and failed to engage their opinion.

WHAT TO DO?

The onus can remain on the individual to adapt. Brent found that whistling Vivaldi often reduced his stereotype threat. It could have been any classical music that was more familiar to many white people. When he signalled 'white music', white people didn't cross the road. Black colleagues have used other strategies to allay stereotype signals.

Or the onus could be on all of us. To build an inclusive organization, we try to further change the culture to be more inclusive, rather than expecting individuals to do all the heavy lifting and fit in. For example, we could support networks that offer mentoring and profile-building opportunities that many of us not in networks take for granted. We could all cross the road, but to join, rather than run away.

Of course it's not black and white, no pun intended. It's necessarily a blend. We want individuals of whatever colour, shape, and background to make an effort to 'fit in', to contribute, to support the team, just not to feel they have to go beyond the bounds of their selves to do so. Whatever tune they are whistling, we could do more to listen, reach out and include.

UNLOCKING THE PROBLEM: SEE NO EVIL, HEAR NO EVIL, SPEAK NO EVIL

We are trying to solve a problem of adaptation. Majority groups need to find ways to adapt to minorities instead of forcing a level of assimilation that makes minorities feel like they can't be themselves. Is this what most people currently understand diversity and inclusion to be?

Google had a mantra – 'don't be evil' – introduced in 2000 as part of its first corporate code of conduct. In 2004 the founders Larry Page and Sergey Brin wrote in a letter for the Initial Public Offering, 'Google users trust our systems to help them with important decisions: medical, financial and many others. Our search results are the best we know how to produce. They are unbiased and objective…'.[4]

We now know it's impossible to be completely unbiased and objective in any scenario. Bias is a natural part of the human condition and an essential component in how we judge situations and make decisions. Larry and Sergey's intention was good, 'don't be evil'. But it suggests passiveness – don't do bad things – rather than action – do good things. The well-intentioned desire to do no evil actually prevents us from seeing the problem.

The Japanese proverb san'en or sanzaru embodies the mantra *see no evil, hear no evil, speak no evil*. In Buddhist tradition the idea is to avoid dwelling on evil thoughts. In Western tradition it's more about turning a blind eye to bad things.

Not wanting to dwell on evil thoughts is perhaps desirable, but ignoring the real issue in the pretence that nothing is wrong is perhaps undesirable. Organizations spend considerable effort thinking they are tackling D&I; however, it is often masking the real problem because rather than seeking to actively create inclusive cultures – rather than adapting – most D&I programmes focus simply on avoiding doing harmful things. But this isn't enough to create inclusion. It's just the bare minimum.

SEEING THE PROBLEM IN THE FIRST PLACE

You may not be aware how few minorities you have in your organization. When Steve worked with the partners at KPMG UK in 2014 the data showed that, among other things, there were few Black leaders in the business, with just one Black partner and a small number of Black colleagues at director and senior manager levels. Is the onus on them to fit in? Or on all of us to be more inclusive?

Similarly, the tech industry is so male-dominated that men unconsciously benefit from network effects and women are penalized by them. Men in tech rarely have to walk into a room of women talking about stereotypically female issues, but the opposite is true in most women's daily lived experience. When you are an outsider it requires more effort just to attain the same norms. We can call this *minority stress*, something majority groups never have to endure. It is why a culture change is needed.

To see more diversity (representation) organizations need to increase inclusion through a more welcoming culture, which will attract, promote and retain different people.

HEARING THE PROBLEM

When trying to diagnose the extent of the culture problem in an organization, pulse surveys and engagement surveys can be useful. They help us understand if people like coming to work, enjoy the atmosphere and their colleagues, are challenged and fulfilled by their jobs, and feel like they are valued by and contribute to the company. All of these outcomes are correlated with an inclusive workplace culture, and they should be measured.

Some organizations also ask the questions explicitly: 'Is this an inclusive organization?'; 'Do you think the organization values diversity and inclusion?' These surveys can give us a good idea of the overall workplace atmosphere, especially once the results are disaggregated by demographic group. However, while that information is useful it's not enough. It only indicates the extent of the problem, not the cause; nor does it point towards a solution.

FEELING THE PROBLEM

The next step, then, is to figure out the cause of your engagement scores. What is making people feel more or less included? What behaviours and processes are your company engaging in that are alienating people, and who are they alienating? Only when we answer these questions can we formulate an effective response. In other words, we need to more accurately diagnose the problem in order to find the right solution. We need to run an Inclusion Diagnostic on the organization.

When Raafi was doing his Master's, this was the problem he focused on – finding a way to measure an inclusive culture by measuring the perceived frequency of behaviours that affect inclusion. Working with a client of ours, Wellcome, the world's second-largest funder of health research, he combed the existing academic literature and organizational best practices around inclusion and developed an Inclusion Diagnostic based on inclusive behaviours. These included perceptions of transparency and objectivity of personnel or salary decisions, psychological safety, microaggressions, negotiations, work flexibility, and other factors.

For example, we asked questions like, 'How often are your ideas attributed to other people?' and 'How much do you agree or disagree that using flexible work policies will hinder your salary or advancement opportunities?'

The reality of how much using flexible work might hinder advancement is important, but what is equally important yet often ignored is the *perception* that this is the case. If people feel that these non-inclusive behaviours are occurring, then they'll feel less included. It is this feeling that we measure when running an Inclusion Diagnostic.

What we found, perhaps unsurprisingly, was that different behaviours affect different groups to different extents. For example, LGBT+ employees particularly felt that more diverse recruiting sources were needed. Disabled employees felt that they needed to be more empowered to use flexible work policies. What's useful about this information is that it points towards specific solutions to bring people in and improve workplace culture.

For our LGBT+ example, having more LGBT+ recruiters, or having the LGBT+ employee resource group featured in recruiting can be an effective way of increasing the number of LGBT+ applicants whilst simultaneously showing support for current LGBT+ employees. Had this issue been about hiring more ethnic minority employees, we likely would not have made this recommendation because the evidence of its effectiveness is mixed on race.[5] However, there have been positive effects for LGBT+ people so in this case it may help.

For the example of disabled employees, making work flexibility the default rather than something you have to seek permission to do can signal that using flexible ways of working will not impede job progression. This not only helps disabled workers, but also helps working parents and people with other caring responsibilities.

These solutions may help your own organization's inclusion, but they may not. Until you run an Inclusion Diagnostic to establish the specific needs within the context of your organization yourself, you won't be able to know for sure.

FUTURE-SCOPE THE PROBLEM: DIVERSITY IS DIGITAL

We are living through a fundamental (as opposed to incremental) techno-logical revolution. The UK government understands the digital revolution to be one of the principal two trends affecting the nature of government in the 21st century. In 2000, e-mail was still being introduced to UK workplaces. By 2010 it was ubiquitous. It has completely transformed how we work in less than a decade.

Technology's disruptive power affects everything from the automation and changed delivery of key public sector services to the empowerment of citizens and their ability to hold leaders to account. But whilst we have witnessed an accelerated response to the technological revolution, we have not responded with anything like the same urgency to the diversity revolution.

In both 2000 and 2010 women made the majority of purchasing decisions across sectors[6] but they are still not in the equivalent corporate decision-making positions they ought to be. In 2014, more non-white babies were born annually in the United States than white babies[7] but there is still an ethnic penalty to getting a job,[8] being promoted[9] and chances of incarceration.[10]

Whilst we increasingly accept (if not totally understand) how the technological revolution is changing the nature of our work and lives, we have been comparatively slow to understand how diversity is.

TOO MUCH INFORMATION, NOT ENOUGH KNOWLEDGE

The data revolution has led to exponentially diminishing costs for generating, storing and processing data. Very roughly speaking, every five years the costs of storing data are one order of magnitude cheaper, and we have one order of magnitude more data to store.[11] Silicon Valley is pushing this trend as part of the elastic business model – more data to profile and optimize advertisements and operations.

Processing all that data generates lots of information and content. As such there is a race for customizing and contextualizing the user experience. As technology optimizes to our behaviour, we encounter less and less friction to consume a river of bite-sized content that caters to our beliefs and opinions.

Thus, this contextual information is inherently biased. We get what we like, in very effective silos, far away from a comprehensive view of the world's happenings. And we get an infinite buffet of catchy bite-sized content that displaces any other appetite for richer, more diverse content. It is in this very situation that fake news thrives, that biases can be activated, that polarization can be furthered and exploited.

With ever decreasing friction in accessing information, and ever refined personalization of what we consume, we are getting further and further away from genuine knowledge. Knowledge creation is the deliberate process of concentrating, filtering and absorbing information and constructing logic, the underpinnings that explain the information we get. Knowledge creation is based on diverse inputs, but we are filtering them out.

We are letting technology drive this consumer process and are insufficiently managing it. We get an 'optimized' view of the world and our networks, driven by an infrastructure that favours herd behaviour and shallow constant streams processed by machines that are actually learning. There is a risk we are leaving our brains out of the process.

The same is happening in organizations – we are not taking an active role in creating the diverse institutions or teams that we need in order to thrive. Instead, we are forcing workers to either assimilate or leave, which only leads to creating more silos. Just like with technology, in organizations we have misdiagnosed the problem.

MISDIAGNOSING THE SOLUTION: TECH IS NOT A CURE-ALL

The idea of leveraging technology to help de-bias our decision making is tempting, and many organizations are increasingly seeking to do this. However, we're now at a point where we may have gone too far in our assumptions of the objectivity of machines. While we may think artificial intelligence and computer programs will make us more objective, these programs are written by humans that are subject to bias. Relying too heavily on this technology, then, especially when tech is such a homogeneous field, can have drastic consequences.

For example, ProPublica, a think tank, analysed an algorithm called COMPAS which was used to predict the likelihood of criminal defendants reoffending in Florida. They found that it is twice as likely to misclassify Black defendants as more likely to reoffend than their white counterparts.[12]

This is not to say that we shouldn't use technology at all. Indeed, programs that de-bias our job advertising language or anonymize CVs for us can be extremely helpful. But the case of Florida highlights the importance of not relying too heavily on technology to do our thinking for us, and also of having diverse people involved in the development of new science and technology in order to help us notice our blind spots.

This doesn't mean that we shouldn't try to leverage technology at all when trying to increase inclusion in organizations, as we will see later in the book, especially Chapter 13. We just have to make sure we're using it cautiously and deliberately to supplement our inclusive activities rather than just blindly using it as a way to solve all our problems.

For example, take a tool like Textio. This web-based platform allows a company to input its job advertisements and descriptions, and it identifies words and phrases, as well as aspects of how the job description is organized (including the number of requirements) that might turn off members of more marginalized groups from applying. Their tool is based entirely on academic research, and then leverages machine learning to supplement that with their own findings, and is a really helpful way of encouraging a more diverse group of people to apply. But again, this is a supplement to help hiring managers mitigate their bias, and is not a cure-all. It is simply an effective way to leverage technology.

Another example of an effective use of technology in this space is Nottx. One of the biggest arguments we often get from clients when we suggest that they anonymize job applications is that it would take too much time and effort. Nottx attempts to solve this problem by doing the anonymization for you. Thus, no additional time or effort is needed – you just have to upload the applications you receive to their platform and they'll give you anonymized versions for you to review. Again, this is a way of leveraging technology rather than relying on it to solve all our inclusion problems.

As for leveraging Artificial Intelligence and other machine-learning technology for inclusion, there may be ways to use it effectively. But the key is not relying on it entirely. We cannot absolve ourselves of all responsibility when it comes to inclusion, we need to be a part of it. Technology can help us, but relying on it means falling prey to the same problem as we always have: applying a technical solution to a cultural problem.

LIMITS OF PSYCHOMETRIC TESTING

Another way organizations have become increasingly reliant on data to de-bias decisions is by having employees and applicants do extensive psychometric testing. Like technology, psychometric testing can be useful to help us understand different people's areas of strength or ways of working. But there are important pitfalls that organizations must avoid in order to leverage psychometrics properly.

First, ensure you're measuring something useful. Trying to understand if an employee is introverted can be helpful, for example, because it means that actively making space for and seeking out their opinion in one-on-one situations is more likely to get them to speak their mind than only speaking to them in large meetings. However, unless you are working in something that involves construction or design, an employee's visual-spatial skills may not be all that important. Measurement can be helpful, but measurement for measurement's sake is wasteful and only creates more opportunities for our biases to enter our decisions.

Second, your measurement tool must be right. Use scientifically validated tools like the Big 5 personality index instead of popular but unscientific tools like the MBTI. Non-validated tests only provide unreliable metrics.

Third, use test results to put different people together on teams. Often, organizations use these tests to weed out people who score differently than successful managers or partners at their firms. However, this is precisely the opposite of what they should be doing. Hiring for difference on teams means coworkers will have complementary skills and knowledge – they'll be able to spot each other's blind spots. Hiring for sameness results in groupthink.

Again, psychometric testing should not replace all evaluation. We must still employ critical thought to their results. Using psychometrics responsibly, though, can help us avoid some of our biases.

In order to harness this data, technology, and new metrics properly and in a way that will actually help us do better work and be more diverse and inclusive, though, we need a clear understanding of what biases are and how they work. As we will explore in more detail in Chapter 5, if we can understand the ways in which our subconscious sometimes reacts incorrectly, and importantly when we are more susceptible to these reactions, we can ensure that the way we are using data and technology actually helps solve our problems rather than exacerbating them.

DEEDS ARE GREATER THAN WORDS

When organizations adopt a Diversity 2.0 model based on marketing, as we discussed in Chapter 2, there can be some benefit from the actions that come from that. People certainly appreciate when an organization affirms its commitment to inclusion. However, people appreciate it even more when it acts on those words. And the more an organization talks about inclusion without following those words up with concrete actions and policies, the more those words ring hollow. That can make an organization's reputation even worse.

What's more, it means that while those words might get someone in the door they aren't enough to keep them in the room. In practical terms, those words might get someone to apply for a job, or maybe even take a position, but your attrition rate will be the real KPI of your level of inclusion.

The real challenge organizations face is about changing workplace cultures to adapt to those usually considered 'the other'. And if you want to truly solve this problem, you can't just blindly rely on technology, you can't expect things to change on their own, you can't be satisfied with 'doing no evil'. You need inclusive actions to keep people, to motivate people, and to create an environment where your employees and your organization thrive. And to make those inclusive actions effective and sustainable, we need to understand the biases that keep us from doing them in the first place. We will explore that bias more in the next chapter.

TAKEAWAYS

1 Appreciate how many organizations misdiagnose the real challenge in the first place – it's about organizational performance, not a segregated diversity work stream.

2 See, hear and feel the problem as much as you can to increase your understanding of the challenge.

3 Understand the importance of measurement and inclusion diagnostics to track your improvement.

4 Don't over-rely on tech and AI; use it judiciously to supplement your work.

5 Deeds are greater than words.

ENDNOTES

1 https://www.seattletimes.com/business/microsoft/i-felt-so-alone-what-women-at-microsoft-face-and-why-many-leave/

2 https://gender-pay-gap.service.gov.uk/Viewing/search-results

3 Steele, C M (2010) *Whistling Vivaldi: How stereotypes affect us and what we can do*, WW Norton & Co

4 https://www.nytimes.com/2004/04/29/business/letter-from-the-founders.html

5 Avery, D R and McKay, P F (2006) Target practice: an organizational impression management approach to attracting minority and female job applicants, *Personnel Psychology*, **59** (1), pp 157–87

6 https://hbr.org/2009/09/the-female-economy; https://www.forbes.com/sites/michelleking/2017/05/24/want-a-piece-of-the-18-trillion-dollar-female-economy-start-with-gender-bias/#6d3475d06123; https://www.forbes.com/sites/bridgetbrennan/2015/01/21/top-10-things-everyone-should-know-about-women-consumers/#38a435b96a8b

7 https://www.npr.org/sections/ed/2016/07/01/484325664/babies-of-color-are-now-the-majority-census-says

8 http://www.pewresearch.org/fact-tank/2016/07/01/racial-gender-wage-gaps-persist-in-u-s-despite-some-progress/

9 Beattie, G and Johnson, P (2012) Possible unconscious bias in recruitment and promotion and the need to promote equality, *Perspectives: Policy and Practice in Higher Education*, **16** (1), pp 7–13

10 https://www.sentencingproject.org/publications/color-of-justice-racial-and-ethnic-disparity-in-state-prisons/

11 http://www.datacenterjournal.com/cost-data-storage-management-headed-2016/

12 https://www.theguardian.com/commentisfree/2016/jun/26/algorithms-racial-bias-offenders-florida

5

EMBRACING AND
CHALLENGING BIAS

The first televised political debate in the United States was between John F Kennedy and Richard Nixon on 26 September 1960. Until then, all debates were aired to the public via radio – which many still used. And, just like in current debates, the media polled the public afterwards to ask them whom they thought had won. The vast majority of citizens who listened to the debate on the radio said that Nixon had got the better of Kennedy. However, those who watched the debate on TV agreed that Kennedy had just destroyed Nixon completely.

Famously, Kennedy was prepared for the spotlight. He was young and good-looking, his team had put make-up on him so his skin wouldn't reflect the light, and he wore lighter clothing so he wouldn't get too hot under the lights. Nixon on the other hand was sweaty, wore no make-up, and was just not as prepared for how he might look on TV. In the end, looks mattered in deciding the winner.[1]

This is not a unique experience. Alexander Todorov and his colleagues at Princeton University showed study participants two black-and-white portraits side by side for one second. For each picture, the participant was asked to select which of the two people in the pictures 'looked more competent' based on that one-second look at their photos. In each case, the participants were – unbeknownst to them – picking between two opposing candidates in the most recent US Congressional election. In the end, the candidate that participants thought 'looked more competent' was also the candidate that won the election 70 per cent of the time.[2]

Examples of this subconscious influence are not limited by industry or location either. Research published by the *Harvard Business Review* showed that in the Arab Gulf, men who looked like local middle-class men were less likely to be hired or given a promotion in a private company than those who looked 'international'. They also experienced negative social backlash when negotiating for pay similar to the experiences of women in the workplace in many North American and European countries.[3]

What these examples show us is that no matter how much we feel like we are making important decisions – like who to vote for or who to hire – based on objective criteria, we're not. Even though we think we are judging who supports the policies we like, who has the skills we think are useful, or who has the best plan to make the changes we want to see, the fact is that we are often making decisions based on irrelevant characteristics such as how a person looks.

This is what it means to be biased – to make judgments and decisions based on personal opinions that maybe shouldn't matter. Biases are some-thing we all have, and they're based on a long history of what we have heard, seen, and experienced throughout our lives.

TYPES OF BIAS: POSITIVE AS WELL AS NEGATIVE, CONSCIOUS AS WELL AS UNCONSCIOUS

Biases aren't always negative. In fact, they are often helpful in ensuring we get through the day without agonizing over every decision. For example, when we drink tea or coffee, we automatically opt to use a mug over a regu-lar disposable cup – we're using what Daniel Kahneman calls System 1 thinking. This is because we grew up subconsciously noticing that a handle was useful in handling hot beverages. We might have even learned this by burning ourselves, making us mentally associate hot drinks in mugs being good and hot drinks in cups being bad. And now, since we know this automatically, we don't have to run through a cost-benefit analysis or reason more deeply – what Kahneman calls System 2 thinking – about what container to use every morning because we already know the answer. Evolution has trained us to learn from our experiences and be able to be more efficient later on.

However, problems occur when we make inaccurate associations and apply these quick judgments in the wrong places.

This starts with explicit bias, which is not at all unconscious. It might manifest in the form of segregated schools in the United States in the mid-20th century, apartheid politics in South Africa pre-1994, women not being allowed to drive in Saudi Arabia until 2017, or LGBT+ people being imprisoned or sentenced to death. Explicit bias is a result of conscious choices based on clear beliefs that someone different from you for a specific reason is worse than you. We increasingly meet people in organizations undertaking 'unconscious bias' training, when in fact part of the problem may be conscious bias and we need to call that out and not simply hide behind 'unconscious' when we know full well that what they are doing is problematic.

However, much more common in the 21st century is implicit or unconscious bias, which is much more insidious. This is the type of bias exhibited in the examples at the beginning of this chapter. We think we're not being biased and actually making rational decisions, but non-rational beliefs that we don't even realize we have are influencing us. For example, take someone who was raised in a community where everyone was white, and the only images they saw of Black people portrayed them as violent thugs. It then starts to make sense that when that person sees a Black person in real life it might scare them – even if they don't think the reason they're scared is because that person is Black.

As another example, take the maxim about the surgeon and the car crash. A father and a son are involved in a fatal accident. The driver (the father) is killed instantly. The passenger (the son) is rushed to hospital. The surgical team, led by the surgeon, are gathered around the boy in a critical condition and about to start the emergency operation when the surgeon says, 'Stop! I can't possibly operate on this boy, he is my son!' How can that be?

Most people are confused or simply don't know. A few assume it is a stepfather. Some younger people we have tested this on suggest it is his same-sex partner. But very few people consider the possibility that the surgeon could be a woman, his mother. The stereotype (and our assumption) due to the norm presented to many of us by society, culture, and media is that surgeons are male.

This isn't the only way unconscious bias manifests. There are all kinds of biases that affect us in many ways. Catalyst identified 175 types of bias ranging from confirmation bias (seeking evidence that confirms our previously held belief rather than seeking evidence of the truth) to stereotype threat (irrational behaviour based on stereotyped identity, including of oneself).[4] The ones most relevant to the workplace are summarized in Table 5.1.[5] Most often, these biases tend to occur when we're tired, hungry, stressed, or otherwise preoccupied. We'll talk more about this later in the chapter, but for now suffice it to say that having bias is inevitable. It's in how and if we manage those biases that we have a choice.

HOW TO MANAGE YOUR BIASES

If you Google 'three black teenagers' you will get some criminal-looking mug shots. If you Google 'three white teenagers' you will get some smiley happy young people playing sport. This sums up yet another everyday example of how we are all deeply biased.

Google acts as a window into our soul – a mirror to our unconscious. One of the reasons bias runs rampant is because we are not even aware how biased we are in the first place. We assume our view is 'normal', our decisions are rational and our view of the world is *the* view of the world. That level of egocentrism may not cause problems to us personally when we are working with our in-group, who likely have a similar view of the world to us. However, it can cause problems for ourselves and for others when we interact with members of our out-group, like at work. Managed properly, though, these unhelpful biases could, in certain circumstances, be harnessed in a positive way.

For example, we might assume that women are introverted and less likely to speak up in a meeting. Regardless of whether or not that is true, it is a

Table 5.1 Types of bias

Type of bias	Definition	How it affects decision making
Unconscious bias	Bias that we are unaware of and which happens outside of our control	Decisions are made instinctively without thought or deliberation
Cognitive dissonance	The state of having inconsistent thoughts, beliefs or attitudes	Decisions are based on behaviours and attitudes, often to reduce tension and avoid conflict
Confirmation bias	The tendency to interpret new evidence as confirmation of one's existing beliefs	Prevents us from considering important information when making a decision
First acceptable option	Feeling compelled to some degree of making a quick decision	Deciding before considering other possibilities
Groupthink	Tendency of humans to agree with each other in order to prevent conflict	Decisions are based on similar or the same thinking
Framing bias	Taking into account contextual features of a situation	Base decisions on interpretation of the background to a situation
Egocentricity	Viewing everything in relation to oneself and being self-centred	Decisions are made on how the person making the decision sees things and not from others' points of view

stereotype that may or may not apply to the women we work with. However, we might leverage that assumption by ensuring we bring in all voices during a meeting – this way, not only might introverted women be helped, but all introverted people. We could easily use that bias against women to not promote them. Instead we reframe the situation and adapt to others. In a hiring context we leverage what we know about the bias to be inclusive.

This is just one example of how working towards mitigating the effects of bias can be helpful to more than just those we think are affected by it. In general, whether we think we have a particular bias or not, whether we feel like that bias is affecting our employees or not, it is important to work towards adapting our behaviours to be as inclusive as possible.

The journey to managing these biases can be thought of as climbing what Noel Burch called the Ladder of Conscious Competence.[6] We start off as unconsciously incompetent, not realizing our biases. We basically have the wrong intuition about how we're making decisions. This is the Google coder who doesn't realize their biases influence the search results for three black vs three white teenagers. This is the hiring manager who thinks they are always hiring the best person for the job and hasn't noticed that 80 per cent of new hires have been white despite living in a diverse area.

However, once we begin to understand our biases we then move to conscious incompetence. We understand that we have bias, but we haven't done anything to change that either because we aren't willing to or because we don't know how yet. The coder notices the difference in search results, the hiring manager realizes the prevailing whiteness of the people they've hired. This can be a particularly low point for leaders trying to be inclusive because they realize they may not have the right skills to solve the problem. However, this can spur us on to learn how to consciously change our behaviours and the organizational systems in place to be more inclusive.

At this point, we have moved to conscious competence, when we have begun to develop the skills and techniques to mitigate the effects of our bias or change our behaviours so that our biases have less chance to influence our decisions. The coder ensures people of other races are on their team. The hiring manager anonymizes CVs and consciously creates diverse interview panels.

Finally, when we continue to perform these inclusive behaviours repeatedly over time, we can move towards unconscious competence – doing the right thing without even thinking about it. The coder's team is diverse without even trying; the hiring manager's interview panel is automatically representative of the firm's diversity.

Below are three steps that follow Burch's ladder, showing us how to manage some of the most common biases we all share.

1. BIAS IS NATURALLY OCCURRING

First, acknowledge that bias exists and we are all subject to it. Reflect on our past experiences when we were less aware. For example, we might publicly state that we don't see colour. However, reflecting on our behaviour it becomes clear we do (and many people will tell you that they want you to notice their race or ethnicity because it is a part of who they are – they just don't want you to discriminate against them as a result). This goes back to the point about egocentrism that we made earlier: when we state that we don't see colour, it's more about us defending ourselves than really being honest. It centres the conversation about race on our reaction rather than others' experience.

Additionally, this is an example of cognitive dissonance (the difference between our stated intention and actual behaviour), which we mentioned in the table earlier in this chapter. We'll explore this concept and how to confront it more in Chapter 6 as well as in the case studies in Part Three but it is at the heart of making workplaces more inclusive. Moreover, it is at the heart of making ourselves more inclusive as individuals, and it is important to note how it manifests in each of us.

As we discussed earlier, problems occur in the workplace when we are over-reliant on System 1 thinking, especially when dealing with people. And we are more likely to do this under strenuous conditions.

For example, when we are under what Kahneman and other psychologists call 'high cognitive load' – when we are hungry, tired, stressed, under time pressure, or preoccupied – we tend to rely on our gut instincts, our System 1 thinking, more than our carefully reasoned thought. One example of how this manifests is a study about Israeli judges who give more lenient sentences after lunch when they aren't hungry rather than right before lunch when they are.[7] But this happens in all kinds of decisions in all kinds of workplaces; when we have to decide quickly who should work on a particular project, or when we are trying to get through a giant stack of job applications for only one or two positions.

What would be better is if we used Kahneman's System 2 thinking in all these decisions. So when we are deciding who should work on a project, we lay out the tasks to be accomplished and the times the organization has done those well in the past and simply select the people involved in those. When we are going through applications, we can ensure they are anonymized so that irrelevant characteristics like race or gender don't distract us from the more important criteria. These types of processes help us get past some of our biases, but what's important is to realize that we all have them and so we all need help.

2. BIAS IS PERSONAL

Second, become personally aware of your own biases. Only through becoming aware can we understand how those biases play out in reality. Try doing some of the activities we discussed in earlier chapters. Take the implicit association test (IAT) at www.implicit.harvard.edu to measure your implicit associations of people and stereotypes and benchmark yourself against the rest of the population. Determine your 'in-group' by writing down your closest friends, colleagues, partner and neighbours. Then consider who is not in this group – that's your 'out-group'. What are you doing to reach out to them? Finally, consider the simplicity of eliciting feedback from your colleagues, senior and junior, friend and foe. Making this personally relevant can be key not only for your own self-improvement, but also for bringing others on board. We'll discuss this in more detail in Chapter 6 on getting buy-in.

3. NEGATIVE BIAS CAN BE REDUCED

Third, now you are aware of some of your own biases, work out how you can minimize the negative ones. This is about becoming more consciously competent. Take an extra few seconds to breathe, count to 10, and shift your mind from System 1 to System 2 thinking. Move from unconscious knee-jerk reactions to more conscious reasoning. Get to know your out-group. Grab coffee, have lunch, join an employee network, change your hot desk location. Try to get to know others and change your frame of reference. Finally, walk in someone else's shoes – rotate the chair in meetings, take on the role of devil's advocate for a meeting, or simply listen to more/different perspectives.

Remember, understanding your bias is useful, but it's only the first step. To make any progress, you have to do something with that knowledge. The real value of that understanding is in how you apply it over time – to mitigate the negatives and make better decisions for you and your organization.

SELF

'COVERING' – WHEN WE CAN'T BE OUR FULL SELVES

Part of the issue with bias, especially for those of us who are minorities in some way, is that we know people are biased against certain aspects of who we are. But while these aspects might be more apparent for some minorities, certainly there are things we might be biased against in all people – for example, accent, weight, or introversion. Not everyone has bias against these parts of ourselves, but the risk that they do means that we will hide those parts of us that could be judged. Not feeling like we need to hide aspects of ourselves is likely what we mean when we talk about 'bringing your whole self to work' but how does this really work in practice and how can it apply to everyone?

'Covering' is the idea that we all conceal aspects of our identity or personality to fit in with the prevailing norm. In his 2006 book, Kenji Yoshino, Professor at NYU Law School in the United States, demonstrated that 45 per cent of straight white men 'covered'.[8] Rather than this being a minority issue (gay people not being 'out' at work, for example) even those who are generally considered not 'diverse' were affected by this.

Examples given ranged from stigma surrounding the need to leave work early to collect the kids from school, to discussion about mental health issues. Childcare, for example, is still traditionally seen as a female responsibility. Indeed, in parts of Southern Germany, the term *rabenmutter (raven mother)*, remains widespread, stigmatizing any woman that abandoned her 'nest' in order to pursue a career. Yet in addition to disadvantaging women through stereotype and confirmation bias (see Table 5.1 again), this situation also stigmatizes the man who wants to act outside the perceived male norm and actually just collect his kids from school.

Women often cover their femininity in order to fit in to a male norm and are thus disadvantaged as a result because they are not male. We know that in some of our client organizations there may be pressure for women to be more masculine to show that they have 'presence' and 'impact'. Indeed, Stephen was once told about a case where the proposed solution from one male partner to a quieter woman seeking promotion was to send her on an 'impact course'.

When women have to earn the respect of colleagues by acting masculine, we get into risky territory. For example, Ann Hopkins sued the professional services firm PwC when she was asked to cover. Her delivery suffered and her nomination for the partnership was taken away. She later went on to win this case and was the first person admitted into the partnership by court order.[9]

This case illustrates what is often called the double bind for women at work. When women aren't making it to the top in organizations, what's often blamed is that they aren't exhibiting the leadership qualities that the men are, like being staunch in one's views and being a strong negotiator. However, we now know that when women do exhibit those qualities they're seen as cold and uncaring, like Ann Hopkins might have been. This double bind is a big reason why gender pay gaps still exist. It's hard for women to be both liked and perceived as competent at the same time.

While somewhat less problematic than the double bind, men are often not able to act in stereotypically female ways either lest they feel backlash. To combat this issue, leaders have to be willing to take risks and be vulnerable. One of the most impressive things we have seen with one client is when two male leaders talked about their mental health issues in the internal magazine. You could also start by asking yourself whether you cover, what aspects of your 'self' you hide, and what you might want to do about it.

When you meet clients, and when you engage colleagues, ask yourself whether they are covering. By you explicitly talking about inclusion and your work in this area, you create a more inclusive environment that may allow them to uncover and to be themselves – to bring their whole self to that situation.

As inclusive leaders, we have a simple job that sometimes feels brave and is always significant. The positive power of disclosure lies in the very vulnerability you might feel while doing it. By talking about your own story, you create a more inclusive environment that gives others the permission to uncover and convey real honesty. That not only benefits them, it benefits the organization, client relationships and de-risks the environment.

Moreover, thinking about the way we and those closest to us cover can help us understand what others go through when they cover. This leads to increased empathy, and can help us be more inclusive as leaders.

ROLE

LEADING FROM THE BACK

In his 2014 book, *Lanterne Rouge*, Max Leonard[10] researched all the losers of the Tour de France cycle race since it started, in 1903.

Whilst we award a yellow jersey to the rider at the front, we also 'award' a red lantern to the cyclist at the back.

But consider, if you will, that the 'loser' has to psychologically work harder, physically ride longer and by the time they eventually finish they will have endured a lot more than the 'winner'. They may have 'lost', but they may have performed better than the yellow jersey would have were they in last place. In a different situation, the red lantern's skills in endurance and psychology might have turned out to be more valuable.

In our organizations, we need both: the yellow jersey can help the red lantern by going up front and creating a slipstream in which to follow at reduced wind resistance, making cycling easier and more efficient. Yet any yellow jersey also relies on a team that can take over the lead rider position from time to time to give them a chance for rest and renewal. Every member of the team has a role, and any individual glory is predicated on a team behind them.

Over the century of *Le Tour*, the gap between the first- and last-placed riders has narrowed. In 1903 the last-placed rider, Arsene Millocheau, finished 64 hours, 57 minutes and eight seconds behind the winner Maurice Garin. In 2017, Luke Rowe finished in last place only four-and-a-half hours behind his first-placed teammate Chris Froome.

The warning though is that this increasing homogenization of *Le Tour* mirrors increasing homogenization inside companies. A narrower time gap is viewed as a good thing, but actually it just means we are all more alike. We have a team of people with very similar backgrounds, skills, and experiences playing very different roles that they may not be best suited for. A few more Arsene Millocheaus would not necessarily be a bad thing.

The founder of the Tour de France, Henri Desgrange, said 'the ideal Tour would be one in which a single rider succeeded in completing the challenge'. This model of leadership was set forth in 1903 but it still prevails too often today. That is, our current model of becoming a leader focuses mostly on increasing individual skill sets. But we're in an era where the team and being able to flex our roles to bring the best out of each other as a team is much more important and effective.

So acknowledge the red lanterns in your team. They are an essential ingredient in our collective success. That's not just empathy, it's also inclusive leadership – we need endurance as well as speed.

FROM TRANSACTIONAL TO PERSONAL

Part of being an inclusive leader is recalling the areas in which we are the red lantern – the times in which we have felt excluded (recall our discussion of covering) – and using that to empathize with other team members or clients. Here are a few examples and ways this can help build relationships and make them more personal:

1 **By deepening relationships and building trust.**
   Recently, a director was terrified of the consequences of disclosing his mental health situation to a client. In fact, framed effectively, it made the client relationship stronger. The client responded with the fact that a family member had also suffered from depression.

2 **By increasing the touch points.**
   One of the ways London beat Paris in the bidding for the 2012 Olympics and Paralympics was because London concentrated on the smaller countries that the big countries (most notably France) ignored. They had a vote too. Steve recalls one time we had a board-level dinner with a client. At the end of the evening, comparing notes, some people had some good data on sales performance, M&A and current pipeline challenges. Others knew that the CEO's second son was autistic and he was deeply passionate about disability in the workplace, and having a perspective on disability inclusion was another way to reach the client.

3 By reaching the parts that others can't reach.

In one client example, a partner was struggling to gain traction with two new board members of a bank. Together, we crafted a note and an introduction – diversity was the secret sauce that allowed him to have a conversation and initiate relationships where previously the door had been shut. On another occasion, Steve held a networking dinner with a major insurance client, bringing together several African Caribbean networks. The energy in the room by the end of the evening was palpable and many new relationships have been initiated as a direct result.

Diversity and inclusion can be another tool in your toolbox – flexing your self and empathizing with those of others to reach them on a personal level, making your relationships that much stronger.

Understanding bias and knowing how to mitigate its effects is a key part of embedding inclusion in the workplace. And by working at embedding it, we can begin to climb the ladder of conscious competence so that eventually it becomes a natural habit. When we are able to do that, we and those around us will not have to cover as much, making it much easier to bring all aspects of our perspective to work. This is what will allow us to leverage diversity.

TAKEAWAYS

1 Bias underlies our inclusion problem – understand it and learn how to work against the negative aspects of it.

2 Bias is naturally occurring, it can be positive and negative and conscious and unconscious – but we can adapt to capitalize or counter it as needed.

3 Climb the ladder of conscious competence to become more self-aware and make more informed, accurate decisions.

4 Be your true 'self', role model, and help others feel like they don't have to cover.

5 Flex your role and build empathy, allowing others to bring their whole 'self' to work.

ENDNOTES

1 Druckman, J N (2003) The power of television images: the first Kennedy-Nixon debate revisited, *Journal of Politics*, **65** (2), pp 559–71

2 Todorov, A, et al (2005) Inferences of competence from faces predict election outcomes, *Science*, **308** (5728), pp 1623–26

3 Thomason, B, Bowles, H R and Al Dabbagh, M (2017) When men have lower status at work, they're less likely to negotiate, *Harvard Business Review*, 8 September

4 Catalyst Inc, http://www.catalyst.org/be-inclusive/unconscious-bias

5 Frost, S and Kalman, D (2016) *Inclusive Talent Management: How business can thrive in an age of diversity*, Kogan Page Publishers

6 Burch, N (nd) Four stages for learning any new skill, Gordon Training International

7 Danziger, S, Levav, J and Avnaim-Pesso, L (2011) Extraneous factors in judicial decisions, *Proceedings of the National Academy of Sciences*, **108** (17), pp 6889–92

8 Yoshino, K (2007) *Covering: The hidden assault on our civil rights*, Random House Trade Paperbacks

9 Sachs, A (2001) A slap at sex stereotypes, *Time*, 24 June

10 Leonard, M (2015) *Lanterne Rouge*, Pegasus Books, New York

PART TWO

LEAD

6

GETTING BUY-IN

At a diversity conference, the CEO opening the session read from a prepared script. He talked about why diversity was important to the bank that he ran. He quoted all the latest research. The diligence of his research team was evident. But the message didn't land with the audience.

The reason the message didn't land was because the message was generic. Any studious professional can amass a business case for diversity. But nobody in the audience really believed the CEO's words were genuine. If diversity was so important why did he need to read from a script? What was his personal view on it? Above all, why was diversity important to him?

There is no silver bullet to getting buy-in for building an inclusive organization. The nearest we can get is to make the case as personal as possible. Instead of a 'business case' this chapter focuses on the personal case. Whilst people may care about diversity and they may care about the greater good, they are busy with limited additional cognitive space available. As we discussed in Chapter 3, we need to make this personally relevant to them. So that they listen. And so that they ultimately 'get it'.

We need to know which buttons to press and in which order. We need to learn how to have empathy for those who might not appear to have empathy for us. And we need to be courageous and resilient, because this can be hard work. What follows is our experience of how to best create buy-in.

THIS IS NOT JUST AN HR ISSUE

Often, HR is not accorded high status in the organization. As such, HR professionals are often insecure about their status vis a vis 'the business'. Rather than challenge this, HR professionals often try to be 'business savvy' and curry favour with their internal stakeholders.

Of course it's important to be business-led and only undertake work that will add value to the organization. However, HR is business and business is about people. Rather than seeing HR as devolved from the business, it is key to see HR as an integral part of the business. Rather than just trying to be 'business savvy' remember, as CIPD CEO Peter Cheese said, that business also needs to be 'people savvy'.[1]

When diversity becomes a subset of HR and HR is itself insecure about its status in 'the business' you are admitting defeat before you've even started. As the Indian writer Sarojini Sahoo reminds us, it's important to simply be as we wish to be, rather than reinforcing an unequal power structure by playing into it.[2] So if we really understand diversity and the critical value it can provide for a business, we need to see it as a strategic resource that opens the door, rather than an issue that further reinforces HR segregation.

It is in this context that diversity is not just an 'HR issue' – it is a business matter. And by educating the business you are doing them a favour, not the other way around. This is the point you need to land with the people at the top of the organization – that you are there to help the organization run more smoothly and get the work done more efficiently and effectively. Diversity and inclusion can only do that if it is embedded in the whole company.

FIGURE OUT THE BEST WAY IN

D&I work can often be extremely difficult – it requires being willing to challenge people at the top, often including those who control your salary and determine whether you keep your job. What's more, it often requires challenging the very norms and systems in the organization that have helped it reach the point it is at now. Thus, we recognize that doing this work can take a lot of courage.

It also takes a lot of creativity to figure out how to bring people on board and how to solve the problems that exist in a way that is sustainable and effective within the parameters and capacities of the organization. With the right mindset of offering help and advice to the business it's then important to determine the best route to take. We suggest two routes.

1. STRATEGY ALIGNMENT WORKSHOPS

The first is an approach we have trialled with several clients to great effect. In order to circumvent the hierarchy evident in an organization, we assemble the key decision makers in one room for a joint session. We lead them through a process of understanding the business problem we are collectively trying to solve and how inclusion and diversity might help. In essence, we cover three agenda points. What is the problem we are trying to solve? What levers do we have at our disposal? What is the order in which we pull them?

Table 6.1 How to align your strategy

Goal	Question
Common definition	What is the problem we are trying to solve?
Resources available	What levers do we have at our disposal?
Plan of action	In which order do we pull the levers?

Sometimes when we do this, we find that the problem leaders think they are trying to solve is really just the surface-level issue – we don't have enough women, all the minorities are leaving, no young people want to join. But the real problem we're trying to solve is the underlying issue – our workplace culture just doesn't work for those people. And it's important that the leaders come to this conclusion themselves, even if you help guide them there. This is important to get the most powerful decision makers in the organization to actually own the challenge from the outset. And then with greater appreciation for the challenge and how we might go about solving it, they are more likely to be supportive during the subsequent journey.

We continue to see colleagues who struggle on, hitting brick wall after brick wall. It is much more efficient to get the senior people and decision makers to own the problem from the outset. This will not only educate them – it will also increase their empathy towards you as the person leading the change.

2. INCLUSIVE LEADERSHIP PROGRAMME

This programme is deliberately designed on a 'little and often' basis which has been shown to be a far more effective learning method than 'one-off' diversity training.

Table 6.2 Inclusive Leadership Programme overview

Stage	Input
Marshalling the evidence	Organizational data framed in an effective way. Individual data to hold up the mirror.
Group session 1	Reframe diversity and inclusion as a leadership issue.
Feedback and prep for 1-1	Chance to reflect.
1-1	Exploring cognitive dissonance.
Feedback and prep for Group session 2	Chance to reflect and plan actions.
Group session 2	Sharing of actions.
Ongoing actions	Being held accountable.

First, marshal the evidence for change in the form of organizational data and frame it in an arresting way. For example, rather than just list the gender or racial diversity by department, order the departments from most to least diverse to positively frame the information. Ideally, construct a dynamic projection model showing the consequences of their recruitment, promotion and retention decisions (or lack of decision) on the population diversity in two to three years' time. This proved very effective at KPMG, Virgin Atlantic, Harper Collins and in other organizations we have worked with.

It is also important to bring to the fore individuals' own personal data on their own leadership style, biases and goals. Due to resource constraints you may only be able to do this with the senior decision makers but that's a great start. We have them fill out a simple diagnostic survey on their understanding of the issues and their self-awareness of their own leadership style. We also explore their biases by having them take the implicit association tests described in Chapter 5.

For people who have never confronted such issues before this can be a challenge. They may need time to reflect and to process. Giving them the opportunity to have a coaching session to privately explore their results and understand them can be invaluable. By reframing diversity for them as a leadership issue and then exploring cognitive dissonance (the difference between what they say and do, for example) we can lead them to determine their own actions to close the gap.

For example, the CEO who reads out a speech on diversity and publicly rates it business-critical might in private think it is a low priority linked to lack of understanding or care. The gap between intention and action is why most diversity programmes fail. Privately, when it is easier for people to admit ignorance or be vulnerable, we can explore how to close that gap.

A final session on actions is important to begin the process of holding people accountable. It is important that these actions be concrete, specific, and achievable, but also that they not be so small that they feel they can do them in a week. Often, if one of the actions is a behaviour to turn into a habit, other participants can hold them accountable and support them in achieving that goal. This leadership programme invariably ends up with people in a much more positive place than after conventional training. Instead of the trainer telling an unreceptive audience, the audience is co-creating their own leadership actions, in an informed and sustainable manner.

What this journey of seven touchpoints achieves is a game changer compared with standalone unconscious bias training or diversity training. That's because you can't change habits in three hours. You can't even change habits in a few days. It of course varies by task and by individual but 66 days-plus is often cited as the minimum required to see behavioural change.[3] Little and often, the chance to go on a journey, and above all the chance to personalize the journey to make it individually relevant results in far greater buy-in.

REDEFINE DIVERSITY AND INCLUSION

If you ask someone how they identify in terms of diversity they may be slightly shocked by the question. On reflection, you may get demographic data such as their gender or race. This would fit with most legislative environments that have some form of 'protected characteristics'.

On further reflection you may start to get less obvious data such as any hidden disability, or sexual orientation. These may also be covered by legislation, though it is far less ubiquitous than race and gender. Should you go even deeper you may end up learning about personality type, political view, or significant historical background or life events. The point of this exercise is for both of you to appreciate that diversity is infinite.

There are of course important patterns of similarity, such as race, often linked to systemic forms of discrimination and bias. But ultimately, diversity is infinite and as such is actually quite an inclusive concept. We are all unique, something we have in common. This can help us avoid tokenism. It's not just about recruiting more women, for example. 'Women' are diverse (just like men). Some women and men are feminists, some are not. Some white people are racial equality activists, and some are not. No two people are the same, and it is this diversity of people and their perspectives that makes it valuable.

The importance of this can be seen in overcoming the 'othering' tendency of many (male) executives that diversity is about somebody else. It is actually about all of us.

REFRAME THE CONVERSATION

With a fresh perspective on the subject matter it is important to reframe the conversation. If you ask people to care about diversity or help you, you risk activating confirmation bias by reinforcing the negative stereotype many people hold about D&I initiatives. If you reverse the power dynamic and ask how you can help them, you start in a different place.

If you ask someone to tell you about a time they have felt excluded, you may get a couple of reactions. First, you may get people who never feel they have been. However, on further probing most of us (even the dominant group) have experienced exclusion – just not as often or as systematically or as seriously as others. But this appreciation is an important start. We witness male executives who feel they have been passed over for promotion, or left out of an important meeting, or not invited to a function. This, on one level, is exclusion.

A second reaction might be a real sharing of vulnerability about a serious case of exclusion.

In both cases, it is important to empathize with the fact that people have experienced exclusion and then, if possible, to translate this to how other people have also been excluded; to build empathy between different people who have both experienced the same feeling.

Asking people to recall a potentially painful event or memory is a risk. So it's important to follow up with a supportive question that lowers the temperature. Once you have asked them how they felt, move them onto what could you have done about it? Is there anyone around you now who might feel similar? How could you include them? How could they include you? If you can push it further onto the subject of adaptation, great, remembering the platinum rule we discussed in Chapter 2 – treat others as *they* wish to be treated.

BUILDING EMPATHY (ACROSS THE DIVIDE)

People who might be dreading a conversation on D&I may be pleasantly surprised if you start by asking them how they are doing. Being an executive today is significantly harder than it was even 10 years ago, and one of the primary reasons is stress related to high cognitive load.

We pay people to process data, turn it into information and generate organizational knowledge. We are expected to process data and information and use it to reason and make good decisions in the interest of the organization. The challenge is that we are now living in an age of near-ubiquitous data and infinite information. The amount of information is increasing at an exponential rate. However, our ability to process that information is not. We have to pick and choose which information we see and, as we discussed in Chapter 1, we aren't always doing a good job of that if the goal is to build knowledge.

Advances in machine learning have fostered incredible content curation. Yes, it's easier for us to access content we like, but it's also easier to avoid content that challenges us. Machine learning has come at the expense of human learning. They take in all the information they can, from all sides of an argument, and are able to turn that into useful knowledge. We humans, on the other hand, are heading deeper into our own bubbles through the advent of things like social media and aren't able to challenge our arguments as strongly. So the gap between the expectation and our ability to make (good) decisions is getting wider by the day.

Start your conversation with empathy for the person confronting this new reality. They are almost impossibly stressed. That also means their ability or desire to entertain a conversation on D&I which they may immediately perceive as a threat or at best an opportunity cost, will be limited.

So say you understand and explain the above. Then ask them how they are coping with it, what their plan might be. And offer them the two choices we described earlier:

1 Option one: get an executive coach, a mentor, a counsellor, or other support to try to help them process a huge amount of information and help them with their decision making.

2 Option two: look around and include as much diversity as you can handle. If you let different people speak, they can help calibrate your thinking.

It is also important to appreciate that their understanding of bias, inclusion, and the other concepts we've discussed may not be at the same level as yours. Their understanding of the systemic issues facing minorities that lead to inequality may not be at the point where they've confronted the manifestation of those systems in their own behaviour. They may understand how inequalities exist in the very structures of society, yet they may also still fail to see that they play a role in upholding that unequal structure, as we all do.

Consider what has brought you to where you are – how much thinking, reading and self-reflection has gone into your own journey. It is unreasonable to think that if they are just starting they'll be convinced or jump on board right away. Thus, appreciate that they might be just at the beginning of their journey, and try to meet them where they are. It may help them realize that if used effectively, diversity is free and in infinite supply. The key dependency is leadership style.

REFRAME INCLUSION AS A LEADERSHIP CONCEPT TO DRAW OUT ITS BENEFITS

Including people with different perspectives can also mitigate risk by challenging bad decisions, groupthink and bias. You don't need to pay people more money for them to have a different viewpoint, perspective or skill set. But you need to include them to benefit from this difference.

Including people by allowing them to bring their whole selves to work can increase their productivity. We know that people perform better when they can be themselves. In a small company, like ours, people often get more job satisfaction from being able to be themselves and have more direct responsibility and client contact. This is a free way to retain people and motivate them to deliver excellent client service.

Including difference also increases the resilience of firms. Think of your company as a toolbox. When faced with a problem to solve or a solution to build would you rather have a toolbox of hammers, or a toolbox of different equipment that allowed you to get the job done quicker, and with more resources and options at your disposal?

We spoke earlier in this chapter about the need to create knowledge and ensure we aren't just letting technology filter out challenging information. Leadership is needed to bring different (biased) people together to create knowledge and applied solutions to our global and local problems. We need to rethink how technology can support thinking, not replace it. Mentally, the consequence of information selection is that we only consume what we believe in and we filter out challenge. Without challenge, we are less likely to engage in conscious reasoning. Without conscious reasoning, we are at risk of becoming even less diverse in our thinking.

Increased awareness of the digital revolution therefore goes hand in hand with increased awareness of diversity and bias. Only by remaining curious of both can we fully capitalize on the phenomenal opportunities that exist all around us. Whilst this change is in some ways terrifying, the positive potential of diversity remains there for the taking.

INCREASE SELF-AWARENESS AND HELP OTHERS INCREASE THEIRS

As we discussed in Chapter 5, if you say, 'I don't see gender, I just treat everyone the same', then you probably need to become aware of your own bias. Challenge others in your workplace to do so as well. They don't necessarily need to share their learning or test results with anyone, but it can help them reflect on their behaviours and experiences.

Remember that conference you went to? If you are a man, perhaps you were oblivious to the fact it was all guys in blue suits slapping each other on the back and talking football. Go to a women's conference, such as FT Women at the Top or Catalyst and see how it feels to be one of the only men in a sea full of women. We have both been in those situations before, and it's difficult, exhausting, and even sometimes humiliating to have to justify your presence at every turn. Realizing that can help you empathize as a leader and understand what you might be able to do to include your more marginalized team members.

EXPLAIN CONCEPTS LIKE SYSTEM 1 AND SYSTEM 2 THINKING

In Chapter 5 we discussed Daniel Kahneman's concept of System 1 vs System 2 thinking – our quick, instinctual reactions vs our slower, more reasoned decisions. We have found that explaining bias with this framework helps many people understand the concept much better and makes them much more receptive to solutions since it is not predicated on them being bad people.

One helpful illustration of this is an awareness test video: in the most common version, two teams of people, one in black uniforms and one in white, pass around a ball while moving around each other. We as observers are asked to count the number of passes the team in white makes. While the teams are passing and we are counting, a person in a bear or gorilla costume walks into the frame, dances a bit, and then exits. What is amazing is that if we are focusing on counting the number of passes – the task to which we were assigned – we don't even notice the bear or gorilla at all. It's easy to miss what you're not looking for. And even if one has seen this video, there are other versions where multiple things change like the colour of the background or the number of team members, making it even harder to notice everything that changes.

When we are concentrating on a specific task, we are often so focused that we miss the more important event. We all have blind spots that become exacerbated when our System 1 thinking tells us to ignore anything not specific to the task at hand, but these blind spots can be overcome with more diverse viewpoints – different people notice different things and they can calibrate our thinking, pushing us into System 2 when necessary.

MIMICRY AND SENSE OF RESPONSIBILITY

In Chapter 1 we mentioned the role of mimicry in workplace inclusion efforts, and how people tend to mimic those in power. If the people with the most power exhibit inclusive behaviours, especially if they are open about the fact that they know they have biases and are working to fix them, and give specific examples of what they plan to do, they will affect everyone below them in the organization as well. This can be a powerful tool to convince those at the top of your organization to be more conscious of whether or not their behaviour is inclusive. Not only might it appeal to their sense of responsibility, but it can change the entire tone of the D&I conversation across the organization.

DELIVER: SHOW THE PROMISED LAND

Appealing to leaders' sense of responsibility dovetails nicely into another way of getting buy-in – helping them see their personal win. When we work with HR or diversity teams in organizations, they often ask us to help them convince the C-suite by giving them statistics about how D&I efforts can help the organization. While we are able to provide evidence showing that diverse and inclusive teams are more engaged, perform better, make better decisions and more accurate predictions, and ultimately tend to make the organization more money, we also often explain that these arguments will only get them partway towards their goal.

This evidence helps people understand cognitively why they ought to be more inclusive, but it often is not enough of a motivator to affect what they actually do day to day. What really helps change minds, hearts, and more importantly behaviours – what gets people to bridge the intention-action gap and fix their cognitive dissonance – is helping them see how they personally, individually, can benefit from diversity.

Explaining to leaders how D&I can help them personally be more efficient at their jobs by having a greater number of perspectives at their disposal gives them something personal at stake. Framing the lack of diversity as a lost opportunity for making a better decision may help give them a bit more skin in the game. Reminding them that the workforce is becoming increasingly diverse and that being more consciously inclusive now puts them a step ahead of the competition can increase the likelihood that they will buy in.

HeForShe interview

The following interview was conducted on 13 July 2017 by WeAreTheCity, a UK-based organization that helps companies find female talent. They were specifically asking us questions about our feelings regarding HeForShe, the UN Women campaign to bring together men fighting for gender equality across the globe.

Why do you support the HeForShe campaign? For example, do you have a daughter or have you witnessed the benefits that diversity can bring to a workplace?

Gender is by definition about both men and women. All of us are under pressure, all of us are facing unprecedented professional challenges, and all of us need all the help we can get. We support the HeForShe campaign because, as men, it's in our own self-interest to have greater gender equality as well as being the morally right thing to do. Morals are a personal choice and we find sexism deeply unjust and distasteful. But above, and perhaps beyond, the moral case we like to base our arguments in evidence and all the evidence we have reviewed over years in our profession has led us to conclude that there is a meaningful correlation between diversity and performance.

How welcome are men in the gender equality conversation currently?

It varies. Steve was speaking as the 'token male' (the moderator's words, not ours) at a recent *Financial Times* 'Women at the Top' conference in London. He made the point that (caveat, he was a man) people, men and women, cannot bring their full selves to work. By only focusing on a narrow definition of what it means to be 'women' there was a risk that we were promoting those women that most fitted the existing male-dominated culture.

Half the room really appreciated this point. Half the room didn't. Women who are fitting in to a male culture, rather like gay people in the closet, or disabled people hiding their disability, might be most threatened by men who care about gender equality. Men who care about gender equality are important allies and they need to be embraced and supported.

It's harder for men to admit weakness in a male-dominated stereotypical culture and they need to be encouraged – particularly by other men – to come to such conferences and encouraged to speak out.

Do you think groups/networks that include the words 'women in...' or 'females in...' make men feel like gender equality isn't really their problem or something they need to help with?

There is a risk of that. Of course there's a need for any 'minority' group to network proactively in a majority culture because otherwise the network effects are stacked against them. But if it's only about fixing the minority then it does remove the responsibility for the majority group or the system to self-correct.

What can businesses do to encourage more men to feel welcome enough to get involved in the gender debate?

Focus less on language and technical issues and more on encouraging conversation. Make it clear there is an issue of self-interest at stake here. We are not seeking charity, we are seeking performance. The notion that we are all working in perfectly functioning meritocracies is fanciful. Gender inequality is a market failure. Any senior male leader in business should be concerned about that, be concerned about economic inefficiency and seek to correct it to improve business performance.

We spend a significant part of our professional lives training men to reframe diversity as a personal leadership issue that can actually help them and their business. So business can instigate inclusive leadership programmes, even keynotes, that particularly target the men.

Do you currently mentor any women or have you in the past?

Yes. We both have women as mentors and we mentor them too. It's important to point out that it shouldn't just be men mentoring women; that could just compound the problem. Reciprocal mentoring, reverse mentoring, active sponsorship, two-way education and female role models are all important.

Have you noticed any difference in mentoring women – for example, are women less likely to put themselves forward for jobs that are out of their comfort zones or are women less likely to identify senior roles that they would be suited for?

Yes. On average, women tend to self-select out more and men tend to self-select in more. So we know that on average men tend to put themselves forward for promotion when they can fulfil half the criteria for a job whereas a woman would hold back until she could fulfil 90 per cent of the criteria. We know that men are more likely to be vocal about pay and negotiate when dissatisfied, while women are more likely to keep quiet and just leave rather than negotiate (since negotiating puts them in the double bind we discussed in Chapter 5). These are patterns professionals should be aware of. Our job is then to offer tools and solutions to help them lead effectively.

HELPING MEN (AND OTHERS IN POWER) TAKE ACTION

One of the difficulties we often encounter – with male leaders in particular – is that once they've bought into the idea that inclusion can be good for them they don't see what they can do themselves. They just don't know where to start. Instead, they simply apologize for the problems that exist. Giving them some concrete actions can be extremely helpful in getting their buy-in and having D&I land as a personal leadership issue. Chapter 7 has some insights and practical actions that people could take.

TAILORING THE ARGUMENT TO THE AUDIENCE

Not every technique we've discussed here will help D&I land with every group. The arguments that will bring executives on board will not necessarily work for entry-level staff. However, to change company culture and embed inclusion throughout the organization, everyone should engage in inclusive leadership and practice inclusive behaviours. And that means bringing everyone on board.

For executives and upper-level managers, workshops on inclusive leadership that touch on the topics we've discussed like unconscious bias and making inclusion personal can be very effective. Our own Inclusive Leadership Programme which we described earlier has shown great results, in particular because it involves multiple approaches at multiple points over multiple months.

For employees that are less senior, bringing them in through embedding inclusive practice in the organization's processes and procedures, transparency about why diversity is important, keynote addresses, and shorter workshops and training sessions on the same topics over longer periods of time are great for showing that D&I is important to the organization.

DEALING WITH BACKLASH – POLITICAL CORRECTNESS AND POSITIVE DISCRIMINATION

Political correctness was a term coined in the 1970s as a completely understandable and, we would argue, justifiable response to downright dangerous and offensive language regarding minorities by people who sought to maintain sameness in their lives and countries.[4] However, it has since acquired negativity of its own, and is still often used to discredit anything that might challenge the norm that has served some people very well.

Now we have 'positive discrimination', a term that is the weapon of choice to discredit any action that might be completely justified in combating an inefficient labour market, or an unjust hiring decision.

An example would be female promotions. In a recent round of promotions at a professional services firm, some brilliant women made it through the selection process and were promoted to partner. In fact, of all promotions in the firm, 33 per cent were female, above its current female population of 14 per cent. When the norm is 86 per cent male, anything that challenges that norm can be discredited as 'positive discrimination', even though every one of the women promoted was better than other men (or women).

So, while positive discrimination is in most cases disagreeable, the term can also be a lazy crutch, used as a label to discredit selection and promotion decisions we disagree with. If we really want the best, then we should have no problem with a wider talent pool, more competition, or challenging our norms and current world view.

Diversity is no bed of roses. It means more, not less, competition. But it also makes for stronger, more resilient organizations, more productive workforces (when led well) and less risky decision making. Above all, diversity is the enemy of mediocrity.

INCLUSION IS FOR EVERYONE

In the end, the way to make D&I land is by reconciling self-interest with collective interest. We have to make the case for having some 'skin in the game'.

We can point out the dangers of sameness, noting that homogeneous teams can be more susceptible to risk and endure lower resilience and lower productivity over the medium to long term. No manager wants their team to be a failure. We can also point out the benefits of diversity to all when properly led. Managers want their teams to thrive.

But it's important to remember that embedding inclusion is a long-term process, and it often isn't easy. As much as we remain optimists, the world is in a pretty dangerous place right now and being drawn to sameness, not difference, is the default position. That's why we will never outgrow the need for a diversity strategy. As long as human beings keep associating with similar people, then appreciating difference will always need to be encouraged and taught.

TAKEAWAYS

1 Reframe this as a personal and business issue (not an HR issue).

2 Think about your approach – strategy alignment workshop, Inclusive Leadership Programme, and remember why 'one-offs' don't work.

3 Redefine D&I and reframe the conversation – this is about you adapting rather than expecting they will.

4 Build empathy and increase self-awareness – think about your in- and out-groups.

5 Think of some practical examples like #HeForShe that could help you act on and test out your new understanding.

ENDNOTES

1   Closing keynote speech, Peter Cheese, CEO, CIPD, Manchester, Annual Conference, November 2016

2   Sahoo, S (2010) *Sensible Sensuality*, Authors Press

3   https://www.spring.org.uk/2009/09/how-long-to-form-a-habit.php

4   Hamilton, C (2015) Political correctness: its origins and the backlash against it, *The Conversation*, 30 August

7

DESIGNING A PLAN
THAT WILL WORK

At this point, we've discussed the context in which we are attempting to do this diversity and inclusion work at the societal, organizational, and personal levels. We've then talked about why past efforts so far have been unsuccessful, and how we are misdiagnosing the problem we're facing. Understanding what has gone wrong, and what we're working with to try to get it right, is crucial to making sure our efforts are effective.

Likewise, it is important to understand the psychological mechanisms that underpin our behaviours, like the biases we discussed in Chapter 5. Finally, we discussed how once we understand all these things we can bring others into our plans and get buy-in to set ourselves up for success. What follows here is how we actually design our plan once we have the organization on board; the next chapter will discuss making it sustainable.

HOW TO BUILD A MERITOCRACY

Often, we think of D&I as something to do on the side. But really, all we are trying to do with D&I work is make sure teams have the best people to do the job, and that leaders are able to bring the best out in their team members. It is simply a plan to build a meritocracy, not a segregated plan for a D&I initiative.

If you're a male-dominated organization, especially at the top, you're probably not a true meritocracy. People towards the top of the tree are more likely to believe their organization is already a meritocracy. This is often based on an egotistical analysis of how they got there. However, take a random poll from people at all levels in the same organization and the result might be slightly different.

True meritocracies don't just happen. They need to be built. Building meritocracies often meets resistance from people who think they are already the product of the meritocracy. They don't want to upset the apple cart. Any intervention may therefore be perceived as a Stalinist intervention in an otherwise perfectly functioning labour market.

But to build a meritocracy we do need to upset the apple cart. Repeatedly. Disruptively. To build a meritocracy we have to first open up the supply of talent to raise standards through open competition. Then we need to increase demand for all talent, whatever it looks like, and subject our talent decisions to rigour and transparency. For specific examples of how an organization might do this, see Chapter 8, with specific case studies of how they worked in Part 3.

DEVELOPING YOUR PLAN

To successfully build an inclusive organization, you need a plan. It needs to guide you and your colleagues to define the tasks necessary to enact the overall strategy and in what order. The plan should be framed in an Inclusion 3.0 fashion, aiming at embedding inclusive decision making in the key systems, processes and leaders in the organization.

The plan will benefit from five key areas of focus:

Figure 7.1 Key parts of your plan

We will go into detail on each of these areas below.

STRATEGY

What is your overall approach? The D&I strategy is simply about strengthening the organization and achieving the overall mission. So first, you need to define your goal. With one firm we worked with that goal was higher productivity of teams (critical to the financial and overall performance of the organization). Inclusive leadership permits greater team productivity. With another organization it was to create a consistent culture of inclusion, which:

1 encourages higher performance and motivation, especially in the leadership;

2 calibrates, challenges and refines decision making;

3 challenges and stimulates sluggish areas;

4 encourages confidence and bravery;

5 is better for talent attraction, promotion and retention;

6 increases well-being;

7 contributes to consistent customer and client experience;

8 contributes to growth, new business and clients.

DEFINING YOUR GOAL

You might benefit from using phraseology from existing organizational plans and strategies. What language does the business already understand? Is there an existing strategy you can embed your D&I strategy into? For example, we have worked with government agencies in several countries whose laudable goal is to keep their country safe. By embedding inclusion in the organization they can increase loyalty and engagement of existing staff and recruit from all communities. The D&I goal is therefore the same as the organization goal – safety through inclusion.

On other occasions we worked with banks, whose goal is financial returns. Often the diversity work is seen as a cost and therefore counter to the overall driver present in the organization. The goal needs to be embedded, so in this case what are all the ways inclusion could contribute to the goal of financial returns? Through talent acquisition, promotion and retention? Through risk mitigation? Through stakeholder relations and entering new markets? The goal needs to be interrogated, agreed to, and stated clearly up front.

Your goal may include diversity (representation), particularly of female and ethnic minority talent. This is laudable because representation is important, especially role models at senior levels, ideally being representative of all available talent in the market. However, try to push this further. What about disability, LGBT+, other under-represented groups. Push it further to consider cognitive diversity, introversion and social mobility. However far you push representation, remember that it is not a zero-sum game and should never be allowed to be framed as such. It must be additive, not exclusionary. You can't start aiming for cognitive diversity and forget about race and gender. This is all part of the same idea.

However, your goal, ideally, should also include inclusion. This is about leveraging diversity for innovation and all the business case reasons we have stated. And without inclusion, increased diversity likely won't yield many positive benefits. The goal is really that everyone in the organization 'gets it' in terms of articulating why D&I matters to them and the organization and actually lives it as demonstrated through behaviours. You could argue that if you start with inclusion, diversity will follow. But if you only focus on representation, you might actually be missing the real value-adding work.

BUY-IN AND POWER DYNAMICS

Thinking about buy-in, start with aligning the key decision makers behind a shared understanding of your approach to prevent problems down the line. Not doing so could lead to those decision makers wanting to make changes that are key to your plan. Additionally, if they feel like they aren't part of the process, they may be less willing to put the plan into effect or less trusting of the plan's effectiveness. The process we have used successfully in several organizations has been the understand, lead, deliver model we trialled at the London Olympics and Paralympics in 2012 and have discussed in earlier works (The Inclusion Imperative, Inclusive Talent Management).

Another important consideration when designing your strategy is ensuring that the bulk of the onus is placed on the people with power. When it comes to gender equality, for example, this means making sure that the programmes you design are focused mainly on the things men can do to be more inclusive of women for organizations in which men dominate positions of power. While we might have some aspects of a gender equality programme in the workplace that encourage women to lean in, it is even more important to design and implement programmes that encourage men to lean back and create the space for women to participate more fully.

SCOPE AND PROCESS

It's important to define your scope and the process you intend to follow. Throughout our work we have recommended you make the scope as wide as you can support. It starts with people (HR) and should cover the key steps of the people journey (at minimum recruitment, promotion and retention). You can then think about procurement and client service, besides additional functions such as legal, communications and marketing.

If you are resource-constrained, you might want to limit yourself to parts of HR and demonstrate a real difference in a focused area. However, even here you will need to at least be aware of other areas in that they impact and are impacted by recruitment and promotion decisions, for example. In terms of looking at the organization overall, focus on those areas that most impact the overall goal of the organization. In professional services you have to look at client relations. In manufacturing you have to look at production. In tech, you have to look at coding as well as support services.

Consider the geographical reach of your plan. Is it just one office, one country, one market or global? How are you defining the regions? Could you focus on the high-growth areas that are more likely to have the biggest recruitment and talent needs?

In terms of process, it is important to appreciate this is a journey, not a series of events. Think about the ladder of conscious competence and where your colleagues currently are. They need to understand the basic ideas in this book, they need to lead as a personal responsibility, and they need to be held accountable for delivery. This is an iterative process over years but it can be condensed into a one-year cycle in a three-year plan. To see a real example of what this might look like when bringing together all five areas of focus, see Appendix 1.

COMMUNICATION AND ENGAGEMENT

Finally, when you are ready to roll out your strategy, it is imperative that you communicate well with everyone in the organization. All employees are stakeholders in developing a more inclusive workplace, and it is important that they know they have input, and that the goal is to create a better workplace for everyone. Communicating the benefits of more diverse and inclusive workplaces is key, but we have also found that also key is communicating the reasons why particular interventions have been chosen. Being able to back up these decisions with the data you gathered as well as the research underpinning the intervention can be very effective for this purpose.

Another way to communicate your strategy and increase engagement with your D&I initiatives is to leverage your organization's employee resource groups. By going to those groups' meetings and explaining how you plan to be more inclusive and how you came to those decisions can be a very effective way of getting employees on board. It is important that you are transparent about what you are seeing in the data and how you're interpreting it, and check in with them to make sure you're interpreting the data as accurately as possible. This will also ensure that these groups, who often feel marginalized, are heard, and that in itself could actually help them feel more included.

DATA

What is your overall baseline and how will you measure change? We suggest you undertake an inclusion diagnostic, like the one we described in Chapter 4, to get an accurate sense of what is going on in your organization that is creating your workplace culture. We also suggest you make the scope as wide as possible given resource restrictions and differing legal jurisdictions. Define your baseline and then calculate your targets, ideally using a dynamic projection model. Get key people to understand the modelling and the realistic expectations they should have about the journey ahead.

GATHERING DATA

The first step is to actually monitor your organization's diversity. Most organizations monitor some protected characteristics like sex and age, and in some parts of the world it is common to have everyone's ethnicity data as well. However, it is important that organizations go beyond this because there are many groups that are often discriminated against in the workplace.

Any characteristic protected by law against discrimination should be measured, including sexual orientation, gender reassignment, parental status, and disability. However, you should also consider going further to monitor characteristics like socio-economic background and level of introversion.

One issue we hear often is that employees don't want to disclose their diversity characteristics. Our suggestion is that you change the framing of the questions and the collection method to elicit a higher response rate. For example, if you phrase the questionnaire along the lines of 'whilst this is voluntary, most people share the data in order to allow us to measure our success in creating an inclusive environment', it can elicit a higher response than 'the below is voluntary'. In addition, if you frame the collection as an 'opt out', ie the expectation is that you complete it, like you would bank details in order to get paid, this can elicit a higher response than an 'opt in' method, where you have to convince people to take part in the first place. Finally, be sure to gather this data through an anonymous survey, which could make many employees more comfortable since the information would not be tied directly to them.

At KPMG, a 93 per cent response rate was achieved through linking the questionnaire to the point where they filled out timesheets. Everyone had to complete timesheets and a pop-up window at that moment nudged people to complete the diversity information. Whilst this was of course voluntary, you had to at least acknowledge the questionnaire by preferring not to say before you could progress to complete timesheets.

The next step is to measure your pay gaps. Many organizations, particularly those in the UK, have published their gender pay gaps and it has brought to light potential discrimination that many may not have realized was going on. However, it is important also to analyse pay gaps along other diversity metrics as well, and where possible to measure the pay gaps at the intersections of diversity characteristics. For example, how does the pay of white men compare to that of white women, Black men and Black women?

Many pay gaps are in part a result of marginalized groups not being promoted in the organization, so the next step is to develop a diversity projection model to see what your organization will look like at different levels of seniority in one, three, and five years. By looking at your joiner and leaver rates by demographics at different levels, and your promotion rates at each of those levels, you can see what the future of your organization looks like. You can then adjust those rates for future years to see what might happen if you, say, increase the promotion rate for women by 25 per cent and decrease the leaver rate for women by 15 per cent in the next year. This can help you understand what reasonable expectations might be for your organization's diversity.

Finally, you should measure how inclusive your workplace culture is. As we will explain in more detail in Chapter 8, culture is what you do – it is a product of behaviours. So consider the various behaviours that might be contributing to or detracting from inclusion in the workplace, and ask employees how often they feel these behaviours occur.

LEVERAGING YOUR DATA

Once you've gathered all this data, you will be well set up to choose the right interventions for leadership and nudges in your organization. Use the data from your diversity monitoring and diversity projection model to help set targets and benchmarks for you to reach. Ideally, you should have one set of benchmarks that are realistic and achievable, another set that are still achievable but might be a stretch goal, and a final set that are your ideal targets (we often use proportionality with the general population as the ideal target). You should then do your best to implement interventions that reach for those ideals, and even if they are not immediately achievable, this at least gives you a long-term goal.

You can also use your pay gap data and inclusion diagnostic data to choose particular areas of focus. One option is to focus on particular demographic groups, and often interventions that are designed to help include one group can actually be really effective for all employees. Another option, though, is to focus on particular behaviours.

Using the data from your inclusion diagnostic, you can see which behaviours are detracting from inclusion the most, and can implement leadership training as well as embed nudges in the organization's policies that are specifically targeted at changing those behaviours. For example, if you see in the data that employees with young children feel like their needs aren't being taken into account when planning meeting times around school runs, consider making it easier for people to join meetings virtually or set a precedent that agendas should be passed around a day or two in advance so that those who can't attend have an opportunity to give input even though they can't be there in person.

Data can be extraordinarily powerful if leveraged properly. By using the data you gather to develop more specific, targeted interventions, you will create much more sustainable and effective change.

GOVERNANCE

How will you manage the change programme and hold people accountable? Define your key stakeholders and prioritize them with a management plan. Who has the most to gain or lose through your plan? Who might feel like they have a lot to gain or lose? Perception can sometimes be as important as reality when trying to get a new strategy off the ground. Moreover, who are the key people whose names will be on the line at the end of the day? This could range from the CEO down to the bottom of the ladder. Whomever you decide the key stakeholders are, you should map them out and prioritize who you will bring on board for governance of your strategy.

Next, decide your communications approach to them including method and frequency. Will you meet in person regularly, or communicate via other channels? How often is that feasible, especially if you are all dispersed across the globe? How far in advance will you share your plans, and should you include pre-reading materials like academic papers that speak to the topic at hand?

Resource your team, both immediate and wider, understanding what talents you can draw upon to execute. Just like your organization, you want a diverse team with a variety of skills and knowledge. This will allow you to have multiple tools at your disposal when implementing your strategy. Moreover, having a diverse group at the helm of working on D&I ensures there won't be a backlash about the irony of a D&I team not being very diverse.

Remember to account for official power as well as unofficial influence. People from 'the business', people at a variety of grades, in a variety of departments, in a variety of roles. Who is in your out-group that you need to include in order to make this plan watertight? Who will be productive contributors who could best cover your blind spots? Who will be the strongest advocates of the plan post creation? It is crucial to engage with a diverse group to ensure buy-in and success across the organization.

CREATING A GOVERNING BODY

Implementing all these nudges and trainings is a difficult and time-consuming task. Moreover, trying to impose them on people can often cause backlash and disengagement. As such, it is important to create a steering group in charge of choosing the interventions and tailoring them to the organization's needs. You should also discuss the order in which these interventions should be done, creating short-, medium- and long-term plans for increasing D&I, as discussed above. Having a clearly laid-out strategy can help keep the organization on track and hold the steering group accountable to themselves and the benchmarks they set.

A good rule of thumb is for the board to own the strategy and hold the Executive accountable for delivery. The trick is to get the Executive to agree to this. They may decide to co-opt a Diversity Council to run it and update them. If this is the case, think about existing scope – are there any bodies in operation already, even if a collection of enthusiastic amateurs? Perhaps they are regional, department or even office based.

Additionally, by engaging with leaders from different parts of the organization in this way, you can bring them on board early, and have them bring their teams on board as well, creating broader ownership of the initiative. This can help to ensure that your interventions are more likely to be successful. Moreover, by bringing in a diverse cohort to help you design, implement and oversee your strategy will help guard you against your blind spots and provide different perspectives, ensuring that your strategy is as effective as possible.

Establish a Diversity Council or steering group including key decision makers and establish or co-opt employee resource groups. You need to decide specifically which key people you need on your team to ensure success. These could include members of the teams in charge of each of the areas under your scope (recruitment, promotion, retention, legal, etc). Alternatively, you may decide that because of how your organization is structured you may wish to include representation from each of your regional offices. You may also decide that you need someone on the team with greater access to the executive leadership or board, or someone from each of your employee resource groups.

STAKEHOLDER MAPPING, USING YOUR TEAM WISELY, AND CREATING ACCOUNTABILITY

Map out your key stakeholders. There are various frameworks to help you do this, but think about official decision-making capacity and unofficial power and influence. You need to map the key people and assess where they are on the journey. At the professional services firm we mentioned earlier, we used a red, amber, green rating system to assess level of buy-in amongst the 600 partners. Upon feedback (largely from partners in the majority) we changed this to bronze, silver, gold, so everyone was a winner and no fragile egos were offended. A table like Figure 7.2 can be helpful.

Figure 7.2 Stakeholder mapping framework

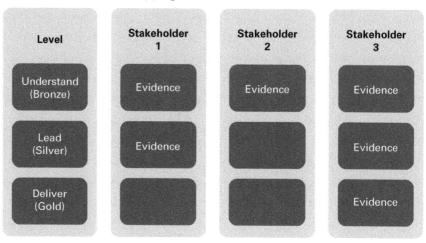

You can determine the key players and their current level of understanding and buy-in around D&I. Let's label them Stakeholder 1, 2, 3 and so on, along the top horizontal axis. Are they at an understanding stage? If so, we could categorize them as 'bronze' on the left vertical axis. Are they advocating and leading on inclusion? If so, we could categorize them as silver. Have they achieved tangible results? If so, we could label them gold. In all cases, look for clear evidence. Then, once you have defined your key stakeholders and ascertained how many different types of medal winners you are starting with, you can prioritize them with a management plan.

Think about your team and the resource you need to execute the plan. It might just be one person, or even part of one job. In this extreme situation, your relationships with the key stakeholders will be even more critical as you will be asking them to commit time and resources to help you. If you are lucky enough to have a team, think about how you most effectively allocate the work. Traditionally, it has been on 'strand' basis, one on gender, one on LGBT+ etc, but this is increasingly obsolete if we are focusing on inclusion. Think about the overall business plan. See if you can allocate people to work on diversity/inclusion relating to the work streams of the business in general, so workforce, procurement, clients for example to tie in with the overall process.

In terms of accountability, you want to ensure as much accountability as the powerful decision makers will embrace (or tolerate). Hence the importance of getting your stakeholder mapping and governance structures aligned behind the plan. Implementation is where plans fall down and accountability on D&I is as close as you can get to a silver bullet.

Consider how you embed inclusive behaviours in competence assessments and 360 feedback. One professional services firm has now linked 360 performance to remuneration which provides a very clear link between desired behaviours and reward. Anyone in the organization could provide valid input to any partner or director in the firm. Transparency minimizes malicious comments. One construction company linked 50 per cent of bonuses to 360 performance. The reported changes in behaviour were significant and almost immediate.

EMPLOYEE RESOURCE GROUPS (ERGS)

These can be incredibly useful if the terms of reference are clear and the Chairs have clear and transparent job descriptions. Not only do these networks provide support and advocacy for employees from marginalized groups, but they can be your natural strategic allies in getting buy-in and communicating your plan. Further, if you involve these groups (or at least the Chairs) in the design of your interventions, they will be even more on board and you will have begun to create a coalition of like-minded colleagues in the organization.

Additionally, when analysing your data you should be transparent with employee resource groups about what you are seeing in the data and how you're interpreting it. They might see patterns you don't or confirm suspicions you're unsure of. Check in with them to make sure you're interpreting the data as accurately as possible. This will also ensure that these groups, who often feel marginalized, are heard, and that in itself could actually help them feel more included.

Furthermore, ERGs can be a great hub through which your interventions are run. It can be the origin point of your programmes. As we will discuss in Chapter 11 on the tech industry, some organizations have found that when they run their D&I programming through ERGs the whole can be greater than the sum of the parts. For example, when interviewing candidates who are members of a marginalized group, you could put them in touch with ERG Chairs so they can know what it's like to work at your organization as someone with that identity. This would help the candidate feel like your organization truly cares about their well-being, the candidate can feel like they won't be alone, and you will have another way to convince people to join your company.

However, if you don't get ERGs on board with your plan early, they may be reluctant to help you implement your interventions. In the end, consulting with ERGs about your plan is a good way to ensure that the people you will be affecting most have some level of ownership of the plan, that they will be willing to help you when you need it, and will help you cover your blind spots.

LEADERSHIP

How will you gain buy-in from the key influencers in the organization? Bearing in mind the limitations of traditional diversity training and unconscious bias training, define your approach to ongoing education and support to your stakeholders, as we described in Chapter 6. We recommend keynotes followed by work such as an inclusive leadership programme or a series of labs. It's an ongoing journey, not an event.

INCLUSIVE LEADERSHIP

One of the issues we often discuss with our clients is that the biggest difficulty isn't necessarily writing more inclusive policies and procedures (though that is a difficulty). The biggest difficulty is ensuring that those policies and procedures are implemented and followed. We can very easily work with an organization to compile best practices of how to run inclusive meetings and set out those guidelines for managers, but often those managers don't follow those guidelines – either because they forget or because they actively think they aren't worth it. They filter out the content (or policies and procedures) they don't like.

And when leaders exemplify those inclusive behaviours and follow those guidelines and best practices for inclusion, other employees follow. That's when the information we give to an organization becomes knowledge that is embedded in that organization's way of working. It's part of the ethos of the organization. That's why the first step in designing a plan that works is to get leadership on board.

One example of where this has worked is Wellcome – an organization we discussed earlier in the book where we ran the inclusion diagnostic. We mentioned that one of the aspects of inclusion that we measured in the inclusion diagnostic is psychological safety. In essence, psychological safety in the workplace is the concept that one feels comfortable expressing disagreement and dissent with one's teams or supervisors, offering a controversial or unpopular opinion or idea, taking measured risks (often to innovate), or potentially making mistakes.

Much of the time, those who do not fit the norm of society or of the organization – that is, people from marginalized groups – feel like just being their authentic selves bucks the norm so much that there might be backlash, and so they don't feel psychologically safe because they fear further rocking an already rocky boat. Making all workers feel psychologically safe, then, would make them more comfortable being who they are, and so more included.

When we first discussed this concept with Wellcome's diversity and inclusion team, they really liked the idea and wanted it to be part of the culture they fostered there. However, it wasn't until the D&I team discussed it with the leadership team that it really took off as a more widely known concept there. Wellcome's leaders, when they heard about psychological safety, what it was, and how their employees felt about it at Wellcome, really latched onto it as an idea. It was a concept that really resonated with them. As such, these leaders started talking about it more and more, in their meetings, in their intranet publications, in their communications.

Now, more than a year later, the term psychological safety is understood and used by many staff at all levels. In this way, the information we gave over a year ago has now become organizational knowledge. But it could not have happened if it had not resonated with the leaders and they had not exemplified its importance by consciously discussing it widely.

Without leadership, information does not become knowledge. The information remains shallow and biased. And knowledge creation only works if the incentives for creation and management are aligned with the core values of an organization. HR could encourage cross-functional collaboration, perhaps by creating secondment opportunities from one function to another. This would allow employees to notice places of overlap in work and come up with more creative solutions that cross the organization. You could also check how you allocate work by checking in with those who you manage to see the kinds of projects they've been on and the people they've worked with to ensure diverse teams.

Embed inclusive leadership as a standard leadership competency. For example, leaders need to be aware of their in- and out-groups, and actively diversify the circles they move in and recruit from. Make that unconscious behaviour more conscious. As we have discussed already, we are governed by norms, and these are directly related to leadership behaviours. As we discussed in Chapter 1, inclusive leaders have to constantly review:

1 which norms are enabling and we want to preserve;

2 which norms are limiting and we want to challenge;

3 which norms are in the 'too difficult' box and we leave for another day.

At a financial services client, we surveyed the entire Top 150 leadership group and asked them for examples from each of the three categories above. We came up with some fantastic insights, generated by the leaders themselves, that we could play back to them. They could then see what behaviours they needed to amplify and which ones they needed to address.

At some of the organizations with the smallest gender pay gaps, we have recently conducted inclusive leadership programmes with largely male teams. The purpose of this is to hold up the mirror (to the men in particular) and reframe diversity as a leadership issue (for them personally). By taking them on a journey over a period of months we can avoid the usual failing of 'diversity training', which is usually restricted to an individual session or short series of sessions, and instead focus on repeated behaviours that sink in over the course of the programme. People internalize diversity as a good thing in their own self-interest and are far more receptive to seeking it out as a result. This has resulted in more men stepping up and calling out behaviours and practices that would disadvantage female progression and inclusion.

SYSTEMS

How will you embed inclusion in the processes of the organization to support all the above? Start with the overall organization business model and work backwards from what the organization is trying to achieve. Identify the key processes such as recruitment, talent management, marketing and business/client delivery and who owns them. Work with the owners to analyse the processes end to end, identify areas of bias and then prioritize your interventions accordingly.

Redesign your systems and processes such as recruitment, promotion and marketing. Regardless of individual world-view, people can act more inclusively by default through using nudges and behavioural economics to influence behaviour. For example, hiring teams over individuals can result in a more meritocratic and more diverse cohort. Use principles of behavioural economics, or nudges, to subtly alter the remaining unconscious behaviour so that the organization becomes inclusive more organically. We'll discuss this methodology in more depth in Chapter 8 and provide examples that have worked with our clients.

We deploy nudges throughout HR processes and systems. We analyse a system (let's say promotions) and we identify the gaps and biases in it. Then we prioritize which ones to intervene in, and de-bias them by implementing process changes (nudges). These are often low-cost or even no-cost changes that make organizations more inclusive.

Recent examples include presenting anonymized CVs side by side, implementing mixed panels, and recruiting and assessing groups of individuals at the same time, not individuals one by one. While these may seem like rather simplistic solutions, they have been shown to have outsized effects. That's the beauty of this approach – nudges are designed to be easy to implement, cost-effective, and still make a difference.

Another example: at one client, we led a series of sessions involving all regional Chairs to map the three-year talent pipeline for the business.

They placed their initial candidates' names on a large whiteboard in red ink by groups of one, two and three years away from promotion. Then they rewrote female names in green. This showed that women had been de-prioritized in the process to date. Candidate by candidate they discussed the business case and the reasons for each candidate's position and slowly but surely many women started to advance from three years out to two years out to 'promotion ready'.

We were leading a process to point out the group's collective blind spots. None of them were maliciously sexist or consciously discriminatory. But all of them had been susceptible to the blind spots that come from 1–1 promotions, without the big picture view of group aggregation. They simply didn't know the women as well as the men and the women hadn't put themselves forward as obviously as the men. This process resulted in more competition, more rigour in decision making, and more diversity in promotions. We will go more in depth on systems in Chapter 8 of the book.

ENSURING SUSTAINABILITY: DEEDS, NOT WORDS

There will never be enough time or money and you have to prioritize. We highly recommend you focus on Inclusion 3.0 leadership and systems work that will make a difference. If you really want to promote more diverse talent, continue your supply-side work but focus a lot more on the demand side. Ensure not only that you are recruiting more diversity, but make sure those in your organization understand the benefits of diversity and demand it. And by all means continue your unconscious bias training, but focus a lot more on the real unconscious behaviour going on below the surface.

As Bob Diamond said, 'Culture is what you do when nobody is watching'.[1] Now they are. You can't apply a technical fix to a cultural problem and expect to solve the problem. If you really want to build an inclusive organization, follow the steps outlined here. Make sure your plan has a clearly defined scope and process, and brings in the right people to help you define those. Together, you and your team can collect and analyse your data to decide the specific interventions in your plan.

Focus on the interventions that will reduce the risk of your own biases coming into play in your decision making. Focus on embedding those practices in your everyday work. Include interventions that don't just involve changing your processes and procedures, but also getting your leaders, especially your male leaders and other leaders from less marginalized groups, to be exemplars of inclusive behaviour. Creating a plan in this way will help create a sustainably inclusive culture, something we will explore in more depth in Chapter 8.

TAKEAWAYS

1 Frame your plan: diversity and inclusion is about building a meritocracy. Define the scope and the process carefully.

2 Acquire, analyse and leverage data effectively to gain insights, set targets and measure progress.

3 Think carefully about your governance – stakeholders, communications, your team, a council and employee networks – how will you hold people accountable?

4 Consider your leadership engagement plan to create ongoing buy-in (and deal with backlash).

5 Think about the systems you want to influence and who controls the processes you need to de-bias.

ENDNOTE

1   Diamond, B (2011, 3 November) *Today Business Lecture, 2011*, BBC Radio 4, London

8

HOW TO MAKE
IT STICK

CULTURE IS WHAT YOU DO

In the early 1930s, Danish carpenter Ole Kirk Christiansen decided to branch out from making furniture to start making wooden toys. His company – founded on the principle of bringing joy to people's lives – was named after the Danish phrase *leg godt* meaning 'play well', hence the name Lego. He based his entire company's way of working on this idea of playing well, bringing joy, and never promoting the opposite. This governed the products they made, the way they worked, who they employed, and how they expanded. It came to be known in the company as 'The System'. Sticking to these principles and creating a company culture based on them served Christiansen and Lego well for a long time.

When the Second World War began, and many toy makers started to profit from making weapons, Lego stuck to their guns of never promoting the opposite of joy and only made toys that promoted peace. While they didn't expand quickly during the war, having their products reflect a culture of peace and joy helped them do extremely well during less popular wars like those in Korea and Vietnam.

However, the advent of video games in the 1990s started to make Lego obsolete. They needed to find a new way to engage their market. Ole's grandson, now at the helm, saw an opportunity in Bionicle – action figure-style toys that fought with weapons. He departed from The System and started building toys based on fighting. It was innocent at first, and led to an increase in profits, but not everyone at Lego was on board. Part of what many employees loved about the company was The System – they were dedicated to it and felt that this was a departure from their identity.

Over time, Lego dove increasingly deep into this new market. They built fighter jets, and spaceships that could shoot projectiles, and other sorts of weapons. This made them money for a while, but employees became even more concerned about where the company was going – things had changed at Lego. People felt like they didn't know whether they'd get fired, or even if entire departments might get eliminated. The System might have truly been lost, and the company culture had changed.

In 2004, most of Lego's revenue was coming from fighting scenes from only two movie franchises, but that year neither of the franchises released a new movie. As such, people weren't as interested in those products. Lego nearly went bankrupt. Their overreliance on short-term moneymaking had now not only changed the culture of the company but had potentially sunk the family business.

After speaking to company employees, they finally saw just how much the culture had changed at Lego. People weren't as dedicated as they used to be. People felt afraid. When Lego had changed its products and behaviours for profit, it had changed the culture. And in a culture of fear, nobody had room to innovate.

So, they went back to The System. They focused on updated versions of their old toys and became less reliant on toys based around fighting. They built toys that told stories and then built stories to make people laugh. And the market responded. Their profits skyrocketed to 125 per cent of the previous year, and by 2011 Lego had become the largest toy company in the world.[1]

When leaders of the company who lived through that time were interviewed, they often spoke about the importance The System – that culture matters, and behaviours create culture. The same is true of any organization. Earlier we mentioned the quote by Bob Diamond, 'Culture is what you do when nobody is watching'. While what often gets attention is the 'when nobody is watching' part, an equally important part of the quote that gets less attention is, 'Culture is what you do'. Culture is what you *do* – it is active, it is a product of our behaviours.

To change a company culture, then, we must change behaviours. If we want to build a more inclusive culture, we must make our behaviours more inclusive. This chapter will provide a methodology to support and create sustainable, effective behaviour change that will drive a more inclusive culture. Additionally, this chapter will provide some examples of effective interventions to embed inclusion in your organization.

THE FALSE PROMISE OF UNCONSCIOUS BIAS TRAINING

Diversity trainings have been around for a long time, and most commonly in the past they came in the form of a one-hour or at most a half-day session, which maybe happened once per year. People in HR knew that people needed to change the way they acted, and they thought that if they told people what not to do and how they could get in trouble if they didn't heed that advice, then they wouldn't do it. The idea was based on the assumption that discriminatory or offensive acts were conscious behaviours that offenders knew they were doing.

And yet, unfortunately, this discriminatory behaviour continued. Indeed, one study conducted in 2006 looking at more than 700 workplaces from 1971 to 2002 showed that having diversity sensitivity training had almost no correlation with increasing diversity, and in some cases actually had a negative effect due to adverse reactions to mandatory trainings.[2] Clearly, this method was not working.

More recently, practitioners and academics alike learned that most behaviour that led to a lack of inclusion – that offended marginalized groups or made people feel like their voice didn't matter – was actually unconscious.[3] The offenders didn't realize that their behaviour was offensive in the first place, and even if they did realize that such behaviour detracted from inclusion they often didn't even realize they were doing it at all. What's more, these practitioners and academics realized that everyone has bias towards some group or another, and more often than not that bias was directed towards the same groups – women, ethnic minorities, disabled persons, introverts, and other marginalized people. So the answer seemed quite simple: get people to realize what they're doing, and they'll be able to stop it!

Thus began the advent of unconscious bias training. This is probably the most common form of diversity and inclusion training in organizations now, and those that are doing it seem to feel like this is the most cutting-edge, effective training they can do to help make them more inclusive. The problem is, we've known since at least 2016 that unconscious bias training on its own doesn't work either.

Harvard University professor Frank Dobbin and his colleague at Tel Aviv University, Alexandra Kalev, published research showing that just doing unconscious bias training does not actually make much difference in actually making people behave more inclusively.[4] In fact, they found that when people learned about the concept of unconscious bias, that everyone has it, and that it's a product of growing up in our current societies, many people attending these trainings not only felt helpless to change it but also that it wasn't their fault and so not their responsibility. As a result, they stopped being apologetic about engaging in subtly discriminatory remarks and behaviours, and just leaned into those biases.[5] This is actually such a common reaction that behavioural psychologists have a name for it: Moral Licensing.

If you think about it, though, it makes sense that just doing this type of training doesn't work. Just because someone is made aware of the fact that they're doing something wrong doesn't mean they are actually able to stop doing it. They need to have the skills to stop doing it. This is why, when we run unconscious bias trainings, we insist on people – at a minimum – doing a fair bit of pre- and post-work to help them gain skills to act on what they've learned. Better yet, while they build those skills we could put in place systems that would help to reduce the frequency of opportunities for bias in the first place. This model, we suggest, is the way forward to make truly effective and sustainable change. In fact, this is how we change everyday behaviours. Changing behaviours is how we change organizational culture.

NUDGES

In Chapter 5 we discussed bias and how it often manifests in all of us, and for good reason – we need to be able to jump to conclusions quickly and subconsciously in order to deal with all the decisions we make on a daily basis. And we develop our ability to make those quick, subconscious decisions by observing the world around us. However, we also discussed that when used incorrectly these biases can lead us astray and push us to make irrational and suboptimal decisions. What's worse, these biases are so deeply ingrained in us that they are extremely hard, if not impossible, to get rid of.

But there is good news in all of this: while we humans may often be irrational, we are, as Duke University psychologist Dan Ariely puts it, 'predictably irrational'.[6] That is, while certain signifiers may cause us to behave sub-optimally, those behaviours are consistent. For example, we humans are extremely suggestible by orders in lists. One example where we see this is that when people are in a restaurant they are significantly more likely to order the first or last item on a menu.[7] This might seem somewhat trivial – and in the context of a restaurant it might be – but consider how many lists you see every day, and how important a role they play in decision making.

Possibly one of the most important contexts in which this plays a role is in the most sacred duty of any citizen of a democracy: voting. It turns out that the order in which the candidates appear on the list has a significant effect on how many votes each candidate gets. This name-order effect is such a well-known phenomenon that we can actually quantify the extra benefit a candidate gets from being at the top of the ballot. Political scientists Saad Gulzar from Stanford University and Nelson Ruiz from the London School of Economics calculated that being the first name on the election ballot increases your share of the votes by 6.6 per cent on average.[8]

What's great about this is that if certain aspects of our environment can consistently predict our behaviour, we can frame that environment to increase the likelihood that we engage in behaviours that we want. In other words, rather than trying to accomplish the potentially impossible task of eliminating our biases we can use our biases and heuristics to our advantage to help us make better decisions. When we do this to help us make more inclusive decisions or act in more inclusive ways, it can help us make more inclusive cultures more broadly. In essence, this can be a way towards cultural change.

In our restaurant example, let us say we want people to eat more healthily. Rather than try to convince customers that they should order the salad or grilled chicken, we can simply place those items strategically on the menu so that they are more likely to be ordered. In our voting example, if the goal is for all candidates to have an equal opportunity (as much as possible) to be elected, we can randomize the order in which candidates appear on each ballot so that different voters see the candidates in different orders.

These subtle changes to help us make better decisions are what behavioural scientists call nudges. And since there are, as we saw earlier, so many ways in which humans can exhibit bias, there are equally so many ways to nudge ourselves. In fact, nudges have been shown to be effective in an incredible number of contexts and fields – from public health to environmental sustainability, from saving for retirement to donating to charity, from increasing cleanliness to not snoozing the alarm in the morning. And yes, this has also been shown to work in diversity and inclusion.

NUDGING FOR INCLUSION

When thinking about how using nudges might be a useful methodology to create more inclusive workplaces, it's easy to see the benefits it provides. Unconscious bias training can provide a solid foundation to bring awareness about our biased behaviour, and the leadership work we discussed in earlier chapters can help us understand and make commitments to the personal work we can do to develop the skills we need to be more actively inclusive.

Nudges, though, can help us make sure that while we are in the process of building those skills we've built our organizational environments up in a way that sets us up for succeeding in practising those skills. In other words, these nudges act as a form of cultural support, helping to facilitate and encourage our desired more inclusive behaviours to create a more inclusive workplace. Additionally, nudges tend to have little to no cost, are relatively simple to implement, and can be embedded in organizational policies and practices, making them sustainable. The next sections focus on examples of what some of those nudges might be.

NUDGES FOR MEETINGS AND OTHER INTERPERSONAL INTERACTIONS

One very subtle but common type of unconscious behaviour that leads to the exclusion of marginalized groups is microaggressions, which can be defined as 'the constant and continuing everyday reality of slights, insults, invalidations and indignities visited upon marginalized groups by well-intentioned [people they interact with]'.[9] Microaggressions often go unnoticed by those who perpetrate them, and can have negative consequences for work performance, job satisfaction, employee engagement[10] and mental health.[11]

We know from research that many employees from marginalized groups, particularly women and ethnic minorities, are more likely to be interrupted, talked over, or have their ideas attributed to others in meetings by higher-status individuals.[12] This leads the lower-status employees to be less likely to contribute to conversations, voice dissent, or feel as though their work and opinions are valued by their team and the organization more broadly. Therefore, it is clearly very important to reduce the frequency of microaggressions when colleagues are interacting with each other.

Two potential nudges to reduce microaggressions are:

1 **Set language and behaviour norms.**
   One of the biggest microbehaviour contributors to non-inclusive environments is the language used in that place. By setting language norms at meetings that promote inclusivity, employees will feel like the organization values inclusivity more, are more likely to speak up in meetings, and will come up with more creative and innovative solutions to problems. Specifically, the research shows that stating at the beginning of a meeting that there is a norm of not using sexist language can have these positive inclusive outcomes.[13]

2 **Hang photos of counter-stereotypical high achievers on walls and in meeting rooms.**
   Attitudes and stereotypes about what types of people are good at particular activities can affect not just those with whom we interact, but also our own performance. Exposing minority groups to images of successful members of their group can counter these negative stereotypes, increase performance, and promote inclusion.[14] Most of the research on this intervention has been done on gender biases, but the

theoretical underpinning of these studies[15] was originally done on race, and has been extended to apply to other marginalized groups as well.[16] This indicates that the intervention could work for implicit racial bias and bias against other groups also.

Another way to be more inclusive in meetings and other interpersonal interactions in the workplace is to attempt to increase the level of psychological safety. As we have previously explored, psychological safety refers to how comfortable people feel to express dissent and disagreement, to innovate and potentially make mistakes, or to bring up potentially unpopular opinions or ideas. When people feel that they are different or have different opinions from the majority for whatever reason (maybe their race or gender has meant they experienced the world differently and so they have a different perspective on the issue), feeling that they cannot express that difference for fear of retribution would mean that an aspect of their identity is not welcome at work, and thus they are less included.

Three potential nudges to increase psychological safety are:

1 Assign a devil's advocate.

When working in teams, assigning a person to play devil's advocate can help people feel more comfortable with voicing dissent, rotating who plays the role so that no one individual is always the devil's advocate. This has been shown to breed true inclusion in an organization and reduces bias in meeting dynamics and decision making.[17]

2 Create a formal dissent channel.

Dissent channels are officially sanctioned spaces where employees can voice their dissent without fear of backlash. These can be anonymous at first, so that people are not afraid of using the space, but there is mixed evidence of whether or not this is necessary. Dissent channels have proven useful even for solving enormous policy problems due to the more creative solutions developed through these channels. For example, the dissent channel created in the US State Department is credited with being a big reason the Dayton Accords (ending the war in Bosnia in 1992) were brought about.[18] Creating a space where critique and dissent are not just tolerated but encouraged can be really helpful in reducing the risk of groupthink and encouraging people to bring their entire selves to work.

3 **Rotate the chairperson for meetings**.

When working in teams, rotating which team member acts as the chairperson of the meeting helps to bring into the conversation people who sometimes don't feel like they can get a word in. This is particularly helpful in pointing out interruptions, and reducing the number of interruptions that occur.

NUDGES FOR TALENT MANAGEMENT

A big part of an organization becoming more diverse and inclusive is ensuring that all candidates have an equal opportunity to join and progress through that organization and that the talent management processes have as few opportunities for bias to creep in as possible. Three nudges that can make recruitment processes more inclusive are:

1 **Recruit from diverse pools, but pool diverse recruits**.

When advertising for jobs, continue to advertise in current locations but also start to advertise in locations where you may not normally do so – for example, on websites that are more targeted to gay or lesbian applicants, or at universities you do not usually recruit from. This type of targeting increases the rates of applications from targeted groups. Moreover, it increases in applicants the sense that the company values diversity of experiences and thought. However, be mindful that when evaluating recruits/applicants, pool all of them together regardless of which recruitment method they went through to apply. Pooling them together will reduce the bias that might come from noticing where they were recruited from, for example.[19]

2 **Review applications in groups**.

When reviewing options individually, we are more prone to be influenced by social information. When reviewing the same options jointly with each other, we focus more on the actual desired outcome. This certainly applies to reducing potential gender bias, and can result in more objective, merit-based and diverse decisions,[20] but could also have effects for race, sexual orientation, and other personal characteristics since joint evaluation has been found to more generally reduce reliance on social cues and focus more on the things that actually matter to the job.[21]

3　Use strictly structured interviews.

Rely on a very structured interview that standardizes the process among candidates. Pose the same set of questions, in the same order, to all candidates (despite the awkward flow of the conversation). Score each answer immediately after it is provided. When reviewing the responses of interviewees, compare horizontally – compare responses to question 1 among all candidates, then question 2 among all candidates, etc, rather than comparing collective answers of one candidate to another. If there are multiple interviewers, have each interview the candidates separately and have each submit their reviews individually before meeting. All of these reduce bias and the influence of unimportant characteristics, leading to better decisions and more diversity.[22]

Once a diverse set of candidates has been recruited, though, that doesn't necessarily mean they'll stay. It's important that there are equal opportunities for advancement as well, and that efforts are made to be inclusive in promotion and retention policies. Three nudges for being more inclusive in promotion and retention practices are:

1　Search for diversity for your team, not cultural fit.

Searching for cultural fit when bringing people onto your team almost always leads to some level of confirmation bias creeping into decision making. Confirmation bias is the natural human tendency to seek out information that confirms our previously held beliefs and avoid or disparage information that conflicts with those beliefs. Similarly, hiring for cultural fit tends to make us hire people that are like us, making us pay less attention to the qualities that matter most to getting the job done right, and leads to less diversity and more bias. Hiring to get the most diversity of thought in a team is a better solution.[23]

2　Use proportionality to benchmark.

When promoting from one level to another, keep in mind the proportions of different groups in each level. For example, if you are concerned about gender equality at different levels in your company and you are promoting employees from level A to level B, check to see if the proportion of female promotes is roughly equal to the proportion of females in level A. While adhering to strict proportionality may not be best (for legal reasons, for example), it provides a benchmark by which to check whether bias might be at play. We expect proportional promotions from one level to another, and this is often used as a benchmark to check if discrimination might be occurring (for example, this is used in UK court cases and with the European Commission).[24] To give this a few more teeth, you can also tie compensation to these benchmarks using a comply-or-explain approach, where all managers have to either promote proportionally, or have to give a legitimate explanation as to why they didn't reach their target. If that explanation is not sufficient, that could affect their compensation.

3 **Make work flexibility the default.**

Niall FitzGerald, former co-chair of Unilever, explained this standard saying, 'In principle, every job can be operated in a flexible manner unless it can demonstrably be shown to be otherwise'.[25] This basically changes the default setting, which can dramatically impact employees' comfort with taking advantage of work flexibility,[26] leading to increased inclusion. This has been used to great effect with some of our own client organizations, and has helped create more inclusive workplace cultures, in particular for people with disabilities and those with caring responsibilities.

TRANSPARENCY AND ACCOUNTABILITY

One common issue we find with our clients is that employees don't feel like the reasons for personnel or salary decisions are clear and transparent. A lack of transparency has been shown to be highly correlated with a lack of feeling included in organizations,[27] so it is important for organizations to make very clear the reasons for why certain people get promoted or get paid a certain amount. Moreover, when biased decisions are made or discriminatory behaviour occurs, often what makes people feel excluded is when the offenders are not held accountable. It is important that if an organization creates policies to limit discrimination there are actually consequences for continuing to behave in an unacceptable manner. Thus, three nudges to improve inclusion through increasing transparency and accountability are:

1 Establish transparent, inclusive talent pathways, with a diverse group of mentors.

Having professional development programmes that focus on members of minority groups can help ensure pathways for diversity at higher levels of the organization. Having role models certainly helps, but having mentors, or clear rotation, secondment, or management training programmes can also be beneficial to workplace inclusion.[28] Additionally, when employees feel clear about what they need to do to move upward in the organization, they are more likely to feel that promotion decisions are meritocratic.

Making it clear, then, what skills and experience are needed for different positions can help people plan their career paths and make them feel like the organization wants them to succeed. Moreover, having a diversity of people in higher positions that are aspired to by more junior members of the organization provides inspiration as well as a true belief that the organization is actually meritocratic and inclusive, and can help to improve overall performance and commitment.[29]

2 Internally publish all employee salaries.

While many countries have laws against pay discrimination, this is very hard to enforce. Most of the time, organizations do not want to be paying one group of people less money than another group for the same work. However, due to implicit bias, this happens quite frequently. By internally publishing employee salaries, an organization can be held accountable if they are paying unequally for the same work, and can have the opportunity to show employees why they might be earning different amounts due to different responsibilities.

Moreover, if an employee is negotiating during a promotion, this gives both sides objective criteria on which to base salary negotiations, limiting the discrimination that so often plagues negotiations. On the other hand, if an employee can see that they are making the same amount of money as their colleagues doing the same work, their perception that the company is objective in salary decisions will likely increase and help them feel more included.[30] It is important to note that publishing specific individual salaries, not just pay bands, is important for this to work. It is this level of specificity that holds managers and decision makers accountable, and also allows employees to see that bias does or does not exist.

3 Call out bad behaviour.

Often, when offensive and non-inclusive behaviour is exhibited in the workplace, people are reluctant to call it out. However, when someone models calling out bad behaviour, particularly if that person is high-ranking in the organization, more people feel willing to call out others and it can change behaviour in the organization broadly.[31] As we explained when we discussed the concept of mimicry, leading by example is a powerful message, when done both subtly and more publicly and clearly.

CHOOSING THE RIGHT NUDGES

Now that you have a few nudges you could potentially use, the next step is to decide which ones are most likely to be effective in your organization. It's often easy to see that *something* is wrong, but what is more difficult is figuring out precisely what is causing things to go wrong. But this diagnosis is essential when trying to create more inclusive workplaces. By knowing more precisely what actions or policies are making people feel excluded, we can more effectively curate the best interventions to solve those specific problems.

To come to this understanding, you need to gather data. Use the methods described in Chapter 7 – gather diversity data, calculate pay gaps, and run inclusion diagnostics. Once you've done this, and analysed that data, you'll have a clearer idea of what particular behaviours need to be changed, and what to be careful to keep intact. Importantly, this analysis will also help you prioritize nudges that will be the most impactful.

That prioritization will help you truly change behaviours. It will support your employees as they acquire the skills to mitigate the effects of their unconscious biases by focusing on the behaviours most harmful to your workplace culture. And in the end, that's the whole point – to create more inclusive cultures. These nudges, combined with the inclusive leadership development we've described throughout this book, will help you get there.

Of course, the effectiveness of all these nudges is dependent on context. The next chapters will describe how different organizations in different sectors have worked to become more inclusive, providing case studies for best (and worst) practices.

TAKEAWAYS

1 Culture is what you do. It's a product of behaviours, so to change your culture you need to change behaviours.

2 Unconscious bias training isn't enough on its own because it simply makes us aware of our problematic behaviours. It doesn't give us the skills to change.

3 Nudges can help us change behaviour and act as a form of cultural support to create more inclusive workplaces.

4 In particular, nudges can help us tackle microaggressions, increase psychological safety, and improve accountability.

5 Collect and leverage data to choose the right nudges for your context, and measure their effectiveness over time to demonstrate change.

ENDNOTES

1 Lego [Television series episode] (2018) *The Toys That Made Us*, Netflix

2 Kalev, A, Kelly, E and Dobbin, F (2006) Best practices or best guesses? Assessing the efficacy of corporate affirmative diversity policies, *American Sociological Review*, **71** (4), pp 589–617

3 Beattie, G and Johnson, P (2012) Possible unconscious bias in recruitment and promotion and the need to promote equality, *Perspectives: Policy and Practice in Higher Education*, **16** (1), pp 7–13

4 https://hbr.org/2016/07/why-diversity-programs-fail

5 Ibid

6 Ariely, D (2008) *Predictably Irrational*, New York: HarperCollins, p 20

7 Dayan, E and Bar-Hillel, M (2011) Nudge to nobesity II: menu positions influence food orders, *Judgment and Decision Making*, **6** (4), pp 333–42

8 Gulzar, S and Ruiz, N A (2018) Ballot order effects and party responses: evidence from lotteries in Colombia

9 Sue, D W (2010) *Microaggressions in Everyday Life: Race, Gender, and Sexual Orientation*, John Wiley & Sons, Inc, p xv

10 Basford, T E, Offermann, L R and Behrend, T S (2013) Do you see what i see? Perceptions of gender microaggressions in the workplace, *Psychology of Women Quarterly*, **201**, pp 1–10

11 Nadal, K L et al (2014) Racial microaggressions and mental health: counseling clients of color, *Journal of Counseling & Development*, **92**, pp 57–66

12 Schnellmann, J and Gibbons, J L (1984) Microinequities in the classroom: the perception by minorities and women of a less favorable climate in the classroom, paper presented at the Annual Convention of the American Psychological Association, Toronto, ON, 24–28 August; Fox, S and Stallworth, L E (2005) Racial/ethnic bullying: exploring links between bullying and racism in the US workplace, *Journal of Vocational Behavior*, **66** (3), pp 438–56; Cherng, A D and Tate, E A (2007) Microinequities: should employers 'sweat the small stuff'?, *Employment Law Commentary* (Morrison/Foerster), **19** (1), pp 1–4

13 Goncalo, J A et al (2015) Creativity from constraint? How the political correctness norm influences creativity in mixed-sex work groups, *Administrative Science Quarterly*, **60** (1), pp 1–30

14 Cheryan, S et al (2009) Ambient belonging: how stereotypical cues impact gender participation in computer science, *Journal of Personality and Social Psychology*, **97**, pp 1045–60; Latu, I M et al (2013) Successful female leaders empower women's behavior in leadership tasks, *Journal of Experimental Social Psychology*, **49**, pp 444–48

15 Steele, C M and Aronson, J (1995) Stereotype threat and the intellectual test performance of African Americans, *Journal of Personality and Social Psychology*, **69** (5), p 797

16 Croizet, J C and Claire, T (1998) Extending the concept of stereotype threat to social class: the intellectual underperformance of students from low socioeconomic backgrounds, *Personality and Social Psychology Bulletin*, **24** (6), pp 588–94

17 Sunstein, C and Hastie, R (2015) *Wiser: Getting beyond groupthink to make groups smarter*, Harvard Business Review Press

18 Katyal, N (2016) Washington needs more dissent channels, *The New York Times*, 1 July

19 Avery, D R and McKay, P F (2006) Target practice: an organizational impression management approach to attracting minority and female job applicants, *Personnel Psychology*, **59** (1), pp 157–87

20 Bohnet, I, Bazerman, M H and Van Geen, A (2016) 'When performance trumps gender bias: Joint versus separate evaluation, *Management Science*, **62** (5)

21 Bazerman, M H et al (1994) The inconsistent role of comparison others and procedural justice in reactions to hypothetical job descriptions: implications for job acceptance decisions, *Organizational Behavior and Human Decision Processes*, **60** (3), pp 326–52

22 Bohnet, I (2016) How to take the bias out of interviews, *Harvard Business Review*, 18 April

23 Rivera, L (2012) Hiring as cultural matching: the case of elite professional service firms, *American Sociological Review*, **77**, pp 999–1022

24 Barmes, L (2003) The diversity approach to achieving equality: potential and pitfalls, *Industrial Law Journal*, **32** (4), pp 274–96

25 Bohnet, I (2016) *What Works: Gender Equality by Design*, Harvard University Press, p 156

26 Ibid, p 157

27 Sabharwal, M (2014) Is diversity management sufficient? Organizational inclusion to further performance, *Public Personnel Management*, **43** (2) pp 197–217

28 Salisbury, C et al (2001) Pathways to inclusive practices: systems oriented, policy-linked, and research-based strategies that work, Consortium on Inclusive Schooling Practices; Frost, S and Kalman, D (2016) *Inclusive Talent Management*, Kogan Page

29 Kurtulus, F and Tomaskovic-Devey, D (2012) Do female top managers help women to advance? A panel study using EEO-1 records, *ANNALS of the American Academy of Political and Social Science*, **639**, pp 136–69; Mollerstrom, J (2014) Favoritism reduces cooperation, working paper, George Mason University

30 White House Office of the Press Secretary (2018) President Memorandum: advancing pay equality through compensation data collection, 8 April; Jones, S (2014) Valerie Jarrett: wage 'transparency' will help employers 'avoid lawsuits', CNS News, 8 April; Bohnet, I (2016) *What Works*, pp 277–79

31 Jensen, R and Oster, E (2009) The power of TV: cable television and women's status in India, *Quarterly Journal of Economics*, **124**, pp 1057–94

PART THREE

DELIVER

9

CURATING CREATIVITY: HOW TO BUILD AN INCLUSIVE ORGANIZATION IN THE CREATIVE SECTOR

INTRODUCTION TO THE CREATIVE SECTOR

The creative sector can be defined as those industries such as TV, film, music, fashion and the arts. With technological change, the boundaries are blurring. So, for example, digital and gaming could be argued to be tech or arts. For the purposes of this chapter we will focus on the TV and film industry and the classical music sector. These are both areas we have worked extensively in, and they also provide fascinating insight into how the creative sector is adapting to a changing world.

The creative sector is more important than those outside (or inside) the sector may currently appreciate. In the UK, it is worth over £90 billion per annum to the economy, contributing in the region of 5 per cent of Gross Value Added products.[1] Furthermore, the sector is growing at twice the rate of the economy overall.[2] Most importantly of all, however, the sector produces content representing us all. In this sense, the people working in the sector, and creating the content we all consume, are pivotal in defining how society views itself. They are instruments of cultural definition and change.

It is worth pointing out at this juncture that the diversity of the people creating art is not representative of the people being influenced by the art – the population at large. In the UK, for example, white men make up more than 60 per cent of jobs in the creative sector, versus less than 55 per cent of jobs overall.[3] As such, there has been a drive from the UK Arts Council to reach more diverse audiences so that public money is being spent for all.

A stereotype of the industry is that it is populated by progressive types who would be politically left-leaning and socially liberal. Whilst there is some truth in stereotypes, it's our experience that it's actually more difficult to drive and embed change in this sector than most. Largely this is because the creative industries are often made up of freelance workforces who are project driven without a fixed staff base. It is a tricky industry to crack.

The UK television and film industry is regarded as world-class and something of a cultural superpower. However, perhaps because of its success, and certainly because of its informality and the fact that the sector is made up of very small creative entities, all with a very specific character and culture, it has not advanced in diversity and inclusion as much as other sectors.

SECTOR CHALLENGES: TV AND FILM

One of the challenges in the TV and film industry is the informality of virtually everything, because of the freelance, project-driven nature of the industry's workforce. We know that lack of formal processes is one of the biggest areas where bias can creep in. For example, the lack of consistent or transparent recruitment, and the emphasis on relationships and networks are by their very nature exclusive.

For a long time, unpaid internships were the norm. This would exclude people from entering the industry who could not afford London rents, or without parents to subsidize them. Although this is now changing, for many years there was a culture where entry into the industry was through unpaid internships.

Crewing up a production would be a rushed affair, with directors, producers, writers and camera(men) assembled at short notice. We know that accelerated hiring is another challenge to diversity where people tend to rely on who they already know and trust. Furthermore, many of the commissioning broadcasters would stipulate a director they wanted. That director would then probably insist on several colleagues they had already worked with or liked/rated.

Another challenge is the creative process itself, which is not numerically based, or easily measurable. Numbers allow one way of checking bias that is not open to us in appreciation of a piece of art per se. How do you measure an aesthetic? When the creative process is (rightly) prioritized, anything seen as interfering in it is downgraded. To date, this has included 'diversity initiatives', which are often seen as counter to 'talent' and the existing professionals' view of quality or success.

The industry body, the Producers Alliance for Cinema and Television (Pact) asked Frost Included (f(i)) to help them design and deliver a training programme for TV production companies. Having already delivered several keynotes to the BBC, Channel 4 and other film companies, we immersed ourselves in the industry to learn the culture and practices.

We needed to engage a highly intelligent, creative and somewhat cynical group and challenge certain myths head on, such as the conflict between diversity and creativity or talent and the commercial case. We needed to avoid tokenism and make a tangible difference in on-screen as well as off-screen diversity in the industry in a short time frame.

INCLUSIVE LEADERSHIP LAB

In any sector we are mindful of the lessons from Frank Dobbin and others that we discussed in Chapter 8 – diversity training alone doesn't work. In the TV and film sector especially, there is often an allergic reaction to training and a maniacal opposition to anything that may be perceived as interference in the creative process. It is in this context that a version of our Inclusive Leadership Programme offered some way forward.

We worked closely with Anjani Patel, Head of Diversity and Inclusion for Pact, representing the independent TV production companies, or 'indies'. Anjani has to lead carefully, striking the right balance between representing their interests and challenging them to improve their D&I performance. In particular, they have been grappling with how to create impactful change. They want to lead the way with practical solutions which can be embedded into working practices. The challenge is that in their freelance workforce in project-driven environments it can be tricky to drive change. They also needed to accommodate the organic nature of the production and the fact that there isn't a one-size-fits-all approach. The goal is to have a nuanced approach which takes into account all the contexts and genres but still pushes producers to question their default and to embed inclusive practices at all levels.

The buy-in started by reframing any intervention as about representing their interests and about bolstering, not stifling, the creative process.

We met several TV executives and people at various levels within the indies to gauge their drivers for D&I. This resulted in our 'Inclusive Leadership Programme' becoming an 'Inclusive Leadership Lab'.

The lab was designed to:

1 reframe diversity to help executives understand the rationale and benefits of creating a more diverse and inclusive team;

2 help leaders understand and tackle their own unconscious bias;

3 embed D&I in their own decision making on a daily basis;

4 design, articulate and own actions that will make a difference;

5 better disseminate the value of diversity to their teams.

The lab provided a framework for TV executives to create their own personal and corporate diversity strategy, offering practical tips and small changes that collectively had a significant impact. By making it personal and tailored, we headed off the initial scepticism of anything that might damage the creative process. They were in charge of the creative process and this was a new lens through which to view it.

PROCESS

BUILDING THE EVIDENCE BASE

We asked senior executives to undertake some implicit association tests and a simple personal inclusion diagnostic. This was to make a seemingly nebulous subject very real and personal. We were able to gain organizational insights but also very personal insights into the team. We were then able to play this back to the group in a sensitive but challenging manner.

HOLDING UP THE MIRROR: REFRAMING DIVERSITY AS A LEADERSHIP CONCEPT

We then brought the executives together for a three-hour workshop on reframing current understanding of diversity. Using our expertise and the latest research, best practice from other organizations and the data we had collected on their organization and industry, we were able to educate and inspire the team. Crucially, we were able to make the subject relevant to them personally and emotionally, as human beings, as well as logically and commercially, as professionals.

We structured the lab in three parts – the same way we have structured this book.

Understand: diversity is a reality, inclusion is a choice

This introduced participants to the concept of D&I and made it clear that this was about everyone, including them. From this basis of infinite diversity and their own stake in it, we could then progress to discuss systemic patterns of disadvantage. We reframed the business case, based on what they themselves told us about their business and the sector. For example, one drama company we worked with discussed how they were not responding quickly enough to changing audience tastes. We also analysed how in- and out-groups impacted our frame of decision making. TV tends to be very exclusive as a sector – hard to get into and people don't often leave. The in-groups tended to be fairly tight.

The most powerful part of the opening 'understand' session with the teams was the vulnerability exercise – asking people about a time they felt excluded and relating that to their own diversity. We then asked them to empathize with how that might be for others, only the others might experience it even more profoundly and even more frequently.

TV in the UK is still run predominantly by white people. BAME people represent only 12 per cent of employees of the top five main UK broadcasters, and only 6 per cent of those at senior levels.[4] The vulnerability exercise allowed people to relate to others. For example, perhaps their own experience of social mobility and exclusion on the basis of class could be related to exclusion on the basis of race as well as class. It provoked other questions such as, 'Why would extras only be white people?' What about if we mandated 50/50 gender parity in minor roles as a minimum, which would have no negative impact on the creative process but would make a difference? Why wouldn't you include ethnic minority people in casting when there was no valid historical reason not to?

At a minimum, the first part of the lab was about holding up a mirror to their own industry and ways of working. Good people make mistakes when they can't see the bigger picture. In TV people are moving at such speed with such a tight in-group that they are more prone than average to blind spots and groupthink. This is the exact opposite of what the creative process actually needs.

Lead: enlarge the pie

We then collectively defined inclusive leadership – good leadership is inclusive leadership. This is about taking personal responsibility for becoming more conscious of the unconscious decisions we take every day, and reconciling personal interest with collective good. This in turn can be in our own self-interest and can build on what we learned about zero-sum games and enlarging pies.

We discussed the results of their IAT test results in situ. We discussed flexing your role to fit the other person, allowing them to bring more of their self to work. We encouraged people to be more transparent, sharing their own story and making themselves vulnerable, eliciting reciprocal behaviours in others. We discussed power and how the powerful could more easily hold people accountable for their actions. Finally, we discussed who they mentored and asked them if they could be more inclusive in their choices, and even more inclusive in terms of their socializing.

A key part of good leadership is of course awareness of unconscious bias and actions that people can take individually to counter them. Many people didn't even recognize they were biased. Or conversely, they could argue that all artistic output is biased and therefore the question is a moot point.

To persuade people of the need to address bias we came up with examples from within their own industry. For example, we created a short film based on news coverage of the Black British comedian Lenny Henry being awarded a knighthood by the Queen. In the news clip the ITN News network plays a clip of another Black man, not Lenny Henry. This mistake is indicative of a white-dominated newsroom who did not have Black people in their in-group, were not cognizant of their biases and by working to a tight deadline in a high-pressured environment made a mistake.

What makes it even worse is that the news presenter mispronounces Lenny Henry's name. This is yet another indication of bias and typical of microbehaviours that BAME people in TV and film are subject to on a daily basis. Only when the audience could watch it as a third party could they appreciate the gravity of the situation and the need to take pre-emptive action in the future.

We practised mitigating bias in real time, such as through practising conscious questioning rather than unconscious acceptance – a process which involves getting several versions of events including the 'other' perspective. We encouraged people, like others working in high-pressured environments such as healthcare, to proactively and consciously free up space in their minds to help facilitate clear System 2 thinking. In an informal industry we encouraged simple rules of thumb like counting everything – use data to challenge your perception of who 'fits' or is 'best'. We also practised checking language and micromessaging and microbehaviours – checking body language, eye contact, work allocation, praise.

One of the best bias mitigation tools the executives came up with was counter-stereotypical images and positive imagery – for example, in one period drama there was a discussion about why the whole cast was white. The orthodox view was that there were no Black people in Victorian England. However, on deeper fact checking it became clear that this was not the case,[5] and in order to more accurately reflect that fact (actually produce more factually correct and historically authentic TV) an emphasis was placed on more diverse casting. Furthermore, in one episode of 'troy', set in ancient Greece, the executive in charge said that a diverse cast was 'just because'. In other words, they were themselves leading on enhancing their own creative process through diversity. This was a 180-degree reversal from where some of them started.

Deliver: what about diversity and inclusion (WADI)?

This final part was all about embedding the WADI concept in all areas of your business from strategy to recruitment, casting and the creative process. We offered up a checklist that people adapted to their own circumstances. Key areas of focus included communication and measurement.

Communicate your D&I strategy – everyone should be aware of it and why it matters. We explored ways to remind people, from the top of all job descriptions to the backs of toilet doors!

Measure – we took snapshots of the company's showreel before and after to look at on-screen diversity, and of their employee population to look at off-screen diversity (behind the camera).

FIELDWORK

Finally, we gave the participants some set tasks to undertake using the tools we had delivered in the team session. This allowed them to notice bias for themselves, in their daily life. And then we set a date to meet again to see how they had got on.

RESULTS

The lab provoked a lot of conversation within the team. It became a (positive) talking point over coffee or drinks. People had lightbulb moments, adopted key phrases and became more curious. After pre-work, the lab, and homework, in addition to ongoing conversations, we brought the team back together for a second workshop where everyone shared their observations and we planned specific actions to address them. We then discussed these potential interventions as a group and agreed to regroup to measure their effectiveness.

Having taken the executives on a journey we gained buy-in from the top of the organization, we made the subject relevant and personal to leaders in the organization, and we agreed a set of sustainable and measurable actions to make difference.

One TV production company management team agreed the set of individual actions shown in Table 9.1. These are actual ideas and commitments that came from the previously sceptical TV executives themselves. They were undertaken in 2018 and we checked in quarterly to see how they were getting on. They have been anonymized but the roles are accurate.

In addition to the actions shown, there were extra, unintended, outcomes. For example, one senior producer came out about mental health. They had been covering their depression their entire career and it had been debilitating at times. Using the language of the lab, and feeling able to share their vulnerability in an appropriate way, they decided to tell colleagues at work. Colleagues who had also been through the lab were incredibly supportive and shared some of their challenges in return. Being able to be open about an issue that had remained hidden for so long was actually de-burdening. It was the opposite of what the producer had thought the lab would be when they initially took part.

Several executives have now replicated the programme with their own teams. We are seeing a change in on-screen diversity and significant efforts to challenge the closed-shop barriers to getting into the industry in the first place.

Table 9.1 Example management team actions

	CEO	Producer	Producer	People leader	Chief Operating Officer (COO)	Creative lead	Development lead
1	**On-screen diversity targets** Make on-screen diversity a given – set targets for diversity in incidental casting for minor roles	**Crewing** Find as diverse a range of above- and below-the-line crew as possible – especially directors and writers	**Giving a platform to my team** Sponsor x and y and get them recognition, eg representing us at various external meetings	**Formalize recruitment process** Bundle hires of new development execs – actively call for diversity	**Leadership** Encourage an environment where people feel they can bring their 'whole selves' to work (by making myself vulnerable on a specific issue)	**Make nebulous concept real** Visually represent success metrics, eg mentees or new hires from diverse backgrounds	**Formalize the (currently) informal** eg recruitment and JDs of runners. Embed D&I in development
2	**Communicate commitment** to creating diversity on + off screen to all my teams, internal + external – min one diverse talent in each HOD area	**Diverse casting** Not just on gender and ethnic lines but also with ability and background diversity	**Mentor my out-group** Work for Arts Emergency – an organization that helps increase diversity in arts organizations, and provides mentorship for young artists from marginalized groups	**Ask for mixed long lists** from all for on- and off-screen talent	**Create handbook** Synthesize, formalize policies + procedures in a succinct handbook	**Mentor someone from my out group** Move from mentoring to reciprocal mentoring to sponsoring	**Hold people accountable** Review this grid monthly with leadership team
3	**Know my people** Numbers and diversity data as well as sales and financials, and quote it often	**Outreach** Actively seek more diverse range of writers and directors to work with on future projects	**Reciprocal mentoring** with a BAME Director of Production	**Diversity in our writing talent** I am going to make sure I have the figures for that and review often	**Identify ways to embed D&I into our recruitment processes** De-bias the systems. Call out bad behaviours	**Change/adapt visual identify of office** Create and remind people of diversity on a daily basis	**Diarize these diversity commitments** so they actually happen

Diederick Santer, Chief Executive of Kudos, said, 'It's genuinely changed the way I think – and more importantly, what I do – and it's the most compelling thing that I've experienced about inclusion and diversity, both as an employer and a producer.'

SECTOR CHALLENGES: CLASSICAL MUSIC

Classical music is in one sense inherently conservative. Most of the 'great' composers from the previous centuries that we know about are male. The controller of BBC Radio 3, a classical music station, said that greater diversity in classical music was sorely needed if it was to future-proof itself and endure innovation and relevance in the future.[6]

In 2013, the winners of all 13 categories at the British Composer Awards were male, and 12 were white. In 2014, five were female and all were white.[7] In 2015, two were female and all were white. The British Academy of Songwriters, Composers and Authors (BASCA) has decided to tackle this. It has mandated 50 per cent women and BAME inclusion on the judging panel, and introduced an online entry system to monitor and publish the diversity information.[8]

In 2016, BASCA introduced self-nomination to decrease the barriers to entry of having to know the right people in the industry to nominate you. They also introduced anonymous judging, rather like blind CV reviews, to decrease the incidence of unconscious bias.

BASCA undertook some further research that showed that of new commissions, the gender imbalance is actually greater among younger composers than those in the 50+ age group. Six per cent of commissions were from BAME composers (vs a UK population of 14 per cent).[9] Sound and Music, an organization set up to encourage more diversity in the sector, achieves 16 per cent BAME talent on its professional development programmes, showing that the aspiring talent is there. Twenty-one per cent of commissioned composers are female, compared to 51 per cent of the UK population and 36 per cent of all composition students.[10] Over half of commissions were to composers living in London, rather than the rest of the country.

Just as with TV and film, we needed an intervention that would not be rejected as anti-creative. We partnered with London Music Masters, a charity that was set up in 2008 to create more opportunities for primary school students to access music teaching and playing. We worked with Rob Adediran, their CEO, to convene a series of workshops with key people from the industry.

We led them through a series of problem statements from access to training and education, bias in selection, consideration of audiences and marketing, and general HR processes in orchestras and other organizations in the sector. At the end of each workshop we summarized our collective output, agreed the draft and set a date to reconvene. In this sense, what we designed was genuinely co-created with the industry – by the classical music industry, for the classical music industry.

What resulted was the 'I'm In' toolkit that allowed organizations of varying size to assess themselves against a set of co-created criteria tailored to the classical music industry. It then allowed them to assess where they were across a maturity matrix, highlighting any strengths and weaknesses and laying out a roadmap for their future journey to improve their D&I.

THE *I'M IN* TOOLKIT

The questions were ordered in such a way as to guide the participants through an educational as well as a practical process. We started with drivers, to understand why the organization was embarking on this initiative. Then we led them through a series of themes: leadership and accountability, operational responsibility, organizational culture, recruitment, talent management, marketing and branding, customer experience, audience diversity, and procurement.

These are roughly organized as those relating to 'drivers and accountability' such as governance, leadership and responsibility, followed by more systemic themes aimed at assessing processes and culture such as recruitment, talent management and marketing, and finally those that are more externally focused such as customer experience, audience diversity and supplier diversity (procurement).

For example, in the section on recruitment, it started with:

A truly inclusive recruitment process will enable a music organization to create a workforce that is representative of its people and communities. This means being reflective of the people and communities that they create music for. A wide range of people will want to work for an inclusive organization. The sector will be accessible for the diverse populations of the UK (eg all cultural groups, irrespective of class, gender and other factors that might historically limit engagement with the sector).

The sector would itself be valued by all parts of society and be more open and accessible to a wide range of specialties and skills (eg transferable skills from other sectors). Recruitment strategies would be aligned with an organization's governance and business strategy.

After the initial set up, the toolkit then asked organizations to respond to the following statements, with options ranging from 'strongly agree' to 'strongly disagree':

1 Recruitment is aligned with business goals and objectives that articulate long-term strategic plans to address both on-stage and back-office diversity.

2 Recruiting diverse talent is a priority.

3 There is a strong awareness of how to create strategies for diverse talent recruitment.

4 Your organization makes its commitment to D&I clear throughout the recruitment process.

5 Your organization's recruitment process includes creative ways to minimize bias.

6 Your organization promotes activities to widen the business and personal networks of employees, allowing access to a wider talent pool.

7 Diversity is seen as a source of competitive advantage within the organization.

8 Skills and aptitude are prioritized over educational background (school attended, exam success) and employment history (companies worked for) in the recruitment process.

In each section the questions were tailored to the needs of the sector but also guided the participant towards what the best next step might be. For example, when discussing inclusion in customer experience we discussed how creating an inclusive customer retail experience means thinking about all of the 'touch points' a customer has with an organization from the perspective of vastly diverse people. It also means thinking more about creating 'an inclusive experience' than just how one can increase the number of tickets sold.

The tool is still early in its adoption but over 30 organizations signed up and undertook the assessment. We then promoted it at the various classical music conferences such as *Classical Next*. It is an industry first, co-created with the sector for the sector.

Rob Adediran said:

> There have been a ton of diversity and inclusion initiatives in the music industry over the years and very few, if any of them, have had a lasting or transformative effect on the lack of diversity amongst audiences, performers and the workforce. The goal of I'm In is to tackle the root causes of the problem within the music eco-system, not simply to be another initiative without the power to effect change. At its heart, I'm In is a provocation designed to help arts organizations understand how unconscious bias and hidden prejudice – built up over generations – have created an industry that does not reflect our values. It is an audit of the level of true inclusion within our businesses, and ultimately it provides a roadmap towards progress. We need systemic solutions for systemic problems – our hope is that I'm In can provide that for music and the creative industries.

Irfaan Arif, who worked on the project for Frost Included, said:

> As a D&I consultant, working with the classical music sector is fascinating. It provides the ideal platform to showcase how getting D&I right can not only make organizations better places to work or customer experiences more inclusive, but how it can really influence the creative process. Working on the 'I'm In' tool was exciting but also challenging as it required us to think in non-conventional ways. Music organizations weren't 'corporate' and didn't have lots of resources –

instead we needed to think about micro to medium organizations that didn't have high turnover, had informal processes, often small networks, sometimes relied on grants and funding and weren't all profit making. How would inclusion work for these organizations? I believe we developed a tool that will allow these organizations to really assess where they are within their own contexts and create bespoke journeys to inclusion.

TARGETS

The Proms is one of the world's largest music festivals, founded in 1895, and now organized annually by the BBC. It has pledged to achieve gender parity in new composers it commissions. This reflects the challenges in tackling a historical supply side of largely male composers and of not upsetting the apple cart in terms of people who appreciate more conservative classical music.

David Pickard, director of the BBC Proms, said, 'Achieving a 50-50 balance of contemporary composers… is something we have been committed to for some time and consider vital to the creative development of the world's largest classical music festival'.[11]

The music funding charity PRS Foundation has established a Keychange network of female artists and industry professionals. The PRS Foundation has also coordinated a pledge between 45 international music festivals and conferences such as the Manchester Jazz Festival and the Cheltenham Music Festival. Vanessa Reed, Chief Executive, said, 'the Keychange network of female artists and industry professionals and the festival partners' idea of establishing a collective pledge will significantly accelerate change. I hope this will be the start of a more balanced industry which will result in benefits for everyone.'[12]

CONCLUSION

Through designed leadership and systems interventions, we have been able to start to create sustainable change in classical music and TV and film. Of course, challenges remain. In TV, we have been able to impact on-screen diversity much more quickly than off-screen diversity. Affecting casting is easier to do than challenging off-screen working relationships entrenched over decades. However, on-screen diversity is important; it does create role models and cultural representations that are important to all of us. And we have started to affect off-screen diversity, for example with reciprocal mentoring, sponsorship and formalization of previous very informal processes.

Off-screen, the BBC Director General announced some targets in 2018: two members of all executive teams to be from BAME backgrounds by 2020, and at least one BAME candidate on every shortlist for senior roles.[13] Similarly, in classical music we are beginning to affect the pipeline, and there are undoubtedly composers and artists coming through from a variety of backgrounds. The challenge remains finding ways to create interventions and education that can help leaders to embed change into all of their processes and strategies – top down.

We said at the start that a key driver for the creative sector is the creative process itself. When we see creative success allied with diversity we have hit on something important. Rather than a trite 'diversity film' attracting 'diversity audiences' we need to show how embedding diverse thinking in the creative process itself benefits everyone.

It can garner new audiences, as well as bring something fresh to existing audiences. In short it can bring groups together rather than polarizing them. Take for example the TV production company Kudos, who produced 'Boy with the Top Knot' in 2017. This was an authentically told and acted story of a Punjabi family, made by a diverse crew, that went on to garner critical acclaim. Or take for example the hit BBC dramas EastEnders and Holby City that have created their own diverse talent pipelines over recent years. This talent is now bearing fruit with exceptional new voices on and off screen.

Most of all, what our work in TV, film and classical music has shown us is that it is indeed possible to create D&I in a dynamic, fluid, informal sector. It can be done, and it does contribute to creativity that can benefit us all.

Inclusion Rider

In her 2018 Oscars speech, Frances McDormand ended with the words, 'Inclusion Rider'. Immediately after the speech, Google searches and social media posts about 'Inclusion Rider' spiked, with over 7,000 tweets in 20 minutes.[14]

In a pre-recorded video aired during the Oscars, Geena Davis also mentioned that after Thelma and Louise triumphed at the box office in 1991, everyone was talking about the end of male-dominated stories and film in Hollywood.

But that didn't happen.

Three Billboards outside Ebbing, Missouri (starring Frances McDormand) and *Thelma and Louise* (starring Geena Davis) are fantastic films. How come we failed to tackle gender inequality and wider diversity issues after *Thelma and Louise* and what makes us think this time things might be different?

The answer lies in specific, concrete actions and people committed to undertaking them.

A lot has happened in TV and film. We've had #MeToo and Time's Up. Then there was the flood of accusations against so many Hollywood bigwigs like Harvey Weinstein and Kevin Spacey. Then there has been the artistic and commercial success of films and shows that represent the diverse audience that actually consumes the media like Big Little Lies, Wonder Woman and Black Panther. So how, now, at this moment, do we capitalize on the current momentum to spur real change in the industry?

Frances McDormand's Inclusion Rider idea comes from Stacy Smith, a professor at the University of Southern California, and Kalpana Kotagal, a civil rights and employment lawyer. As Smith states, 'the typical feature film has about 40 to 45 speaking characters in it. I would argue that only 8 to 10 of those characters are actually relevant to the story. The remaining 30 or so roles, there's no reason why those minor roles can't match or reflect the demography of where the story is taking place. An equity rider by an A-lister in their contract can stipulate that those roles reflect the world in which we actually live.'[15]

On the one hand, this is one specific, concrete action and I am sure there are numerous actors who can now commit to it.

However, it really only applies to sought-after superstars who can command whatever contract clauses they want. Another drawback is that it doesn't help with casting non-white, non-male people in leading roles, nor does it help tell the stories of a more diverse world. But it's a start.

So why don't we take the idea of Inclusion Rider, and scale it?

Procurement is an often-ignored aspect of D&I but actually the buying power of organizations is more than equivalent to the power of a Hollywood superstar. So think about how you want to use your commercial power to create change.

Say that you will only work with a recruitment agency if they have a guaranteed interview scheme for disabled people and present gender-balanced shortlists. Tell your suppliers that you expect them to undertake Stonewall's Workplace Equality Index or Business in the Community's Race for Opportunity. You can stipulate actions that are minimal additional cost or even cost saving. The only real dependency is your leadership.

Hollywood superstar contracts originated with such ridiculous clauses as the band Van Halen demanding that all the brown M&Ms were taken out of the sweet bowls backstage at their concerts.[16] Your contracts can be more useful and more powerful agents of change. Adopt your own version of an Inclusion Rider for your own company's legitimate benefit – and benefit us all in the process.

TAKEAWAYS

1 While the informal and creative nature of the creative sector makes standardized D&I processes difficult, the process of Understand, Lead and Deliver can still be an effective framework.

2 Use the informal conversations after inclusion programmes to continue the inspiration and enthusiasm, and get people to commit to actions.

3 To ensure your plan isn't rejected as 'anti-creative', co-create as much as possible with your stakeholders.

4 Designing easy-to-implement toolkits can be helpful for disseminating learning throughout multiple organizations within a sector.

5 Ambitious targets can be an extremely good motivator for progress.

ENDNOTES

1   https://www.gov.uk/government/news/creative-industries-record-contribution-to-uk-economy

2   https://www.telegraph.co.uk/news/2017/05/10/britains-creative-industries-success-story-deserves-backing/

3   https://www.gov.uk/government/statistics/dcms-sectors-economic-estimates-2017-employment-and-trade

4   https://www.ofcom.org.uk/about-ofcom/latest/media/media-releases/2017/diversity-uk-television-industry

5   https://www.theguardian.com/artanddesign/2014/sep/15/black-chronicles-ii-victorians-photography-exhibition-rivington-place

6   http://www.classical-music.com/news/disruption-and-diversity-are-key-future-classical-music-says-bbc-radio-3-controller

7   https://www.musicbusinessworldwide.com/classical-music-sectors-lack-of-diversity-laid-bare-by-new-report/

8   https://www.theguardian.com/technology/2015/jul/31/women-technology-gender-equality-50-50-pledge

9   http://soundandmusic.org/projects/news-because-its-2016

10 Ibid

11 https://www.thetimes.co.uk/article/proms-pledges-50-50-gender-split-for-modern-composers-xr0bjjlvc

12 Ibid

13 https://www.theguardian.com/media/2018/jun/20/bbc-vows-to-increase-diversity-of-senior-management-by-2020

14 https://abcnews.go.com/GMA/Culture/frances-mcdormand-found-inclusion-riders-back/story?id=53523044

15 https://www.theguardian.com/film/2018/mar/05/what-is-an-inclusion-rider-frances-mcdormand-oscars-2018

16 https://www.npr.org/sections/therecord/2012/02/14/146880432/the-truth-about-van-halen-and-those-brown-m-ms

10

SAFEGUARDING NORMS, CHALLENGING NORMS: HOW TO CREATE CHANGE IN FINANCE

INTRODUCTION

In his 2014 documentary *Master of the Universe*, Marc Bauder parodied what many in the financial services were said to believe – that they had the power to change the world however they wanted and get rich doing it. It's true that as a sector finance had a disproportionate influence on the rest of the economy and therefore society at large. It has a disproportionate number of highly intelligent, well-paid people. It is also one of the worst-performing sectors when it comes to diversity and inclusion.

However, the sector's confidence (some might say arrogance) was severely challenged in 2008 with the financial crisis. Many questions were asked about governance, accountability and ethics. The crisis demonstrated that a group of highly capable intelligent men could indeed play it disastrously wrong. It was the financial equivalent of Captain Van Zanten.

The literature on the crisis is extensive, from *The Hour Between Dog and Wolf*[1] to *Too Big to Fail*[2] and other excellent reads. However, there was also a diversity dimension to the financial crisis that did not go unnoticed. Discussion ranged from the IMF report on groupthink to questions of whether the crisis would have happened at all if there were more women in finance, such as in the article 'What if Lehman Brothers had been Lehman Sisters?'[3] Diversity could indeed help avert future crises as well as improve performance in the medium and long term.

Some norms in finance are incredibly helpful to diversity and inclusion – the brutal meritocracy of many organizations is genuinely more de-biased than some more cosy sectors. That said, many norms are still unhelpful. Nowadays, it's less the overt displays of sexism (that's now the exception rather than the rule for firms of any significant size with conduct/whistle-blowing/ER practices in place). It's the microaggressions that are the bigger issue. When the discrimination is subtle, it is harder to deal with, first because it is harder to call out, and second because it is often tolerated if the individual in question is delivering results.

SECTOR CHALLENGES

One of the challenges with diversity and inclusion in financial organizations is that it is often not seen as important or relevant to making money. Unlike TV and film, where a lack of formality allows bias free rein, there are now a great number of formal processes in banking. However, these are no guarantee of de-biasing behaviour if the lens has not been applied in the first place.

Even worse, the pitfalls of unconscious bias training are nowhere more evident than in banking, where people who have been trained in a formal process often think they are unbiased. Thus, if they're told their biases are innate, then they are more wont to think they're doing all they can by focusing on pure numbers and policing themselves isn't needed. If moral licence exists anywhere, it is in this sector.

Finance has embraced unconscious bias training like no other sector. However, therein lies part of the problem. The diversity and inclusion challenge in this sector is cultural. It's mainly the behaviours of men and women operating in a male-dominated culture. Training is a technical fix and, as we've shown throughout this book, you can't change culture via a technical fix.

As an example of another technical fix, in 2018 Goldman Sachs started paying for mothers on work trips to courier breast milk back to their babies under an initiative aimed at retaining working parents. Goldman was also one of the first corporate firms to introduce 'lactation rooms'.[4] This might be a helpful intervention, but if there is still a stigma in the organizational culture about taking advantage of these policies, or a feeling of resentment that this is some extra special treatment, then it won't have the intended benefits.

As another example, the highly formalized processes that exist often fall at the last hurdle. For example, whilst remuneration by team is highly correlated with results, and the profits and bonuses are distributed accordingly, it is often the line manager who in the final instance divvies up the pie. That means a person's personal relationship with their immediate superior could be the deciding factor in pay, career progression and overall happiness. That is a long way from the overall meritocratic reputation of the sector.

Another challenge is that customers are often missing as a driver. They are not demanding diversity as they are in other sectors. For example, law firms and professional services firms now face clients demanding diverse teams. This is not happening in financial services. While analysis might be happening on financial products, and a great deal of innovation is underway, we have not witnessed the same focus being applied to understand or address customer diversity.

Any intervention has to be highly regarded, fit within existing formal processes (or be good enough to challenge them), and directly engage intelligent people who already think they have this down.

BUY-IN

As with many other organizations, in many other sectors, it starts with buy-in. Many of the tools and examples we detailed in Chapter 6 come from our work in finance. For example, Steve gave a presentation to the Top 400 leaders at Royal Bank of Canada in Toronto. Much of the content was tailored to banking colleagues to have a better chance of getting engagement. What we have learnt from this, and talks at UBS, HSBC and other banks, is that some examples have particular resonance.

First of all, frame this as 'why wouldn't you?' rather than 'why you should'. In finance, confidence is important, and having the confidence to talk about a body of research that clearly demonstrates a correlation between performance and diversity is compelling. The oft-quoted McKinsey diversity research[5] only goes so far. It's background noise if you like. What adds to this is examples such as why Lehman Brothers failed, how group-think is a source of systemic risk or how similar intelligent people can be outperformed by different mixed-ability groups.

Interventions have not always fitted neatly within existing processes. This is particularly true regarding reputational risk concerns. Many new interventions in financial services have got over the line because they addressed significant reputational risk worries. In addition, some organizations are starting to realize the upside and potential of differentiation from diversity.

Three main ways of gaining buy-in in banking are additional and tailored research, the Inclusive Leadership Programme with a focus on research and decision making, and a focus on cognitive diversity and decision making. We will detail these now, with real examples.

RESEARCH

One of the biggest issues when it comes to D&I work in financial services has been the lack of data and research. Yasmine Chinwala, co-founder of London-based think tank New Financial, discusses the cognitive dissonance between what firms say and what they actually do in diversity and inclusion. While firms often talk about how their organization is about their products and their people, often they don't apply the same level of data-driven, analytical approach to their people as they do to their products.

New Financial has sought to help solve this problem. After the financial crisis, New Financial was founded to make the case for bigger and better capital markets in Europe. A big part of its work is helping the industry make a better case for the value of what it does and how it operates, and to encourage the financial services industry to focus more on outcomes for its customers. In order to make this case effectively, the industry needs to embrace cultural change, and one way to demonstrate a concrete commitment to change is through a greater emphasis on diversity.

Additionally, Chinwala says, the financial services sector thinks of itself as a highly meritocratic industry, if not *the most* meritocratic industry: 'It's all about performance, and the best talent will inevitably make it to the top.' We now know that bias is imbued in all of our decisions, but breaking down this widely held perception that finance is extremely meritocratic can be difficult. One of the things she and her colleagues found is that improving diversity and inclusion can be a fundamental part of that change.

One of the first pieces of research New Financial undertook that helped spur momentum on this issue was to put the hard numbers on the long-suspected problem that there were very few women in the most senior roles on executive committees at banks and other financial services companies. New Financial's 2014 report showed that women made up only 20 per cent of boardrooms, and 15 per cent of executive committees.[6] When people in the industry started to see just how bad the problem was, it really shocked them, Chinwala says. But they just didn't know what to do.

Moreover, Chinwala explains, while each company has specific challenges and is starting from a different place, the reality is that many of the issues around D&I are not unique to individual companies but common to the whole financial services sector. One common issue, for example, is for the industry to understand how diversity and inclusion fits into the strategic agenda for the business. 'It's about having the senior people sit down and talk about why this is important to the business. You need to work out why it's important to your business and to you, otherwise you won't be able to come up with effective plans and you have a much higher risk of failure.'

Their research and reports on issues of diversity, particularly on the lack of senior women in financial services, have helped support steps that banks could take as part of a growing trend towards data-led action. These potential actions include signing the UK Treasury-backed *Women in Finance Charter*. This charter, sponsored by the government with New Financial as a research partner, is voluntary. However, the pressure generated by the data they were able to produce led to nearly 300 signatories across financial services sector firms that employ over 600,000 people between them.[7] Furthermore, the gender pay gap reporting that has been mandated by the UK Government has really lit a fire under financial services firms to tackle the lack of diversity in their organizations.

So now there's more of a push to collect and analyse data about people in financial services, and there are people who understand those numbers and what they mean. Chinwala says this is essential to moving things forward to change the culture of the sector. But what's even better is that while there has been an initial focus on gender diversity, this has led to success in other areas of diversity as well.

What Figure 10.1 shows us is that while gender seems to be a starting point for most firms, they tend to apply similar principles to other aspects of diversity as well. As the title of the first graph says, a rising tide lifts all boats.

MOVING D&I OUT OF HR AND INTO THE EXECUTIVE

What needs to be tackled next, though, is that 'diversity and inclusion' tends to be a subset of HR (often called Human Capital in Banking). The focus is very technical, with a series of initiatives in terms of recruitment, 'talent acquisition' and other extrinsic factors.

However, the real cultural change programme, what the organization understands to be 'culture', sits in the executive office and is seen in terms of 'conduct'. Post crisis, 'conduct' is far higher up the C-suite agenda, whereas D&I is relegated to a subdivision of HR. While attention definitely became more directed at conduct in the C-suite immediately after the financial crisis, these ideas about conduct and D&I are now already moving back into the domain of HR. The challenge is understanding how all of these underlying

Figure 10.1 Including gender diversity helps organizations include other diversity[8]

Correlation between disclosure scores on gender criteria and non-gender criteria

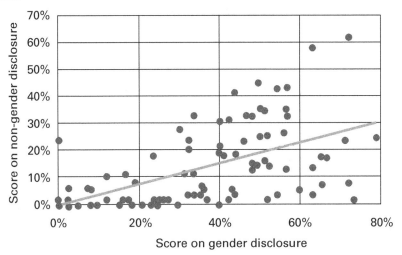

Comparison of organizations that do or do not disclose on any gender criteria and whether they do or do not disclose on any other criteria

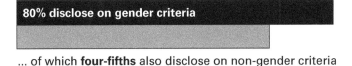

80% disclose on gender criteria

... of which **four-fifths** also disclose on non-gender criteria

20% don't disclose on gender criteria

... of which just **one in five** disclose on non-gender criteria

topics intersect and therefore what leadership and decision making overall should look like going forward.

The most successful initiatives are when this distinction is overcome. Culture and D&I are both integrated into the culture programme of the bank, led from the top. Then it's about going beyond a 101 approach to culture as 'conduct', into a 3.0 approach where culture becomes about leadership and decision making.

INCLUSIVE LEADERSHIP PROGRAMME

With one South African bank, we attempted to tackle the cultural part head-on, not in a segregated fashion, but with an inclusive leadership approach. The bank in question is an investment bank that was founded by two liberal Jewish men in apartheid South Africa. They created a unique and strong culture that fosters entrepreneurship. In one sense it is very inclusive, considering the context in which it was founded, in a nation under apartheid (which is still racially tense[9]), and this has contributed to their strong brand, recognized as a Superbrand by the Centre for Brand Analysis in 2016.[10]

The strong culture is a challenge as well as an opportunity. The South African heritage is palpable in terms of the food served in the canteen, the sense of humour in the office, the sports focus in sponsorship activity. There are no job titles or grades as such. Much about the culture appears, and in many ways genuinely is, incredibly inclusive. However, the appearance of inclusivity can mask a lack of diversity.

Frost Included was asked to help with the sensitive task of educating the leadership and helping to change the organization to be more diverse and inclusive. It was especially sensitive because much of the ethos of the company was indeed inclusive and we didn't want to appear to be slaughtering sacred cows. How could a successful bank become more diverse but remain resolutely South African?

PROCESS

Holding up the mirror

We collated diversity data from across the organization and effectively framed it for the leadership team. We then had the executive team undertake implicit association tests and a simple personal inclusion diagnostic. We were able to gain both organizational insights and also very personal insights into the team. We were then able to play this back to the team in a sensitive but challenging manner.

Reframing diversity as a leadership concept

We brought the executive team together for a three-hour workshop on reframing current understanding of diversity. Using our expertise and the latest research, best practice from other organizations and the data we had collected on the bank, we were able to educate and inspire the team. Crucially, we were able to make the subject relevant to them personally and emotionally, as human beings, as well as logically and commercially, as professionals.

Exploring cognitive dissonance

It's one thing to behave a certain way in a group setting, but this can often be very different from how we behave as individuals, especially when in private. To explore this cognitive dissonance we undertook 1–1 sessions with all executive team members. We explored their personal and professional lives and how they impacted their professional behaviour in terms of diversity and inclusion. We then focused on what actions they might want to undertake to further inclusion at work. It is important to make this personal so that people do not feel as though it is additional work, but instead actions in their own enlightened self-interest.

We know from behavioural science just how powerful an effect small, seemingly insignificant changes can have on our decisions. One example is that reading applications side by side going down a list of criteria rather than one by one going through all the criteria for one applicant followed by another can help the reader focus on more relevant criteria and disregard irrelevant characteristics like race or gender.

THE RESULTS

We brought the team back together for a second workshop where everyone shared their planned actions. We then discussed these potential interventions as a group and then with the diversity and inclusion team to help support their strategy. We determined which of these interventions were most feasible and practical given their constraints such as time, cost and buy-in from the rest of the organization.

There were other results. For example, with another bank, one of the most important executives began discussing his gender identity and began the process of exploring his role in the world. This was significant. Another retail bank undertook some research to explore how they could retain women. What came out of the research was so much more than they had anticipated. They found that part-time working mothers were actually higher performing and achieved higher mortgage and loan sales than their male counterparts. What started as a project to limit the cost of flexible working to the bank, which thought it would be expensive in terms of retaining women, turned into an exploration of how greater flexibility could increase their bottom line.

Buy-in through research and the Inclusive Leadership Programme have all borne fruit. We now give two examples of how we can use cognitive diversity programmes to lead behavioural changes.

COGNITIVE DIVERSITY

We discussed earlier in the chapter about the importance of making the business case for diversity in order to get buy-in. But, particularly in a sector that is so data-heavy, people tend to pick apart the business case by empha-sizing that the studies are only correlations, or that it can't be 'just about race'. What we have found is that by emphasizing that the goal is cognitive diversity we are less likely to be met with defensiveness.

It is important to note that in some firms, using the term 'cognitive diver-sity' has become an excuse to not work on representational diversity, an easy way out of uncomfortable conversations about sexism, racism and homophobia. Thus, when using this approach, it is important to emphasize that these representational aspects of identity do form part of our cognition, as we discussed in Chapter 3. And it is with this level of care that we discussed with the Bank of England their work on cognitive diversity. Thankfully, the bank was not intending for their cognitive diversity work to replace any work on visible diversity. Instead, their aim was to broaden the traditional organizational definition of diversity to make sure they would be including all voices.

Our first step when undergoing this project was to convene a group that represented (and had access to) their stakeholders: Legal, Communications, HR, Data, and Leadership. We then engaged that group in a series of ses-sions about cognitive diversity, inclusion, measurement through an inclusion diagnostic, and interventions. Each session included pre-readings, presenta-tions of concepts or data, and extensive discussion.

The goals of these sessions were to: 1) make sure stakeholders from all relevant departments were bought into the plan; 2) co-develop the plan with stakeholders to increase the sense of ownership of the plan; 3) make sure that the plan was as robust as possible by having as many blind spots covered as possible. Even if you feel you have an amazing plan and know what to do, getting input from people with different approaches than you is crucial for strengthening that plan going forward.

The first session focused on ensuring we all had an understanding of the key concepts we've described in this book: the difference between diversity and inclusion, bias, in- and out-groups, self and role, System 1 and System 2 thinking, etc. We then had a discussion about what cognitive diversity means broadly and in the specific context of the bank – what views are well represented, what is missing, what are the blind spots?

The second session focused on deeper issues of diversity – issues like intersectionality, the importance of inclusion as a bridge between diversity and positive outcomes, and the psychology of how things like gender and race affect the way we think. This allowed the group to consider things like how we needed a high response rate in order to be able to do analysis from an intersectional perspective. We also moved into the more practical side of the project. Led by the member from the communications team, the group created an organization chart to decide which key stakeholders to get on board and define our communications strategy.

When we introduced the Inclusion Diagnostic, the data team member led a discussion on the potential types of analysis we could do and how that might affect the types of questions we asked. Finally, led by the HR team members in the group, we came up with concrete ideas of the aspects of diversity we wanted to measure (we ended up selecting the protected characteristics in the UK plus socio-economic background, level of introversion/extraversion, tenure, scale, and education level).

The third session was a deep dive into the Inclusion Diagnostic, delving into the questions very specifically to make sure the language was appropriate for the context, and any questions we needed to add or remove that were specific to the bank's needs. We also decided on how to measure some of the more complicated diversity metrics – for introversion/extraversion we used the short-form Big Five Inventory,[11] for socio-economic background we used the Bridge Group standards.[12]

The group then launched the Inclusion Diagnostic at the bank, leaving it open for two-and-a-half weeks to collect responses. In the end, over 50 per cent of bank employees filled out the survey. In our analysis, the HR team members were able to check to make sure our respondents were an accurate representation of the bank demographically (they were). Next we performed a factor analysis to see how the responses could be categorized.[13]

We then disaggregated the results by demographic groups (including intersectional groups) to see which groups were most affected by which behaviours, indicating which behaviours were most important to change or keep. Our steering group then came together to review these results and decide what they meant for recommendations and next steps, as well as how to report the results back to the bank.

We decided that to report back, we would first present to the board of governors, as we needed to ensure buy-in from the top before introducing our interventions. We had also decided up front to disseminate the results through the employee networks both to be transparent as well as to ask them for ideas. We then began the process of embedding the results of the Inclusion Diagnostic into existing processes.

There are a few key insights we can glean from this case. First, having a diverse team with representatives from stakeholder departments co-create the plan was key to getting buy-in. It ensured the plan covered potential blind spots. Second, being flexible enough to leverage the skills of those in the team, ensuring that everyone contributed, meant the entire process ran well, from survey design to running the survey, to disseminating the results in a way that would create impact. Third, by clarifying key concepts at the start, the team was able to have the language to articulate the change we wanted to see at the bank.

But what is most interesting about this is that it shows just how important process is. Without defining a clear process in advance of how we were going to bring people in, cover our blind spots, identify stakeholders and get buy-in from them, and all the other considerations we had to make, running this inclusion diagnostic may not have had the success it had.

TRANSPARENCY AND REGULATION

We have long advocated transparency as a way of better ensuring meritocracy. The idea is gaining ground and now several initiatives are underway to call for more transparency in financial institutions. The greatest example of this in recent time is the gender pay gap, detailed in earlier chapters. However, the 30% Club, the Women in Finance Charter and the Hampton-Alexander Review into board and executive pipeline diversity composition are also shining a light on leading practice and those organizations that are straggling.

Finance firms are increasingly turning to new technologies to support their inclusion efforts. Rungway was founded by Julie Chakraverty, a former investment banker, to bring new transparency inside companies by providing an anonymous channel for everyone to access the right advice when they need it.

Julie said:

> The complex nature of finance means a large component of career progression and hence compensation is subjective. Empowering people with in-the-moment advice is crucial for your diverse workforce to have an equal chance to shine. Rungway has found that women tend to comprise one-third of its finance client workforces but ask two-thirds of all anonymous questions. Also, 30 per cent of early posts in finance firms relate to navigating line manager relationships, underscoring the sensitivity of this all-important dynamic.

New technologies can level the playing field, giving everyone access to the advice that will power their career, no matter who they are. Rungway is being embraced by forward-thinking companies who are determined to build and evidence truly inclusive cultures.

Given the push to digital/AI across the sector, the focus areas to date, eg diversity strand development programmes or unconscious bias training, may be considered child's play compared to what the sector will be having to deal with in the future. We discussed in Chapter 4, for example, the issue of a biased AI programme designed to help judges make decisions about sentencing. This is just one example of the potential for diversity bias in the algorithms that will be making all kinds of decisions for people going forward.

How to attract more female talent to finance

Brilliant people instinctively try to 'fix' problems. To address senior female under-representation in financial services, executives often focus on 'getting' more women. This fix of representation over culture is rapidly becoming part of the problem.

The fix is often designed by men, or by women operating in male-dominated environments, and often concerns training women to succeed within that male-dominated environment. So their idea of leadership is often male. This doesn't do much for diversity. The fix involves courses, programmes, initiatives, events, panel discussions, coaching and mentoring.

These can all be helpful, and have a place. But the real problem isn't so much the women (if they are allowed to be their unique diverse selves), it's the male-dominated system. Brilliant people are currently busy prioritizing the wrong thing. The rabbit hole of women's programmes and schemes is distracting us from the real cultural problem in finance.

Companies can say they want women, but the real test is in whether this is a fix or a strategic cultural priority. Do they walk the talk? If they say they do, but their business model is still resistant to flexible working, do they really? If they say they do, but all the female promotions are extroverted characters that better fit in with the men, then do they really?

CONCLUSION

The sector that is most likely to be awarded a 'bad boy' award for diversity and inclusion is also the sector with perhaps the biggest potential to make progress. Many elements of the brutal meritocracy apparent in finance can actually incorporate diversity and inclusion quite easily. The problem is most decision makers view it as a 'soft' subject, but as we have shown diversity is no bed of roses, and managing it takes skill.

There is more buy-in than ever before, some due to the lucidity and framing of the argument in favour of inclusion – keynotes, ILPs and research on cognitive diversity being some of the successful approaches. However, besides the carrots there remain the sticks of regulation and transparency. Transparency is a trend that seems to be heading in one direction at the moment and, as our gender pay gap research showed, has the potential to whip some of the stragglers into line.

FS Focus interview

The following interview was conducted by Rebecca Hobson of *FS Focus*, the financial services magazine published by the Institute of Chartered Accountants in England and Wales (ICAEW) in March 2018.

How would you describe the current situation when it comes to opportunities for men and women working in financial services?

There is a catalytic effect of male-dominated cultures attracting more men because they have to adapt less and can fit in more easily. They unconsciously benefit from network effects. Men are more likely to be promoted and more likely to stay in finance jobs, especially at senior levels. Financial companies often feel male, with macho brand positioning, alpha trading floors, and cavernous receptions – all projections of power.

One of the reasons women are less likely to be promoted is because they are less self-promoting. This is not a deficiency. We know from studies that whilst men are likely to put themselves forward for a promotion when they can do 50 per cent of the job description, women typically wait until they can do 90 per cent before putting their hand up. And the main reason they are more likely to leave is culture.

Were you surprised by the recent report that financial services companies have the highest gender pay gap?

No. The pay gap has many contributing factors but two of the biggest ones are incidence of men and women in highly paid jobs, and the ability to negotiate within the system at each level. In both cases FS is top of the league table – lots more men than women in some of the highest-paying jobs in the economy. And lack of transparency over remuneration combined with network effects and many other variables means men are more likely to receive salary increases compared with women.

Why do you think the gap is larger in FS than in other sectors?

FS has some of the highest-paid jobs in the economy and this, combined with incidence of men and women in those jobs, creates a multiplier effect.

In your experience, what can FS companies do to ensure women employees benefit from the same opportunities as their male counterparts?

1 *Focus on demand, then supply.* Most companies make the mistake of over-reliance on the talent supply side. Yes, the supply of talent is critical for a business and, yes, there are female shortages in STEM subjects. But it's the demand side that can make or break how the supply of talent is included. At London 2012, one breakthrough moment came by changing the interview location from the Canary Wharf office to Mile End Community Centre. By changing the system, not the candidate, we had a far better effect on the demand side and the behaviour and self-awareness of our recruiters. We achieved a step change in diverse recruitment.

2 *Make unconscious behaviour more conscious.* At Investec, Astra Zeneca and BAE Systems, all male-dominated organizations, we have recently conducted inclusive leadership programmes with largely male teams. The purpose of this is to hold up the mirror (to the men in particular) and reframe diversity as a leadership issue (for them personally). By taking them on a journey over a period of weeks we can avoid the usual failing of 'diversity training' programmes. People internalize diversity as a good thing in their own self-interest and are far more receptive to seeking it out as a result.

3 *Nudge the remaining unconscious behaviour.* Up to 97 per cent of our behaviour is unconscious – to tackle the majority of our actual behaviour, we need nudges. We deploy nudges throughout HR processes and systems. We analyse a system (let's say recruitment) and we identify the gaps and biases in it. Then we prioritize which ones to intervene in, and de-bias them by implementing process changes (nudges). Recent examples include presenting anonymized CVs side by side, implementing mixed panels, and recruiting and assessing groups of individuals at the same time, not individuals one by one.

So if you really want to attract more female talent into finance, yes, continue your supply-side work, but focus a lot more on the demand side.

And by all means continue your unconscious bias training, but focus a lot more on the real unconscious behaviour going on below the surface.

As Bob Diamond said, 'culture is what you do when nobody is watching'. You can't apply a technical fix to a cultural problem and expect to solve the problem. If you really want to attract more women into finance, focus on the men.

What measures can they introduce?

Many, but essentially two work streams: conscious behaviour change (leadership) and unconscious system changes (nudges). We work with both and the best results are when a company embraces both, combined with targets and measurement embedded in a scorecard that is reviewed regularly. If you really want to achieve change you need to engage the men and often this can be done through linking explicit desired behaviours to remuneration or whatever drivers they best respond to within the particular company culture.

TAKEAWAYS

1 Financial Services companies often think of themselves as the most meritocratic organizations possible. In this industry in particular, you need to hold up the mirror; showing them the research and data can be particularly effective in making your case.

2 D&I has to become a personal issue to the executives of the firm. Without that, your D&I plan will remain a part of HR and likely not get off the ground as high as it could.

3 Framing your D&I plan as a way to increase cognitive diversity can be a good way to pre-empt backlash. Definitely still include aspects of visible diversity, but expand your definition to include non-protected aspects as well such as introversion and socio-economic background.

4 Having a clear and defined process is key to the success of your plan – it makes sure your stakeholders are brought in properly, your blind spots are covered, and your roll-out and communication are transparent and effective.

5 New technologies to help you in your D&I work can be extremely powerful, but they should be approached with caution. Depending on how they're used, they could level the playing field or simply exacerbate existing biases.

ENDNOTES

1 Coates, J (2012) *The Hour Between Dog and Wolf: How risk taking transforms us, body and mind*, Penguin Books

2 Sorkin, A R (2010) *Too Big to Fail: The inside story of How Wall Street and Washington fought to save the financial system–and themselves*, Penguin Books

3 https://hbr.org/2010/10/what-if-lehman-brothers-had-be

4 https://www.dailymail.co.uk/news/article-6079589/Goldman-Sachs-pay-mothers-work-trips-courier-breast-milk.html

5 Hunt, V, Layton D and Prince, S (2015) *Diversity Matters*, McKinsey & Company

6 https://newfinancial.eu/counting-every-woman-2017-making-progress-gender-diversity-capital-markets/

7 Interview with Yasmine Chinwala, co-founder, New Financial, 16 Aug 2018

8 Chinwala, Y and Bell, K (2015) Diversity disclosure: what the European capital markets industry publicly discloses about diversity, *New Financial*, September (Reproduced with permission of the author)

9 https://www.newsweek.com/2018/06/29/south-africa-cover-story-white-farmers-black-population-economic-collapse-985088.html

10 https://www.rankingthebrands.com/The-Brand-Rankings.aspx?rankingID=57&year=1030

11 The Big Five Inventory is the most statistically validated and widely used psychological measure of personality. It has both a long form and a short form, both of which have been found to be accurate measures of personality characteristics.

12 The Bridge Group has done extensive analysis on measuring social mobility (among other characteristics) and has publicly available sample questions and guidelines for analysis for organizations looking to measure the social mobility of their employees.

13 When there is no similar questionnaire available to compare to a new metric for validation, we perform Exploratory Factor Analysis. This determines which of the questions can be grouped together as measures of the same aspect of the larger idea the entire scale is observing, creating subscales that can each have their own scores. For example, being a 'good student' comprises a variety of factors. Thus some questions may get at a student's intelligence, others may focus on work ethic, and others may look at respect in the classroom. We can create subscales measuring each of these different aspects. A similar approach is taken here for inclusion.

11

RESPONSIBILITY, RE-INVENTION AND REVOLUTION: BUILDING INCLUSION IN THE TECH SECTOR

INTRODUCTION

Raafi grew up reading comic books – everything from comedies like Garfield and Archie to dramatic superhero stories like Batman and Spiderman. Comics have often been used to communicate important ideas and introduce deep philosophical and moral teachings.[1] One particular idea that stuck with Raafi came from an old issue of *Amazing Fantasy* that said, 'With great power comes great responsibility'[2] (to be fair, this phrase actually dates as far back as the French Revolution,[3] but Raafi first learned it from comics).

This phrase has remained with Raafi since childhood, in part because it has been apt in so many situations. The invasions of Iraq and Afghanistan were certainly possible due to the immense power of the United States and its allies, but their military presence in those countries has lasted this long mainly because the use of that power came with a responsibility to rebuild the government. The power that many athletes get from their fame and wealth means they have a responsibility to set examples for others in society.

In a similar way, the tech sector has become incredibly powerful – tech companies control so much of the global economy, people's access to knowledge and information, connections among families, friends and strangers. In fact, the five largest tech companies – Apple, Amazon, Facebook, Alphabet (the parent company of Google) and Microsoft – are collectively worth US $3.5 trillion.[4] For perspective, that's more than the *entire economy of the UK*.[5] Indeed, if finance was once the 'Master of the Universe', that title now goes to the tech sector, as it has the power to influence our very way of thinking and behaving.

Take Facebook, for example. The company may have started as a way to connect people to their friends virtually, but it has become so much more than that now. In fact, 44 per cent of American adults get some of their news from Facebook, and 18 per cent get most of their news that way.[6] As such, Facebook has the power to control what news we see and don't see, affecting our opinions about the world and our knowledge of current events.

However, it wasn't until 2018 that Facebook bosses acknowledged that the level of power they were gaining came with the responsibility to ensure biased information was not being disseminated.[7] Mark Zuckerberg, co-founder and CEO said as much when he testified before the US Senate in April 2018. He stated, 'We didn't take a broad enough view of our responsibility, and that was a big mistake.'[8] Neglecting that responsibility caused problems for Facebook as it gained notoriety for the way biased information spread through the platform may have influenced the 2016 US Presidential election. But it has also caused problems for us as a society in the way it has stoked our fears and divisions and created a more polarized and siloed polity.

Tech companies, therefore, can step up to increase diversity and inclusion in their organizations not just to better their companies and products but also to stem the spread of biased or fake information. More diverse companies can better check that algorithms aren't biased, like the programme in

Florida we discussed in Chapter 4, which inaccurately predicted that Black offenders were more likely to commit another crime than white offenders. More diversity can help ensure image searches don't mistakenly identify Black people as apes, like Google did in the original version of its online search product.[9]

SECTOR CHALLENGES AND ADDRESSING THE PIPELINE PROBLEM

In addition to the responsibility challenge, the next issue we've encountered is unacknowledged bias. Younger people, who dominate the tech sector, sometimes think that issues of racism and sexism and other forms of discrimination are a thing of the past, something their parents and grand-parents dealt with and solved.

As of January 2017, 47 per cent of people under the age of 24 in the United States believe that there isn't much discrimination against women or people of colour.[10] These statistics are beginning to change as a result of current events like the renewed number of white supremacist rallies all over the world, and prominent politicians and celebrities being accused of discrimination and harassment. However, there is still a growing movement in tech in particular saying that diversity programmes have gone too far and that discrimination is now stronger against white men.[11]

It's unclear just how large those groups are, but they have become increasingly vocal of late. For example, in 2017 James Damore, a programmer at Google, wrote a memo suggesting that the disparity between men and women coders was a result of biological differences.[12] When he was fired it emboldened many other men at Google and other tech companies in Silicon Valley to express their similar feelings. This has generated a small but vocal movement against D&I programmes; instituting these programmes in this industry in a particular fashion can result in a strong backlash.

Another challenge to increasing D&I in tech is that working as a programmer requires a large amount of training and education. Whether achieved through formal means such as a university degree or through learning to code on one's own, learning these skills is often required before getting a job. Ben Delk, an equality programmes manager at Salesforce, expressed this as a barrier to inclusion in tech that doesn't exist to the same extent in other industries.[13]

In particular, he explained that marginalized groups have historically been prevented from accessing the specialized skills required for jobs in the tech industry, and that continues today. For large tech companies that have jobs requiring fewer education-based skills like manufacturing, it's easier to increase diversity. But if a company wants to increase diversity in the more technical side of its workforce, they can't really upskill people on the job if there is no baseline level of education in programming.

This has resulted in a third challenge – the pipeline problem. This is the fact that even if companies were to make a concerted effort to hire more women, minorities and other marginalized group members, they as a group are under-represented in computer science programmes. As such, the lack of diversity isn't just a problem at the organization level, but much earlier on in the path towards working in tech.

One way Facebook has now taken it upon itself to ensure more difference enters the tech sector is through its Women in Tech University. This aims to provide support and engage women in tech in universities and among current employees to help build the pipeline. While this is certainly an innovative idea, and addresses the problem much earlier on than when women enter the workforce, this is just the start, and the success of the programme remains to be seen. Microsoft has begun to fund scholarships for under-represented minorities in tech, to help increase access to the education necessary to work in the industry. Sky is similarly funding scholarships in STEM and developing training programmes outside universities to help others gain access to the tech industry.

Another organization working on solving this problem is Learnerbly. Their goal is to 'curate the best learning opportunities to help people grow', by allowing people to direct their own ways of learning. This bottom-up approach caters to diverse people and diverse ways that people access information and knowledge. As such, it is a tool that tech companies could use to their advantage to upskill people who they feel have the right ideas and mindset to work in tech, but maybe not the right skills yet. This would allow those companies to hire from more diverse backgrounds while still ensuring that they have necessary skills. However, until the point where tools like Learnerbly are curated properly for the skills for tech and are more widely used, there will still be a pipeline issue.

However, while this pipeline problem may exist, there is still a dispropor-tionately higher percentage of women and minorities with degrees relevant to tech than actually work in the industry. In the United States for example, women earned 36 per cent of computer science degrees in the 1990s, but still hold less than 25 per cent of computing jobs.[14] Even if we go more broadly than purely computer science, women have made up about 50 per cent of science and engineering degrees since the 1990s (though there was a decreasing trend for many years) but only represent 30 per cent of the science and engineering workforce. For ethnic minorities the statistics are even worse – they represent over 20 per cent of all science and engineering degrees, but only 11 per cent of science and engineering jobs.[15]

There are now many organizations dedicated solely to increasing the numbers of women and minorities in tech and giving them access to organi-zations. Take Girls Who Code, for example. This organization was only founded in 2012 and yet has now reached nearly 90,000 women across the United States to help them learn to code, get support from each other, and begin to understand how to navigate the tech world as a woman. They also put special emphasis on engaging young girls of colour and girls with disabilities. Their continued efforts are affording the United States the possibility of full gender parity in tech by 2027.[16]

OPPORTUNITIES

While there are definitely unique challenges posed by the tech industry to inclusion programmes, it also presents unique opportunities. One study by political scientists at Stanford University showed that workers in tech com-panies are extremely supportive of often-contentious social issues like same-sex marriage, abortion, abolishing the death penalty, increased spending on welfare programmes, and increased taxation of higher-wealth individuals.[17] These types of political leanings might also translate over to issues of D&I.

Additionally, the tech industry has a lot of power to influence. We have already discussed the way it has contributed to polarization in society, but it can also turn that influence on its head to promote more inclusive ideas. For example, a more inclusive coding team could produce a less racially biased sentencing algorithm for Florida and other states. Additionally, a more diverse Google might fix their problem of only coming up with mug shots when searching for images of 'three black teenagers'. Starting with these types of small fixes, we can begin to subtly alter our ingrained stereotypes.

HOW STARTUPS ARE A GREAT OPPORTUNITY FOR INCLUSION: PLASTIQ AS A CASE STUDY

The tech industry is still quite young and new startups are emerging all the time. Globally between 2009 and 2017, more than 43,000 tech companies were founded and received initial rounds of funding.[18] As such, these start-ups can embed D&I right from the start. This is a much easier way to create an inclusive culture than trying to change a culture that already exists. For example, at the US-based tech startup Plastiq, D&I was a consideration right as the company was being founded. As a result, inclusive behaviours are embedded in the company's culture and the way it makes decisions.

One of the company's founders, Eliot Buchanan, explains that this is in part due to the fact that he and his co-founder Dan Choi have diversity in their DNA (Buchanan is an immigrant from Canada while Choi is the son of immigrants from South Korea). But Buchanan says that D&I was impor-tant from the start also because they knew they wanted to have as much debate as possible in order to make sure they were making robust decisions.

The best way to make sure those debates took place was to ensure people were coming from different backgrounds and felt comfortable bringing their different points of view to the table. That definitely meant inclusion of visibly diverse people, but also the inclusion of introverts, for example. To facilitate this, Plastiq has created many different ways of giving feedback that can cater to different people's ways of communicating, including in person, in written form, anonymously, and other methods.[19]

Additionally, inclusion is considered when creating policies. Buchanan explains this through the example of creating a parental leave policy – when two Plastiq employees were about to have children, they approached

Buchanan and his head of HR noting that there was no parental leave policy in place. Buchanan's response was to ask the employees what they wanted, and to solicit their opinions along with those of others in the organization to help craft their policy.

When we asked him why he took this approach rather than looking at what other organizations had done or what the academic research was, he said that doing that type of research is often useful but the most useful thing is to make sure the people who are going to be most affected by the policy have a say. They deserve to be heard, and as imminent parents they have a perspective Buchanan doesn't. Whether the ideas end up making it into the final policy or not, ensuring they have a say allows us to consider things we may not have considered before, which can benefit everyone.

In this way, while Plastiq doesn't have a formal D&I policy yet (Buchanan says there are plans to create one as they scale), it is something that they discuss a lot. It is in the very fabric of what they do and has been from the start. As such, it has been much easier to engender inclusive behaviours and an inclusive culture in the company. But what's most interesting is that so far, Plastiq hasn't needed a formal D&I policy to be an inclusive company. Certainly, as they get bigger this will become more important to ensure consistency across the company, but when inclusion is just part of the way you do business (and indeed a method for doing business better) an inclusive culture and inclusive behaviours flourish. Other startups, then, have the same opportunity to embed inclusion right from the beginning.

TURNING THINGS AROUND? THE CASE OF UBER

If you're working in a larger organization, not a startup like Plastiq, then you have no choice but to work on adapting a culture to be inclusive rather than starting from scratch. This can be a difficult task, as we have explored throughout the book, especially if non-inclusive norms are embedded in the organization. However, some tech companies like this are beginning to show that they are up to this task and willing to try, none more so than Uber.

BACKGROUND

Uber first came into the spotlight around diversity and inclusion because of a public essay that went viral in early 2017, written by a former engineer employee, Susan Fowler.[20] In the essay, Fowler relates her experiences of working at Uber for a year and describes an incredibly toxic and misogynistic culture. Her experiences describe not only regularly experiencing sexual harassment along with more subtle sexism, but also that when she reported even the more outrageous behaviours to HR they did nothing to rectify the situation. Her manager threatened to fire her (despite the fact that firing someone for reporting things to HR is illegal in the United States). In the end, she decided to leave the company and go public with her story.

When the story went viral many other women at the company (and in tech broadly) started to relate similar experiences,[21] and Uber was gaining a reputation as a terrible place for women to work. It eventually contributed to the resignation of Uber CEO Travis Kalanick only five months after the publication of Fowler's essay, and eventually the departure of multiple other executives and board members in the company over the next year. Since then, Uber has been trying to rebuild its reputation and become a more inclusive company.

TURNING OVER A NEW LEAF?

It would be fair to think that Uber would take a very Diversity 2.0 approach – driven by marketing, and simply doing things that earn them good press. However, the company seems to have taken a real turn, instead focusing on actually changing its culture and norms. But this hasn't been the easiest task.

Shruti Kannan, a Diversity and Inclusion Programme Manager at Uber, says that at this point the vast majority of Uber employees mean really well and know it's the right thing intuitively, but don't necessarily know what to do. This group either feels frozen, is scared to engage in conversation and so stays quiet, or tries things that are not the most effective. And this is where Kannan and her colleagues aim to help.

These efforts began with the hiring of Bo Young Lee as the new Chief Diversity and Inclusion Officer. Lee focused strategy on building a more empathetic culture. Instead of centring cultural challenges as a D&I problem, it was about embedding more kindness, compassion and collaboration. Essentially, empathizing with those that are different from you is at the heart of being inclusive, and building that empathy means building in kindness, compassion and collaboration. Without that, D&I work can't take root.

This has been done in a few ways. First, the entire C-suite has undertaken training on bias and the differential impacts of behaviours on different groups, as well as how they have to think of themselves as role models of inclusive behaviour for the entire organization. This helps give the leaders a better idea of what it is like to be a member of a marginalized group at Uber, and the impact their behaviour has on these employees.

According to Kannan, this also helps develop leaders' empathy for that experience 'because people are giving them the context, history and language to understand systemic oppression'. And in 2018 the D&I team is working on ensuring that all members of their executive leadership team worldwide become inclusive leaders through inclusive leadership training, as well as more basic bias training offered to thousands of other Uber employees around the world.

We asked Kannan why Uber hasn't publicized all the work that it is doing – surely it would help with Uber's negative press. She says, 'It feels too soon to pat ourselves on the back. It's a long, heavy, arduous process… There's a lot of work still left to be done, even if we are doing things that I'm proud of.' And she's right. While there still is a lot of work to be done, and while this is a first step, it is a fantastic first step and Uber might just be turning things around.

SALESFORCE'S REVOLUTION: GOING BEYOND D&I TO FIGHT FOR GLOBAL EQUALITY

While some tech companies are trying to turn a corner and enter a new era of inclusion, others are showing us what the future of D&I in organizations could be. One of those companies that is leading in this area is Salesforce.

Many companies have started hiring Chief Diversity Officers or Heads of Diversity, Inclusion and Belonging, or other executives with similar titles. Salesforce has a Chief Equality Officer, Tony Prophet. At first glance, this may seem merely like a meaningless nomenclature – a way of trying to set the company apart in terms of D&I without actually doing anything special. But when asked about this name, Prophet explains that it was about saying Salesforce is trying to go beyond the typical organization's D&I agenda:

> Diversity is absolutely essential... but once you have diversity you're not done. Then you have inclusion, where you're really getting the very best out of every employee... Equality goes beyond that. Equality asks the questions, 'Are you standing for my rights when I step outside my workforce? Are you fighting for equality for me?'[22]

This idea of working on equality is not an entirely new one – in fact, this is where much D&I work started before moving to the language of equal opportunities and then to D&I. However, that was much more about equality at work. Now, Prophet is suggesting we use work to push for equality in society. This view of the role of an organization is certainly a radical one, but it is also a powerful concept. This mindset could completely alter the role of organizations in society as not just drivers of the economy but active drivers of social good.

EMPLOYEE RESOURCE GROUPS (ERGS) AS THE CENTRE POINT

One way that Salesforce is trying to drive equality forward both in the company and in society broadly is by leveraging its ERGs, similar to the way Uber has begun to, as we discussed earlier. Ben Delk, who works in D&I at Salesforce (and who we mentioned earlier in this chapter) says that having D&I work run through ERGs is a natural starting point because all the work intersects there – accountability, subject matter experts, passions.[23] They represent the inclusive nature of a company, it's where people are more likely to feel most heard and at home, and these groups have access to people in the company that may not feel quite at home there yet. Salesforce has really worked on developing its ERGs, giving them the time, space, and resources to create programmes.

They also encourage ERGs to co-programme, which Delk says develops even more inclusion because it helps increase understanding of intersectionality and brings together groups that are similarly marginalized but different from each other. This helps to bridge gaps among all kinds of people at the organization.

Moreover, they also leverage their strong ERG network in the hiring process, by getting their advice to bring in more under-represented candidates, as well as having them help create more diverse interview panels. Additionally, Salesforce is introducing a programme to provide the ERGs as resources to candidates, so they can reach out for information if they want it. This is a great signal that they actually care about the employee experience and want them to feel like they can bring their whole selves to work.

In addition to all these initiatives, they also run training on how to hold inclusive meetings and inclusive leadership broadly, and have a dashboard of their diversity data and pipeline that is public to all leaders in the organization. The former of these helps leaders gain the skills to be more inclusive in their day-to-day behaviours, while the latter helps to hold them accountable for actually using those skills.

Salesforce's approach, therefore, combines some traditional aspects of D&I programmes with some of the more cutting-edge work we have suggested in this book. However, their approach – to use the organization to fight for societal equality – pushes the boundaries of what organizations have done so far in this space. And yet, perhaps that's what we should expect of tech companies. For instance, so much of the industry is based in one location – Silicon Valley. As a result, these communities have been fundamentally changed and not always for the better. With issues like gentrification, the lack of affordable housing, and the rising cost of food being direct effects of the expansion of the tech industry, perhaps it is only right that tech companies be concerned about community. In this way, Salesforce's revolution is really just fulfilling its responsibility.

CONCLUSION

The tech industry has had an incredible impact on inclusion in our society, but in some instances this has served to exacerbate and emphasize differences between people, polarizing society even further. And it might seem difficult to change this, since increasing diversity in tech may be a difficult task with all its particularities. But its ability to influence and innovative startup culture has resulted in many opportunities to get D&I right.

And good work has initiated a virtuous circle. Tech Nation, the UK agency tasked with building and supporting the British tech sector, has run workshops for tech startups on embedding inclusion in their modus operandi. This has created feedback loops in the sector about what works best in practice. On a global platform, Web Summit, held annually in Lisbon, has dedicated more and more programming time to D&I and is trying to embed it in its core curriculum. As it becomes more normal to think pre-emptively about D&I in tech, this can hopefully benefit individual companies, the sector, and society at large.

Whether they're embedding inclusion right from the start, trying to start a new chapter after a period of D&I turmoil, or pushing the limits of what an organization can do to drive inclusion in society, the tech industry has many models that organizations could follow no matter what stage they're at.

TAKEAWAYS

1　The tech industry has a lot of power to influence the way we live our lives, but that comes with a responsibility to not exacerbate our differences.

2　While there are some challenges, such as the pipeline problem, the statistics show that tech organizations still have a lot of work to do to become more diverse and more inclusive based on the talent that is already available.

3　There are many startups in tech, and they have an amazing opportunity to start considering inclusion right from the get-go.

4　Even companies that have struggled with D&I in the past can find ways to reset. While that journey may take a long time, if done right it can really change an organization's culture.

5　The innovative nature of tech companies allows them to push the limits of what organizations can do in terms of D&I. They can fight for equality not just within their own organization, but in society at large.

ENDNOTES

1 Morris, T, Morris, M and Irwin, W (2005) *Superheroes and Philosophy: Truth, justice, and the Socratic Way*, Chicago: Open Court

2 Lee, S (1962) *Spiderman, Amazing Fantasy# 15*, Marvel Comics, New York

3 France Convention Nationale (1793) *Collection générale des décrets rendus par la Convention Nationale* (Vol 33), p 72

4 https://www.inc.com/associated-press/mindblowing-facts-tech-industry-money-amazon-apple-microsoft-facebook-alphabet.html

5 Ibid

6 http://www.slate.com/articles/technology/technology/2016/12/how_many_people_really_get_their_news_from_facebook.html

7 https://www.npr.org/sections/thetwo-way/2018/04/10/599808766/i-m-responsible-for-what-happens-at-facebook-mark-zuckerberg-will-tell-senate

8 Ibid

9 https://www.huffingtonpost.com/2015/07/02/google-black-people-goril_n_7717008.html

10 https://www.prri.org/research/mtv-culture-and-religion/

11 https://www.nytimes.com/2017/09/23/technology/silicon-valley-men-backlash-gender-scandals.html

12 Ibid

13 Interview with Ben Delk, Equality Programs Officer, Salesforce, 21 Aug 2018

14 http://observer.com/2017/06/women-in-tech-statistics/

15 https://www.nsf.gov/statistics/2017/nsf17310/digest/occupation/overall.cfm

16 https://girlswhocode.com/about-us/

17 https://www.vox.com/policy-and-politics/2017/9/6/16260326/tech-entrepreneurs-survey-politics-liberal-regulation-unions

18 https://techcrunch.com/2017/04/19/in-2017-only-17-of-startups-have-a-female-founder/

19 Interview with Eliot Buchanan, Co-founder and CEO, Plastiq, Inc, 21 Aug 2018

20 https://www.susanjfowler.com/blog/2017/2/19/reflecting-on-one-very-strange-year-at-uber

21 https://www.nytimes.com/2017/06/21/technology/uber-ceo-travis-kalanick.html

22 https://www.fastcompany.com/3069082/why-salesforces-new-equality-chief-is-thinking-beyond-diversity

23 Interview with Ben Delk, Equality Programs Officer, Salesforce, 21 Aug 2018

12

CREATING KNOWLEDGE INCLUSIVELY: BUILDING AN INCLUSIVE ORGANIZATION IN ACADEMIA AND FOUNDATIONS

INTRODUCTION TO ACADEMIA AND FOUNDATIONS

Academia can be defined as institutions of higher learning, such as universities, that both teach students as well as perform research to further societal knowledge in various subject areas. Foundations, for the purposes of this discussion, are philanthropic organizations with a specific mission achieved through funding projects. We have decided to look at these two sectors together because they have a lot in common in terms of challenges and opportunities, and so have much in common in terms of how to address inclusion.

Academia and foundations are often seen as isolated and siloed institutions, accessible only to the most elite in society. Indeed, for a foundation to exist it needs a large amount of money (which more often than not means a wealthy funder or set of funders at the helm). Most of academia is dominated by people with Doctorate degrees, which the majority of the population do not have, and many do not even have the opportunity to pursue. However, while most of the population has little interaction with these kinds of institutions aside from attending university, they are hugely influential on the way we live our lives.

Without the initial research by Russian scientists into communication technologies, we would never have had the ARPANET, which eventually became the Internet as we know it today. Without research by chemists and biologists, diseases like smallpox and polio might never have been eradicated. Perhaps the most influential piece of academic research ever done was by Fritz Haber early in the 20th century when he found a way to capture nitrogen from the air and turn it into liquid ammonia, which could be used to create synthetic fertilizers. Without this research, our planet would never have been able to grow enough food to sustain more than 1 billion people. In other words, without academia, about 85 per cent of us likely wouldn't be alive today.[1,2] And foundations play a role at both ends of this, as they fund many academics to undertake their research and also many organizations that put this research into practice.

For example, the Wellcome Trust – which we will discuss later in this chapter – funds research into health and science that has led to advances in vaccines and medication. This includes the vaccine used to stem the spread of Ebola during the outbreak in West Africa and other areas in 2014–2015. The spread of this virus led to over 10,000 deaths; without this successful research, the epidemic may have lasted much longer, leading to even more loss of life. But without funding, the research may never have happened at all.

It is clear then that both academia and foundations are vitally important to our world and the way we experience it. However, like the creative sector, it is possibly in part due to their importance and success that they have largely not paid much attention to issues of diversity and inclusion in the past. Only recently has this come up as an important issue for these sectors, and they have found themselves in a difficult situation of established norms and behaviours that maintain homogeneity and fail to leverage much of the diversity that exists in their institutions.

CURRENT STATE OF D&I, AND RESULTING CHALLENGES

The exclusive nature of academia might be viewed as being in complete opposition to the idea of inclusivity. Indeed, many might equate inclusion with a lowering of standards. Academic institutions seek out the most highly educated or 'high potential' individuals for admission. However, we need to address our unconscious biases. For example, 'high potential' means different things for different people – if we are biased against Black applicants, we might subconsciously require more proof of high potential than we would of white applicants. In this way, D&I is actually in direct support of the nature and mission of these organizations.

One aspect of academia and foundations that the sectors pride themselves on is also one of their biggest barriers to D&I: many of them have been around for so long, sometimes even centuries, and so are used to things being done in a particular way. As such, the way these organizations make decisions around processes like recruitment, hiring, retention and promotion, as well as behaviours like how to run meetings or evaluate progress are almost fundamental to the identities of the institutions. This makes change very difficult. Even when those in power are convinced of the need to make changes it can be very slow moving.

For example, we have known for many years that in US universities there are fewer female and minority professors than male and white professors, particularly tenured or tenure-track professors. As of 2015, white men made up 42 per cent of all faculty and a full 56 per cent of tenured professors across the United States.[3] We also know this has remained true despite more and more women and people of colour studying in graduate school, entering academia, and being put up for tenured positions. What this means is that women and people of colour are making up a relatively static proportion of those who actually get tenure – the apex of the academic ladder. Despite this, though, most institutions are still reluctant to introduce anonymous applications, strictly structured interviews, or other similar interventions that we have mentioned in previous chapters.

Their reticence is partly understandable. Universities pride themselves on being meritocratic organizations. To adapt their processes now could perhaps be seen as an admission they weren't particularly meritocratic before, violating a fundamental aspect of their identities.

Take the Harvard Kennedy School (HKS), our alma mater and a place where Steve has often taught classes and given lectures. In 2005, African Americans made up 6.1 per cent of HKS staff, but by 2015 it was still just 6.6 per cent.[4] Only in 2017 did the school finally commission a task force to research the issue and come up with suggestions. Even then the result was simply that the university would provide 'revised guidance' on hiring. This included material on implicit bias and was distributed to faculty members when they engaged in the hiring or promotion process.[5] While this is a good first step, it seems inadequate, especially for an institution that has known about and acknowledged its diversity problem for over a decade.

Foundations are similar – making decisions based on merit is a core part of their identity. When deciding who to fund and how much funding to give, it is expected both by those applying for the funding as well as the foundation itself that it would make those decisions in an objective manner. As with universities, having to change their decision-making process could be admitting that decisions until this point have not necessarily been as objective as they could have been.

OPPORTUNITIES IN THESE SECTORS

The above discussion shows how D&I work can be challenging in academia and foundations. However, the sectors also provide a unique opportunity not afforded in other sectors.

Specifically, these sectors have a culture of innovation and experimentation. Most other organizations, especially for-profit corporations or organizations that have little money to spend, cannot afford the cost of failed interventions. They want to try interventions they already know have a strong likelihood of success. This means that interventions – while unique in that they are tailored to the specific context of the organization – are largely quite similar to interventions done before at other similar organizations. Hence the obsession with 'copying best practice'.

However, by definition, academia is all about trying new things and testing them to see if they work. It's about 'creating innovative practice'. Foundations similarly look to fund innovative solutions to problems. This means that they are more open to trying new ideas as long as a solid evidence base backs up those ideas.

This is precisely what happened when we worked with Wellcome to develop our initial Inclusion Diagnostic. No tool like this existed – or at least was publicly known and available – when it was developed. However, when we approached Wellcome with the idea of developing the tool and testing it with them, they were completely open to the idea even if the attempt was a failure because it meant they would be contributing to the development of a new method of measurement of organizational culture that could have incredible impact. In this way, new ideas and methods can be tried in this sector in a way that other sectors may not be as willing to do.

INNOVATIVE INTERVENTIONS IN ACADEMIA

Increasing inclusion on university campuses – among staff, faculty and students – has become an important topic in academic institutions. This is in part due to an increase in public awareness of staggering statistics such as 23 per cent of female undergraduates in the United States having experienced rape or sexual assault,[6] or that 20 years after the end of apartheid the university graduation rate of white students in South Africa is on average 50 per cent higher than that of Black students.[7]

Different approaches have been tried, such as training, outreach or creating a position like Chief Diversity Officer, but those alone have not often worked.[8] This is because they are simply technical fixes, not addressing underlying culture. Indeed, one study that interviewed university diversity officers and affirmative action officers stated that they 'expressed frustration in their roles due to uncertainty about the extent to which their work was genuinely supported'.[9] Simply creating these roles without making an effort to change behaviours, or support those tasked with leading change, is not effective.

ATHENA SWAN – A CHANCE FOR ACCOUNTABILITY

Many in academic institutions are now engaging in more innovative ideas. Perhaps the most famous of those innovations in the UK is the Athena SWAN charter. Established in 2005, Athena SWAN (Scientific Women's Academic Network) recognizes organizations that are committed to gender equality. They originally had institutions sign up for the charter and gave awards for equality in science, technology, engineering and mathematics (STEM), but have since broadened their scope to include non-STEM programmes as well.

When institutions sign the Athena SWAN charter, they commit to 10 different principles and commitments regarding gender equality in their institution and academia more broadly. These include action to increase representation of women in senior roles and tenured positions, and addressing the leaky pipeline problem of women (particularly in STEM) dropping out of the academic career pipeline before reaching senior roles.

Athena SWAN publishes the names of those institutions that win Bronze, Silver, or Gold awards each year. This creates public accountability for those institutions that sign onto the charter. It has created some measurable results, including that all staff at the relevant institutions (not just women) were more satisfied with their career performance and development, had more transparency about the promotion process, were more likely to receive awards for their work, and rated their university more highly on promoting equality and diversity.[10]

IMPROVING AND EXPANDING UPON THE ATHENA SWAN MODEL

Athena SWAN also has its limitations. For one thing, it focuses more on gender inequality than on other diversity characteristics. Not only is that inadequate in terms of other aspects of diversity, but it also limits its measurement of gender inequality by not paying attention to the intersection between gender and other identities. For example, the experience of a gay woman may be very different from that of a heterosexual woman. The experience of a white woman in an institution may be very different from that of a Black woman.

To address all of these issues, a US-based project has expanded upon the Athena SWAN model to create its STEM Equity Achievement Change (SEA Change) that it began piloting at the end of 2017. This follows the same premise as Athena SWAN, but expands it to assess inclusion by race, ethnicity, sexual orientation, disability, socio-economic status and other characteristics. It is still in the pilot stage, but it hopes to have similar results to Athena SWAN along multiple diversity identities.

However, both Athena SWAN and SEA Change are based on institutions conducting self-assessments. This is likely better than no assessment at all, but even better than this would be an external audit. While external organizations may not completely understand the context as well as internal staff, they are also more likely to be objective in their evaluations. This, we feel, could really help increase the effectiveness of these tools as accountability mechanisms and make them even more rigorous and robust.

Universities themselves can also institute innovative programmes to increase inclusion. For example, Singapore Management University instituted a lecture series on managing diversity in Asia. It was so popular that it became a recurring course that included experiential learning programmes focused on building empathy for those different from the students. It is now one of the most popular courses and consistently has a waiting list.[11] At New York University's Abu Dhabi campus, the Office of Intercultural Education created a four-part training programme called Intercultural Core Competence, designed to help students understand how to actively create inclusion on an already diverse campus.[12]

These are just some of the innovative ideas that academic institutions and foundations are able to try out. They are all based on the same fundamental ideas we've been discussing throughout this book: education about biases and how inclusion requires action, developing inclusive leadership, creating accountability mechanisms, and designing more inclusive policies and procedures.

PROCESS REVIEWS: THE US–UK FULBRIGHT COMMISSION

Today, when bias is a more well-known topic, many institutions are worried about bias in their procedures because they need to attract the best talent in order to compete, just like any organization. Bias may or may not play a role in their current decision-making processes, but by employing more inclusive procedures, they can protect themselves by being able to conclusively and concretely show they are doing everything they can to remove negative bias from their decisions.

It is also useful to have gone through this process if they are accused of bias, such as the lawsuit against Harvard for systematic discrimination against Asian applicants.[13] Harvard had gone through an audit of their policies to assess for discrimination, essentially ensuring that their policies were legal.[14] However, what would make their argument even stronger would be if they had gone through an audit of their policies for best practices across the board, not just for legality. By following all best practices regarding bias and D&I they could clearly demonstrate intent and minimize any claim against them.

One of the first things we can do is a process review. We undertook this with the US–UK Fulbright Commission, and the process and results were very helpful and insightful for improving their selection process.

For context, the US–UK Fulbright Commission is part of the worldwide Fulbright Program, one of the most prestigious and well-known scholarship programmes. The US–UK scholarships (Fulbright Awards) are given to exceptional students and researchers in the US and UK, to pursue study and meaningful research in each other's countries. The programme rewards outstanding academic prowess and potential, leadership potential and ambassadorial qualities.

To be truly successful in their goals, the Commission seeks to select a cohort that accurately reflects the diversity of its country. This includes diversity in broad terms such as geography, ethnicity, gender identity, age, sexual orientation, field of study, parental status and socio-economic class.

While the Commission can be confident they are selecting phenomenal candidates for their awards, they sought our help to ensure that they were employing all currently known best practices in their selection process for

UK awardees. The Commission run the outreach and the selection process of the UK awards from their UK office; they wanted to be rigorous, consistent and ensure truly diverse cohorts and that the selection process wasn't systematically biased for or against any group of people.

ESTABLISHING A BASELINE

The Commission were able to provide anonymized data on the demographic characteristics of applicants, interviewees and awardees. They had been collecting data for several years, but it wasn't entirely consistent and some of it had been destroyed after the application cycle had been completed and reported on. However, the previous two years of data were much more robust and we were able to make use of it.

While this did give us a partial baseline to work from, it was also a small sample, given how few awards are given out every year, and so statistically significant differences were difficult to show and longitudinal trends hard to establish. We therefore wanted to establish a baseline as soon as possible to build cumulative data (in terms of sample size and longitudinal analysis). We analysed the diversity of cohorts in 2016 and 2017 to understand the extent of what we were trying to solve, and to provide a platform to measure the future effectiveness of interventions we put in place.

While some of the diversity categories showed properly proportional rates of success (what we would expect in an objective process), the success rates of some groups gave us slight pause. While the numbers were small, and statistical significance was difficult to show, it did still indicate some areas to keep an eye on just in case.

UNDERSTANDING THE CURRENT SELECTION PROCESS

Next, we mapped and analysed every step of the selection process. We had extensive conversations with those in charge to go through, step by step, how they make decisions for each stage. This included questions about how they advertise for the awards to solicit applications and the wording and locations of those advertisements, how they receive applications, what those application forms look like, application fees, who reads which applications, how many, and over what period of time, who does interviews, what interviewer instructions are like, what is the interview process, what is the interview scoring process, all the way until final decisions are made.

DESIGNING INTERVENTIONS

As we discussed in Chapter 8, we know from behavioural science just how powerful an effect small, seemingly insignificant changes can have on our decisions. After going through the process in detail, we identified the stages of the process where a different method could yield more meritocratic and organically diverse and inclusive results.

One example is the joint evaluation technique we discussed in Chapter 8. Reading applications side by side, going down a list of criteria, rather than reviewing each candidate in turn, helps the reader focus on more relevant criteria and disregard irrelevant characteristics like race or gender. In other words, be led by the criteria rather than the candidate. We then discussed these potential interventions with the team at the Commission to figure out which were most feasible and practical given their constraints such as time, cost, and buy-in from the rest of the selection committee.

We decided that for the awards given out in 2018, it was best to focus on changes that could be made at the interview stage due to time constraints. Changes in the rest of the process would be taken up the following year.

One aspect of the interview process we noticed that could have the greatest effect was inconsistent questions. Interviewers would ask different questions of each candidate based on how the interview was going or based on their own background in the candidate's field. At first glance, this doesn't seem that bad. In fact, it sounds like a fairly good way of getting to know a candidate better. However, the problem is that when we ask different candidates different questions, we aren't able to compare the candidates equally because we don't have the same information. An interviewer who has a PhD in physics might ask deeper questions of physics candidates than of literature candidates, and then when comparing the two might evaluate the physics candidate as having a more in-depth knowledge of his field. This is not the interviewer's fault per se, but it nonetheless puts the two candidates on unequal ground.

As such, we suggested the Commission introduce strictly structured interviews (based on research by Harvard's Iris Bohnet and others) – a specific set of questions to be asked in the same order to each candidate to ensure consistency – and that scoring was done by question rather than by candidate and done individually before going to the group. This meant that all candidates would be compared in a more equal way and that any systematic biases would be less prevalent.

Another issue that arose when speaking with members of the Commission team was that most of their interviewers had been doing it for so long that they might be sceptical of change. While they certainly want to be objective, in the past changes made to the process hadn't always been followed as closely as the team had wanted them to be. This is an extremely important factor because no matter how good we are at creating the proper processes, if the interviewers themselves don't follow them then it will be all for nought.

For this reason, we implemented two interventions. First, we armed the team with the citations for all the academic research and cases that showed the effectiveness of the interventions we were proposing. This would allow them to make a clearer case as to why the changes in the interview process were being made, so the interviewers would be more willing to follow those new processes. Second, immediately before the interviews each day we had interviewers sign a pledge committing themselves to inclusion and acknowledging unconscious bias. We also reminded them of the wording of that pledge periodically throughout the day (based on research by London Business School's Lisa Shu and her colleagues[15]). This type of intervention has been shown to be effective at getting people to follow the rules and guidelines in a pledge more strictly and closely than they would if they didn't sign a pledge or signed one afterwards.

Other interventions we suggested included giving candidates more specific guidelines on what the interview involved, backgrounds of the interviewers, and more time to prepare. This helped level the playing field for people from less wealthy backgrounds, since more privileged applicants had access to training and practice sessions on how to think on their feet (an imbalance the Commission had been aware of for some time).

MEASUREMENT

With our baseline established, and our first interventions implemented, we were ready to measure the effect going forward and implement more interventions in a controlled way. However, more importantly, the US–UK Fulbright Commission was able to say with confidence that their interview process follows all the best practices and current research available to ensure that their decisions are as merit-based and inclusive as possible.

Amy Moore, Director of Awards at the US–UK Fulbright Commission stated:

> There was no 'rule book' on how to facilitate an inclusive process. Rather, [Raafi] spent a lot of time talking to us, mapping out our selection process, and then made relevant suggestions on small changes we might make, many of which made a big difference. We now feel much more confident in the rationale behind our processes, particularly in the context of inclusion, and will continue to critically assess how we do things in the future.

After learning about the process that we went through with the US–UK Fulbright Commission, other Fulbright commissions such as Germany, Belgium and the Czech Republic have since asked us to help them review their processes as well. While the selection process is largely the same, the different contexts and different committees and cultures will pose different challenges.

For example, in working with the Belgian Fulbright Commission, a big challenge is ensuring language diversity, since primary language is an important aspect of diversity in Belgium. In the Czech Republic, since such a large proportion of the population is white, their issue around race isn't just about ensuring equality in the application process, but rather ensuring that US students who study in the Czech Republic and are not white are comfortable and have access to the resources they need.

While the contexts are different, the work of one institution has cascaded to other members of its network. And while the issues are different in these different places, the same frameworks and process for developing more inclusion can be used, just tailored to the specific needs of that organization. The flexibility of this approach allows Fulbright institutions across localities to learn from each other and improve as a global organization.

INCLUSIVE LEADERSHIP, ORGANIZATIONAL ENGAGEMENT AND MEASURING CHANGE AT THE WELLCOME TRUST

Our work with the Wellcome Trust (Wellcome) has taken a slightly different approach to our work with Fulbright. In part, this is because of the time and resources available at Wellcome that aren't available at Fulbright. However, it is also because Wellcome is a larger organization with a much larger mandate.

Wellcome 'wants to improve health for everyone by helping great ideas to thrive'.[16] In that capacity, they are the world's second-largest funder of health and science research (after the Bill and Melinda Gates Foundation). They give over £1 billion (US $1.28 billion) in funding each year towards academic research around the globe, supporting 14,000 people in more than 70 countries.[17]

They not only fund researchers at universities around the globe, but also fund the Wellcome Sanger Institute (a leading genome research institution) and multiple Wellcome Centres (research centres each with a specific focus area). It also houses the Collection, which seeks to educate the community about science through its exhibits and various talks given there.

D&I was identified as a strategic priority area for Wellcome, acknowledging Wellcome's significant role and influence within the science sector. Led by Lauren Couch, who became Wellcome's Head of Diversity and Inclusion, Frost Included were drawn upon in the development of the inaugural five-year Wellcome D&I strategy. The 'understand, lead, deliver' framework described throughout this book was a particular source of inspiration for the strategy, but Steve and the team also provided tailored advice on specific challenges Wellcome were navigating during the strategy development phase.

The D&I priority area and its strategy were approved by Executive Leadership Team and Board of Governors in November 2016. To help the D&I team address the leadership perspective of their strategy we were commissioned to work with the Executive Leadership Team (ELT) to gain further buy-in and support Director Jeremy Farrar in his goal of creating a more diverse ELT.

The D&I team worked with the Insight and Analysis (I&A) team at Wellcome to develop an outcomes framework. Its purpose was to articulate the change that they would like to achieve through implementing their strategy. Following the development of the outcomes framework the I&A team and D&I team began working together to co-develop approaches to monitor the agreed outcomes. We were able to act as a thought partner to help feed into the development of a measurement approach and helped with the development of measurement tools to track progress towards those outcomes.

WORKING WITH THE ELT: HOLDING UP THE MIRROR AND REFRAMING DIVERSITY

Similar to our work with other leadership teams described in earlier chapters, we began by looking at diversity data from across the organization (which had been previously collected by the Bridge Group, another partner working with Wellcome). When presenting that data to the ELT, we framed it in such a way as to compare it to other similar organizations, as well as the general public that it presumes to serve and would desire to reflect. Like with other executive teams, we then had the ELT undertake implicit association tests and a simple personal inclusion diagnostic and use the results to help make what are sometimes difficult abstract concepts much more concrete, helping the ELT grasp the current state of D&I across the organization.

We then followed the ILP process we've outlined throughout the book, where we reframed diversity as a leadership concept in a group workshop, followed up with 1:1 inclusive coaching sessions to focus on actions and explore their personal connection to inclusion, and then come together again to make commitments and explore how they could support each other.

Having taken the ELT on a journey we gained further buy-in from the top of the organization to support the D&I strategy. We made the subject relevant and personal to leaders in the organization, and began work to agree a set of sustainable actions to help the D&I team achieve their objectives and make Wellcome more inclusive.

MEASUREMENT

As described earlier, Wellcome's Insight and Analysis team and D&I team have been working together to co-develop approaches to monitor the outcomes in their outcomes framework and we have been able to provide support on this. The teams chose to take a mixed methods approach to monitoring the outcomes by collecting and analysing both quantitative and qualitative evidence to enable them to have a more robust and reliable understanding of the changes occurring at Wellcome.

We described in earlier chapters the Inclusion Diagnostic we developed and tested at Wellcome. While this was developed as a diagnostic tool the D&I team at Wellcome were keen to run the survey and analysis annually as part of their measurement strategy, in order to help them monitor the overall culture change at Wellcome. In addition, so far the teams have decided on a preliminary set of measurement methodologies that would be most useful for overall measurement including focus groups, surveys, systematic document review, and key informant interviews.

For each measurement approach the team has worked to design a clear and specific protocol detailing the sampling methodology, the questions to be asked, guidance for the interviewer(s) or facilitator(s), and steps taken to perform the analysis. At Wellcome, this process was led by a member of the Insight and Analysis team and the whole approach was co-developed by D&I and I&A and done in a collaborative way, consulting both internal staff and a range of external experts. Drawing on multiple kinds of expertise and ensuring diverse input led to the co-development of a robust and comprehensive approach.

Our work with Wellcome is ongoing, but we can already say with confidence that their senior people 'get it' and that the D&I team has engaged many throughout the organization. Moreover, they have put in place robust ways to measure the effectiveness of programming and just how the organization's culture changes over time. Clearly, they are beginning not only to reform their own organization but also to act as role models within science and research generally.

MAKING AN IMPACT BEYOND THE ORGANIZATION

What is unique about academia and organizations like Wellcome specifically is that there is the potential to have an incredibly broad impact. Since Wellcome funds so much research and so many labs, it wields the power to mandate more inclusive practices by those labs, something it is considering doing.

Additionally, many of those they fund (and indeed many Wellcome staff) are also peer reviewers for academic journals. For an academic to move upwards in their field and institution, publication in prominent journals is key. However, we know that there is often systemic bias in what research gets published. As a result, delivering unconscious bias training to peer reviewers is an opportunity to affect not just the organization, but the field of science research as a whole. For more traditional academic institutions, implementing interventions like hanging photos of counter-stereotypical role models in classrooms to combat stereotype threat, or providing training for instructors and real-time feedback on potential bias for who is called on in class, can have significant effects on improving performance and increasing diversity among those who study their field.

These are just a few examples, but should academia and foundations follow in the footsteps of Wellcome and Fulbright, they could have a profound impact on inclusion far beyond their individual organizations and truly increase inclusion across entire industries for years to come.

TAKEAWAYS

1 Academia and foundations may seem far removed from most of the public, but they greatly affect our day-to-day lives through the effects of the work they do.

2 Signatory charters can be extremely effective for creating accountability and driving change in organizations.

3 Map out your processes in extreme detail – there may be opportunities for inclusive nudges in ways you didn't expect.

4 Having the language to articulate inclusive behaviours is critical to understanding what D&I means on a practical level.

5 Understand the potential impact you can make beyond just your organization, and design your plan to incorporate the broader societal changes you wish to see.

ENDNOTES

1 Abumrad, J and Krulwich, R (Hosts) (2012, 9 January) *The Bad Show* [Audio podcast]. Retrieved from https://www.wnycstudios.org/story/180092-the-bad-show/

2 It should be noted that Haber was also responsible for the creation of Mustard Gas, used in WWI by Prussian forces, killing nearly 100,000 people.

3 https://nces.ed.gov/fastfacts/display.asp?id=61

4 https://www.thecrimson.com/article/2018/4/3/hks-faculty-diversity-issues/

5 Ibid

6 https://www.rainn.org/statistics/campus-sexual-violence

7 https://www.theguardian.com/global-development/2013/aug/22/south-africa-universities-racially-skewed

8 https://libres.uncg.edu/ir/uncg/f/E_Chun_Creating_2011.pdf

9 Ibid

10 https://www.ecu.ac.uk/wp-content/uploads/external/evaluating-the-effectiveness-and-impact-of-the-athena-swan-charter.pdf

11 https://www.smu.edu.sg/sites/default/files/smu/news_room/smu_in_the_news/2016/Mar2016/Mar28/SUT_20160327_1.pdf

12 https://nyuad.nyu.edu/en/news/latest-news/community-life/2015/october/how-a-diverse-campus-becomes-an-inclusive-community.html

13 https://www.npr.org/2018/06/15/620368377/harvard-accused-of-racial-balancing-lawsuit-says-asian-americans-treated-unfairly

14 Ibid

15 Shu, L L et al (2012) Signing at the beginning makes ethics salient and decreases dishonest self-reports in comparison to signing at the end, *Proceedings of the National Academy of Sciences*, 109 (38), pp 15197–200

16 https://wellcome.ac.uk

17 Ibid

13

TO ALL ORGANIZATIONS: MAKE INCLUSION PART OF YOUR PURPOSE

We have discussed how to build inclusion in TV and film, finance, tech, and academia and foundations. These sectors are changing our world. But most of us don't work in those sectors. What about other nonetheless important companies and organizations that also affect our lives? Moreover, some organizations in less high-profile sectors are actually engaged in cutting-edge work that finance, TV, academia and tech could learn from.

BE THE CHANGE

We work with a wide range of successful companies and organizations across a variety of fields and sectors. What makes these different organizations commonly successful is that they have all capitalized on economic, social and technological change, rather than being subservient to it. As the working world has become more diverse, they have all engaged in improving their performance by including that diversity.

Throughout this book, we have provided you with a roadmap of how to do this in your own organization. We started with an explanation of why diversity and inclusion is an important concept for understanding the world we inhabit, the organizations we work in, and the way we interact with them as individuals. This led us to a new understanding of the real problem we are facing, and that underneath this problem lie our inherent biases. Finally, we have outlined the steps for, and importance of, getting buy-in, designing your plan, and making it stick. We provided examples of organizations in key industries that are doing this.

In reading through this process and these examples, you may be poking holes saying, 'this doesn't work for me, my organization is different'. And in some ways that could be true – trying to copy exactly what Wellcome or Uber or Bank of England have done may not work for the specific context of your organization. But if you take the concepts underlying their interventions, you can adapt them to make them your own. TV and film is an incredibly informal sector. In the absence of processes prevalent in other industries, it relies more on inclusive leadership to achieve inclusion and further the creative process. Finance, on the other hand, is full of process. Financial organizations also rely on inclusive leadership, but more focus can be placed on adapting existing processes through nudges to achieve inclusion.

Overall, though, there is one common factor found in every organization that has been successful in their D&I work: D&I is part of the overall organizational strategy. It can't just be housed as a set of programmes on the side, relegated to the bucket of 'things we'll do if we have time'. It has to be positioned as essential to the business – as a means of keeping up with your customer and client base, improving your overall performance, increasing employee engagement, and earning more revenue. With this framing, you can take the interventions we've described here and make them your own, confident that you have the buy-in of those from whom you'll need support.

ADAPT THESE INTERVENTIONS TO THE SITUATION

JUSTICE

One organization that has tried to adapt these principles to their context is Justice – an all-party organization in the UK with a vision to have fair, accessible, and efficient legal processes to protect individual rights and promote the rule of law. They face the challenge of a non-diverse judiciary and over 1,000 years of tradition. The make-up of the senior judiciary in the UK is primarily white, privately educated, privileged men.[1] In its recent report, Justice's Diversity Working Party makes the case for systemic change to be brought about urgently, as the diversity of the UK judiciary trails significantly behind its European and other common law counterparts. Diversity progress over the past 10 years has been slow, and stagnant at the highest levels.

To rectify this, a Judicial Appointments Commission (JAC) was established, in part to increase judicial diversity. This was a huge change because prior to this, the judicial appointment process relied on a 'tap on the shoulder' by the Lord Chancellor. The establishment of the JAC had real commitment from key actors in the senior judiciary aiming to disrupt this more informal process. However, in reality, the JAC's role in making judicial appointments is overshadowed by ad hoc panels that persist, and which still make appointments for the Court of Appeal, Heads of Division, and the UK Supreme Court. This creates a lack of accountability. We can perhaps all relate to this situation where we have implemented helpful processes, only to be circumvented by senior people in the organization.

To tackle this lack of accountability, where no one body or person can be held accountable for lack of diversity, Justice recommended the creation of 'appointable pools'. These are talent pipelines of people who are deemed to have met the very high standard of appointability to a particular post and are willing to take such an appointment. An appointable pool involves two stages: how people get into the pool, and when people get out. The first stage is focused on the qualities of the individuals applying; the second stage is focused on the needs of the institution.[2] Recruiting from such a pool of objectively measured, highly appointable talent ensures the 'top' talent from a large heterogeneous group (versus the 'top ranked' talent from a small homogeneous group) is available to be appointed to the senior judiciary.

As we discovered in Chapter 8, considering a group as opposed to a series of individuals can also promote heterogeneity over homogeneity. Appointable pools and talent pipelines facilitate batch recruitment. In essence, seeing the pool of top candidates as a group forces you to see the overall diversity of the team. Being able to see that more easily allows recruiters to hire for diversity over 'fit', which we know can lead to bias, as we've discussed throughout this book.

Justice also recommended the creation of inclusive talent pathways. In other chapters we discussed how providing multiple career pathways can help attract and promote diverse talent. Rather than a one-size-fits-all approach, there are usually many ways to be 'senior', and many types of senior roles and responsibilities that can cater to different employees' abilities, skill sets and lifestyles. Having the bar as the main or only route to becoming a judge prioritized not only one pathway, but one particular skill set. In fact, being a judge requires superior listening skills, not highlighted in the barrister route. Opening up other pathways was not 'dumbing down' but rather including much-needed and currently lacking skill sets.

THE COURAGE TO PUSH YOUR LEADERS FURTHER

PROFESSIONAL SERVICES

In Chapter 2, we discussed our D&I maturity model, outlining the three main approaches organizations adopt for D&I work: Diversity 101, which is mainly compliance-based, Diversity 2.0, which is more marketing-based, and Inclusion 3.0, which embeds inclusion into general workplace practices. Many organizations we have worked with have been at either the 101 or 2.0 stage, so we have started with a basic understanding of bias and the business case for inclusion. However, you might feel your organization is further along on its journey and ready for more radical interventions. While we definitely like to be provocative with our clients, we also recognize interventions must be managed with care.

Take, for example, KPMG. The professional services firm has undertaken extensive work on building an inclusive organization for some time. As they are further along in their journey than many other organizations, they have grown in confidence to undertake more hard-hitting inclusion work. At a recent Partners Annual General Meeting they conducted a 'race for privilege' exercise. This has been popularized in social media clips, and involves all participants standing at a starting line and moving forwards or backwards depending on their responses to a series of questions. The questions determine rates of privilege such as whether you had your own bedroom growing up, whether your parents were in work and so forth.

This can be considered a radical exercise for privileged senior people to undertake, as it can be very easy for participants to feel ashamed, discouraged or even angry if their privilege over other colleagues is highlighted. But the goal isn't to instil any negative feelings. Instead, it's to simply bring a heightened awareness of one's privilege relative to others, and to highlight how much harder others may have to work just to get to an equal starting point. When not framed correctly, though, this exercise can go wrong. For example, Raafi recalls one time it was undertaken as part of a Harvard Business School class. Due to poor framing many students described it later as a 'wealth-shaming exercise' rather than an exercise on the awareness of privilege.

For radical exercises to work they need to be managed well. It can be scary to confront those who are more senior than you in your organization. Confronting them in a particularly radical way may require even more courage and even more care. To mitigate this risk, you can make this a collective endeavour – partner with others whom you've brought in, preferably senior people, to help facilitate. This can help to decrease any individual fear as well as personal risk.

When managed properly, these types of exercises can have dramatic effects on the participants. We have seen them work to great effect with this firm, Wellcome and other clients. It's about creating a common reference point and a shared experience that executives still talk about a year after the event. The common language developed at Wellcome, which we referenced in Chapter 7, probed senior leaders to learn more about the subject and develop greater empathy for others.

PRACTISING EMPATHY

When deciding who to promote in an organization, technical skill and individual results are usually prioritized. Managerial and leadership skills, like empathy, are insufficiently taken into account. MIT Professor Emeritus Edgar Schein has shown how this has caused a lack of empathy at the top of organizations.[3] This can make inclusion work difficult because empathy is at the heart of inclusion. To be inclusive, to learn how to bring different people in and help them be themselves, you need to have some level of understanding of why they may not feel they can be themselves now. You need to be able to not just sympathize with their perspective and experience, but to take that perspective on for yourself.

The good news is, according to Schein, that empathy can be learned.[4] Many of the methods we've described will help you do that, such as playing devil's advocate or actively searching for diversity when creating your team rather than just for people that 'fit'. In essence, this means interrupting your System 1 response to a situation and slowing down to use your System 2.

One of our clients, a leading Danish healthcare company, is using this to great effect. One of the main learning points the Executive Management Forum (EMF) told us is that they never fully appreciated the often intimidating atmosphere created in the EMF for more junior people coming to present new research or ideas. Rather than this being a question of having to 'tone it down' and be inauthentic to themselves, their culture, or the Danish spirit of open and honest conversation, many male leaders recognized the inherent benefit of being more aware.

If they wanted to continue to stay ahead of the competition, get the best ideas and challenge their thinking, they would have to create a culture and an atmosphere that allowed the less powerful to challenge the powerful. To directly and personally contribute to that cultural change, they decided to focus on changing their in-the-moment behaviours in the EMF when more junior people came to present. One EMF member said, 'I used to interrupt a presentation when I was frustrated at the pace of delivery and zoom in on a page on the deck that I had already read and wanted to talk about in more detail. I now realize that this is actually playing to my game plan, not theirs, and we could all benefit from letting a different game plan play out and then subjecting it to appropriate challenge.'

These types of in-the-moment behaviour changes offer some of the most effective ways of practising empathy, and so developing an inclusive culture. Of course, it is still important to ensure that policies and procedures are as inclusive and free of negative bias as possible, but these types of small behaviours compound each other to create the culture. Culture is, after all, what you do. And these microbehaviour changes are significant adjustments at key moments in the life of an organization. When an empathetic culture is created, walls come down, differences are celebrated and innovation flourishes.

TO BE INCLUSIVE, BE CREATIVE

We might think creativity is confined to sectors such as TV and film. However, we have found that creativity can exist in many different types of large and small organizations that might not be deemed creative at all.

For example, Lucille Legiewicz and her colleagues at the UK National Health Service (NHS) developed the Forward Thinking Leadership (FTL) initiative. This aimed to develop inclusive leaders to serve the needs of changing communities. While they developed it based on many of the principles we've discussed – data, reframing diversity as a leadership concept, exploring cognitive dissonance and coming up with practical actions – their implementation was unique.

They created a six-day programme that allowed staff the space to talk about their challenges and test practical tools. They involved those who were directly on the frontlines of patient care to be part of the designing of the interventions they would introduce. It was not something that could be 'trained' overnight. Staff needed to know it was a journey, and there was support on an ongoing basis from the team and other resources such as e-learning modules to help them change behaviours over a period of time. Again, this was all done in a collaborative, supportive fashion with the joint focus on the shared outcomes of quality for their staff and patient care.

Perhaps even more surprising than creativity in healthcare is creativity in aerospace and defence. One of our FTSE 100 clients developed 'talent Principles' to inspire middle management at key people decision moments. For example, it included a challenging exercise to consult your out-group before making a promotion decision. It offered a schema for redefining talent in recruitment scenarios. And it offered simple rules of thumb such as proportionality.

This organization was very hierarchical, which made it difficult to challenge authority and feel psychologically safe. The difficulty here was similar to the difficulty at Uber that we discussed in Chapter 11 – people want to be inclusive, they know it's valuable, but they just don't know how. With such a large and dispersed organization, how do you cascade the lessons learned by senior leadership about inclusion down to the whole organization quickly? The answer lay, for them, in creating this specific set of talent principles to which all leaders could be held accountable. Not everyone necessarily had to have the specific inclusion training, but if they followed these principles and embedded them into their day-to-day work then inclusion could flourish.

CHANGE IS ALREADY HERE

In their 2000 paper,[5] Val Singh, Susan Vinnicombe and Phyl Johnson showed the early signs of change at the top of UK organizations. In terms of non-executive senior positions, women increased from holding 3.9 per cent of positions in 1989 to 10.4 per cent in 1995. Things have become more diverse since, with the UK exceeding its voluntary goal of 30 per cent in the FTSE 100 companies.[6] This started as a goal of women occupying 30 per cent of board seats, but now that has been reached the goal has become women occupying 30 per cent of all executive and employee positions. Change is indeed occurring and there is much positive movement in terms of corporate diversity in the boardroom.

However, still too few corporates have mirrored this success in their executive pipeline. In the same way it's easier to achieve quicker change in on-screen diversity than off-screen diversity in TV and film, it is easier to 'fix' board diversity than build a diverse executive pipeline. In 1989, women comprised only 0.5 per cent of executive directors overall. This increased to 1 per cent in 1995[7] and it's now improving (by 2000 that number had already jumped to nearly 30 per cent[8]) but there is still a long way to go. The discussion about race and other minorities, let alone cognitive diversity, is only really just starting.

Technological change and social pressures are making these conversations more urgent. Inclusion practice is evolving at a rapid pace. This makes being proactive about inclusion more important, but in some ways harder. The forces of polarization and appeasing special interest groups under ever increasing media scrutiny and transparent regulation make the work challenging. Our world is more interconnected than ever before, but we are also more interdependent. Including each other, no matter how hard that might be, will be essential for collective future success.

We are often asked for examples of best practice – who are the best organizations at diversity and inclusion? We answer simply that no organization has achieved nirvana. This is for several reasons, not least that inclusion is a journey, not a destination. It is also an iterative journey, not linear, and not one-way. We know several organizations that have regressed, be it due to a change of leadership, crisis management, or diminished resources. However, we also know several organizations that are undertaking excellent inclusion work, many of which we have tried to capture in this book.

Those that we have found to be the most successful have developed detailed and well-thought-out plans. They have considered their strategy and how to get buy-in from all stakeholders, how to best gather and leverage data to their advantage, and how to administer and govern their overall D&I plan. All of this should be planned out thoroughly before moving into the different leadership and systems interventions in order to create effective, sustainable change.

Moreover, many of these organizations have accounted for the particular circumstances of their different offices or locales. Different geographies may require different interventions – being Black in the United States is very different from being Black in Nigeria; being disabled in the UK is a different experience than being disabled in China. However, while a global strategy needs to be locally rooted, many of the concepts outlined in this book are universal. People, no matter where they are based, still operate on System 1 and System 2 thinking, are still biased (even if they don't have the same biases) and still favour their in-groups. So don't shy away from challenging bad practice anywhere and from encouraging good practice everywhere.

And don't give up because of a lack of funding. Budget constraints are the most common reason we hear from clients about why they haven't undertaken significant inclusion work yet. As you have seen, many of the most effective interventions have little or no cost at all. Not only does this mean you can implement inclusion measures no matter how large or small your organization is, it also makes it easier to get senior leaders on board. The cost–benefit ratio of this work can be astronomical. Budget does not have to be a deal-breaker. The only deal-breaker is not following good practice.

What defines 'good practice' in this sense is a measured approach – 3.0, rather than relying solely on 101 and 2.0, combined with tangible measurements to demonstrate progress. To make good practice stick, leadership engagement as well as nudges are required. And targets can be helpful yardsticks, if based on significant data that has been properly modelled and projected. No organization can 'arrive' because as long as homophily triumphs against diversity, diversity will need to be a conscious, continuous workstream. Whilst no organization is the definitive 'best practice' because the work is ongoing, we hope this book has given you insights into the kind of work that can be undertaken to great effect.

Inclusion can be difficult work. But it's often made more difficult than it needs to be when framed in terms of seeking permission. Practitioners too often respond to the question, 'why are we doing this?' If the business case is urgent, the strategy is robust and the data is sound, the question is not 'why?', but 'why not?'. There is important work to do.

We started out with a story of how male leaders, unchecked, caused the worst aircraft disaster of all time. We finish with how we can all achieve the opposite: high-performing organizations, realized through including people, including those we might initially reject.

The deaths of those aboard KLM flight 4805 and Pan Am 1736 were tragic. They were also preventable. Van Zanten's lack of inclusion of those around him, especially those subordinate to him, meant that things were missed, and blind spots weren't covered. While this is an extreme example, and while any of us could fall victim to the same biases, it reminds us how essential it can be to switch our thought processes from System 1 to System 2. It shows us just how important it is to include.

The world, your organization and people around you need your inclusive leadership now more than ever. You and your colleagues can build an inclusive organization. There will never be enough time. There will never be enough resources. But your own ability to lead inclusively is free, in infinite supply and completely within your own control.

Diversity is a reality, inclusion is a choice.

ENDNOTES

1 Justice (2017) Increasing judicial diversity: a report by Justice

2 Ibid, p 48

3 Lambrechts, F et al (2017) Learning to help through humble enquiry and implications for management research, practice and education, Learning & Education, **10** (1)

4 Ibid

5 Singh, V, Vinnicombe, S and Johnson, P (2001) Women directors on top UK boards, Corporate Governance, **9** (3), pp 201–16

6 https://www.gov.uk/government/news/record-number-of-women-on-ftse-100-boards

7 Singh, V, Vinnicombe, S and Johnson, P (2001) Women directors on top UK boards, Corporate Governance, **9** (3), pp 201–16

8 Ibid

APPENDIX 1

EXAMPLE D&I PLAN

Let's look at an example. It's a real plan from a real organization (a professional services firm of 2,000 people). A timeline is provided below, with the specific actions for each month detailed below the timeline – see Figure A1.1.

Figure A1.1 Plan timeline

Action →	1	2	3	4	5	6	7	8	9	10
Month ↓										
Sep	■									
Oct		■	■							
Nov		■	■			■	■	■		
Dec			■					■		
Jan			■					■		
Feb			■	■				■	■	
Mar			■	■	■				■	
Apr				■	■				■	
May									■	
Jun									■	
Jul									■	
Aug										■

Across the horizontal axis of the timeline, you'll see a set of actions to be taken in each month. Below are the actions referred to along this axis.

1 **Agree the strategy and goals and secure resources.**

This might take the form of a strategic alignment workshop like we described in Chapter 6, where you bring the key decision makers in the organization together for half a day and leave with agreement on the plan and the resources to deliver it. In terms of getting resources it might be necessary to wait to make executive decision makers aware of the need for resource until the initial plan is fully formulated, so they can appreciate the extent of the plan.

2 **Collate and frame the data: run an Inclusion Diagnostic.**

Depending on the level of buy-in from leaders and the organization more broadly, the level of current data availability, and the propensity of people in the culture to complete surveys, this may take longer than the suggested two months. These factors should be considered when determining the timing of your plan.

3 **Get buy-in.**

This is an iterative, ongoing process but we have suggested six months to conduct stakeholder mapping and run an inclusive leadership programme for the executive team, culminating in them each committing to three specific, achievable, inclusive actions before the end of the financial year.

4 **Embed the actions in appraisals and create accountability.**

This is about taking the actions that leaders themselves have determined and embedding them in their own evaluations. Link performance of these actions to remuneration and make their commitments to those actions public. Determining the amount of weighting given to these vis-à-vis compensation is a political art and will be wholly related to the level of buy-in achieved in advance. But this is a critical part of the plan – if you can link key behaviours to pay and reward and create more public accountability by committing to those actions in a more public way (for example, through a post on the organization's intranet) then it is a huge incentive to drive behaviour change, and a huge step forward in building an inclusive organization.

5 **Conduct a gap analysis – is anything missing, eg one network is without an executive sponsor.**

Here we have made provision for a mid-year review of any gaps identified so far, with the chance to correct them before progress is halted in key areas of the business. Some gaps that might be identified could be that a specific group is feeling unheard, or that a specific pattern of behaviour has become apparent that you feel must be addressed.

6 **Establish a Diversity Council (including details such as composition, frequency of meetings, Terms of Reference).**

Again, the practical requirement of this will vary and will need to be balanced with the political and management capacity you have to establish it in the first place. But if you are able to create and work with a larger group, getting buy-in and disseminating information will become much easier, and you'll get the chance to surround yourself with a diverse group that can see your blind spots, thus enabling you and your strategy to be more effective.

7 **Establish a communications plan.**

This will be dependent on the level of buy-in you have from communications and marketing, but the sooner you are able to get that buy-in the better able you will be to inform people of progress and remaining challenges. This could be a stand-alone plan or a strand of the existing communications and engagement plan for the organization. One effective way to ensure that communications and marketing are on board from the start is to include them on your Diversity Council. This way, you'll be designing and considering communications as the overall strategy is developed and implemented.

8 **Audit all relevant systems, conduct gap analyses, and assign accountabilities for de-biasing priority areas.**

This relates to the key processes in the organization and their owners, such as recruitment, talent management and so forth as we described in previous chapters. It includes both going over the current policies to ensure they are as inclusive as possible, and also trying to get an idea of whether those policies are actually followed in practice and to what extent.

9 **Complete inclusive leadership/unconscious bias training roll-out to the rest of the firm.**

Once the leadership are on board, this is one suggestion for scaling the training and education out to the rest of the organization. Bear in mind the limitation of training and consider this part of a wider plan that relies on communication, leadership and nudges.

10 **Repeat Inclusion Diagnostic and measure change after one year.**

It will be important to measure and report change to maintain buy-in for the plan. Even if the results are below target, what are the changes? Note changes in representation and declaration as well as the behaviours measured in the actual diagnostic. For example, in terms of LGBT+ declaration, we often find the 'prefer not to say' score diminishing by around 1 per cent per year and the declaration rate increasing. This is important data to encourage ongoing change, and an indication of increased comfort and inclusion in the organization.

APPENDIX 2

ADDITIONAL RESOURCES

This book has provided you with the tools you need to make your organization more inclusive. And while the strategies and interventions we've discussed here are the ones we have found to be the most helpful and relevant in our experience, they are by no means comprehensive of all the knowledge and tools available to you. Should you wish to dive deeper into the many concepts we've discussed, this appendix provides a brief overview of some additional resources that we have found useful in our work and that are also available to you.

TECH APPS FOR DESIGNING MORE INCLUSIVE RECRUITMENT AND PROMOTION PROCESSES

Much of the time when organizations are trying to de-bias their recruitment and promotion processes, they understand the interventions but have trouble putting them in place. This is often in part because they don't have the right tools to prevent the intervention from being a drain on resources, whether those resources are time, money or people. The tech tools below are designed to help solve those problems, making interventions for recruitment and promotion much easier.

NOTTX

One of the most effective and easy-to-grasp interventions that an organization can implement is anonymizing CVs when hiring. However, the problem is that most organizations don't have the software capability to anonymize all the applications themselves. Doing so manually would just take too much time. By uploading the CVs to Nottx, the programme will automatically anonymize all CVs of potentially biasing data such as indicators of gender and race. Organizations can then view the anonymized CVs directly on the Nottx platform or download the anonymized files to their system. Once you've decided who to interview, you can then input the identifying number that Nottx assigned to the CV and only then will it reveal the successful candidate's identity so you can contact them. This is a relatively easy solution to get around the main barrier to organizations adopting an anonymous CV practice.

APPLIED

Borne out of the Behavioural Insights Team in the UK, this app takes all of the established research from behavioural science about de-biasing hiring processes and makes it easy for you to follow them. It will anonymize CVs, help you with scoring mechanisms, and even give you a simple platform for using the joint evaluation technique we described in Chapter 8.

TEXTIO

This web-based tool helps you make your job advertisements and job descriptions more inclusive by identifying words and phrases that we know from academic literature and best practice are more likely to turn off particular groups from applying. It has a simple user interface, and also comes up with suggested replacements for biased language. However, it should be noted that it is geared towards creating more gender equality, and so may not be useful for de-biasing your advertisements for other marginalized groups, although it is adapting.

ATIPICA

This app helps your organization recruit from under-represented groups. Its AI software analyses your data and that of the industry to help identify candidates that have the skills you need and are under-represented in your company. Importantly, Atipica pride themselves on having a diverse team themselves and using diverse data sets to train their machine learning algorithms.

TECH APPS TO DESIGN MORE INCLUSIVE RETENTION SCHEMES

While recruitment is important, without ensuring employees stay, your numbers won't change. To encourage retention, creating an inclusive environment is necessary. The following apps help develop those inclusive environments through mentorship and feedback platforms.

RUNGWAY

Rungway is a web-based community hub for diverse mentorship. Not only can individuals from marginalized groups use this to find mentors for themselves, but organizations can use it as a platform to have larger conversations about diversity and inclusion across the organization and minimize siloed conversations.

CULTURE AMP

One of the difficult issues we come across with clients is that when we suggest conducting 360-degree feedback or organizational feedback from employees, they don't always have a platform on which to collect that feedback. Culture Amp helps with this problem by providing that platform. Moreover, it actually has a database of surveys on employee engagement, effectiveness, dedication, and other indicators of organizational culture that can help you understand some of the actions you might take.

TECH APPS FOR HELPING WITH D&I DATA ANALYTICS

Throughout this book, we have discussed the importance of measurement and data. When used well, they can be extremely powerful and helpful in designing your strategy and interventions to develop inclusion in your organization. However, not all organizations have the capacity or expertise to do this data analysis. The following apps can not only help you collect and analyse your D&I data, but can even help you interpret it and develop interventions.

BLENDOOR

This is another useful tool that can help you anonymize candidate applications, but it also helps you by providing useful diversity analytics. In particular, it allows you to provide diversity data from your organization and can help you create a diversity projection model like the one we described in Chapter 7.

HUMANYZE

One of the big issues for many organizations, particularly smaller organizations, is that even if they gather diversity or inclusion data, they don't have the resources to actually make use of that data. Humanyze seeks to solve this problem by analysing HR data to find solutions that would improve organizational development. That could mean helping analyse an organization's diversity pipeline, or it could mean finding ways to run meetings better, or a whole host of other potential interventions. The unique thing they do is to use people analytics to analyse workplace communications. This helps them understand the culture of an organization, which can be extremely useful for beginning to find and address blind spots that leaders may have about their company.

TECH APPS AND WEBSITES TO FIND IDEAS FOR D&I INTERVENTIONS AND DEVELOP YOUR D&I NETWORK

Often, one of the difficulties faced by those charged with building inclusion in an organization is that they don't necessarily know what interventions have been tried and have been successful. Moreover, they may not even know where to look to find out. We have included some of the organizations doing things well in this book as examples that can be followed. Additionally, though, one of the most useful ways of solving this problem is by turning to others who are in the same boat, and this can be done by developing your D&I network. Not only will this help you in finding potential solutions, but it can also offer support and mentorship.

INCLUSION-NUDGES.ORG

This is a non-profit organization that seeks to share nudges for inclusion that people are trying and testing all over the world. It is also a platform to engage with the global community undertaking diversity and inclusion work through behavioural science. Many of the contributors to this website and community are leaders in the field and are also from leading organizations. It is an extremely useful source for recommendations of nudges to try, useful articles, videos, and podcasts, and opportunities to connect with other practitioners.

ADAPTIVE LEADERSHIP NETWORK

This network is a group of leaders across fields and sectors that convene to support the building of leadership capacity. The network uses the Adaptive Leadership model, which is based on helping leaders become more aware of how they can adapt to those they lead to help bring the collective forward. Specifically, this model suggests that some problems do not have clear technical solutions and require leaders to focus on process and adapt to the particulars of the situation to bring the best out of their team. While this network is not focused on inclusive leadership per se, it can be a helpful place for leaders to learn more about general concepts related to inclusive leadership and adaptation.

HELPFUL ORGANIZATIONS FOR INCLUSIVE PROCUREMENT

Procurement is a common activity of many organizations, particularly larger ones. However, often when deciding on the best service provider we are only choosing among the organizations we already know of. Not knowing what other options are out there inhibits our ability to make the best, most informed decision. Moreover, the organizations that tend to be left out in the procurement process are often organizations owned by women, ethnic minorities, and other members of marginalized groups. The following groups aim to fix this market failure.

WECONNECT INTERNATIONAL

This is an organization that helps create more diverse and inclusive value chains in business processes. Specifically, it aims to help women-owned businesses that are often marginalized gain more visibility with corporations looking to procure services. They not only help these women-owned businesses grow, but they train larger corporations on how to do more inclusive procurement, create connections between businesses to facilitate more inclusive procurement, and perform measurement and data analysis. Moreover, this organization is global, operating in more than 30 countries on every continent.

MSDUK

This is a non-profit organization that promotes inclusive procurement processes in the UK. They help connect buyers with ethnic minority-owned businesses to promote more diverse and inclusive supply chains in both the public and private sectors. Their basic ethos is that a lack of diversity in the supply chain is a market failure that restricts economic growth and opportunities for innovative solutions. Thus, while their goal is to increase inclusive procurement, they do so with competitiveness and the bottom line for companies in mind.

RESOURCES FOR INCLUSIVE CUSTOMER AND SERVICE DELIVERY

A key part of an organization becoming inclusive is not just being inclusive of the people they employ, but also those they serve. It is important, therefore, that one's products are accessible to all, not just the majority group. These organizations are some that focus on expanding the access of service provision.

WORLD ASSOCIATION OF SIGN LANGUAGE INTERPRETERS

This is a non-profit network of sign language interpreters in multiple languages around the world. Not only are they a network for interpreters, but they also help accredit interpreters and are a resource for any organization looking to hire an interpreter for an event. WASLI operates across the globe through their many national chapters and convenes global conferences for interpreters and those looking to understand more about the deaf community.

WORLD BLIND UNION

This is a global organization that seeks to help those who are visually impaired gain more access to independent living, including by helping organizations understand how best to accommodate blind staff. Further, they help connect organizations with qualified visually impaired candidates through their pool. They also serve as a networking, support, and advocacy group for visually impaired people around the world.

INTERNATIONAL LABOUR ORGANIZATION (ILO)

The ILO is an agency of the United Nations dedicated to bringing governments, companies, consumers, and workers together to set labour standards. Not only do they provide industry standards and issue studies on labour practices across the globe, they also have a repository of country reports that include the legal standards within each of their member countries. Moreover, they also develop programmes to promote equitable workplace environments across the world.

RESOURCES FOR SUPPORTING EMPLOYEE RESOURCE GROUPS (ERGS) AND BUILDING INCLUSION AROUND SPECIFIC DIVERSITY CHARACTERISTICS

LGBT+

There are many useful websites with data, indices, and guidance on how to monitor LGBT+ diversity, design LGBT+-inclusive policies, and drive LGBT+ equality. For organizations based in the UK, we recommend the tools and information offered by the Kaleidoscope Trust and Stonewall. Both have not just tools but factsheets, statistics, and places to seek further information.

In the United States, two great sources of information and tools are Gay and Lesbian Advocates and Defenders (GLAAD) and Out and Equal. The former is focused on legal services around LGBT+ discrimination, while the latter is a non-profit focused on creating more workplace equality for LGBT+ individuals. Both provide trainings, leadership development and professional networking.

For more global tools, we suggest the Human Rights Campaign (HRC) and the International Lesbian, Gay, Bisexual, Trans and Intersex Association (ILGA). Both of these provide opportunities for networking, contain country statistics, and offer tools to help build organizations that are more inclusive of LGBT+ workers. Moreover, they provide information and resources for LGBT+ people in countries that are less tolerant of homosexuality.

GENDER

Some of the top places to go for help on creating a more gender-inclusive organization include Catalyst, the 30% Club, and HeForShe. Catalyst is a non-profit organization and has freely available information and tools about gender equality in the workplace across the globe. Importantly, they also have information about laws and protections in various countries. This is extremely useful for global companies in particular. The 30% club is a useful source of information and tools for those trying to increase the number of women on their boards. It started in 2010 as a campaign to increase the number of women on boards of FTSE 100 companies to 30 per cent, and has grown into a wider phenomenon. Finally, HeForShe is a branch of UNWomen dedicated to helping men understand their role in pushing for gender equality and giving them the tools and support network to do so. This is particularly useful for male-dominated organizations looking to take a stand for gender equality.

For those more interested in the latest academic research on gender inequality, including interventions in organizations to promote equality, we suggest using the Gender Action Portal of the Harvard Kennedy School Women and Public Policy Program. This is an up-to-date repository of the top recent academic literature to do with gender inequality around the world.

In East Asia, two organizations focused on increasing gender equality across the region are the Women's Action Network (focused on Japan) and the Working Women's Network (pan-Asia). Both of these organizations are not only networks to support women in the workplace, but also help organizations who are trying to be more inclusive. Moreover, the Working Women's Network contributes to various UN reports on gender equality, and so conducts audits and studies across Asia on the status of working women.

The Businesswoman's Association of South Africa (BWASA) is another network similar to the Women's Action Network in Japan. It helps support women in business in South Africa through lobbying efforts and bringing business issues particular to women to the forefront in South African society. Moreover, it offers training and mentorship opportunities, conducts research on women in business across Africa, and helps connect women in business to funding opportunities to grow their organizations.

RACE

The most effective tool we've seen to help with increasing ethnic diversity is the Rare Contextual Recruitment System. This tool helps by using innovatively contextualizing data and work information to help you mitigate potential biases. In doing so, it has helped companies increase their rates of hiring ethnic minorities by as much as 50 per cent in some cases.

In the UK, Race for Opportunity is a network of organizations dedicated to improving their employment of ethnic minorities. They focus on supporting each other and providing consultation to increase diversity on boards and at senior level, ensure diverse progression at work, and reduce unemployment for ethnic minority youth. Also in the UK, Business In The Community (BITC) is a charity that works on a variety of activities promoting responsible business practices, one of which is the promotion of equality of ethnic minorities at work. Through their awards, they provide incentives for racial equality at work.

In the United States, probably the most famous organizations working towards racial equality are the NAACP and the Urban League. Both of these are non-profits working on a variety of activities to promote racial equality. However, importantly, they both offer platforms for both workers and employers to help connect qualified candidates with good jobs, help organizations be more inclusive, and help ERGs develop their capacity to encourage inclusion in their organizations. While these organizations have historically focused on supporting Black Americans, they now offer support for all people of colour.

A particularly useful source of information and resources in the Pacific is the Diversity Council of Australia. This non-profit organization is focused on helping employers become more diverse and inclusive along a variety of diversity characteristics in Australia. In particular, they have a wealth of information on racial equality and support of indigenous workers.

SOCIAL MOBILITY

Measuring social mobility in a way that is sensitive but still gets the information you need in an accurate way can be difficult. What's more, finding ways to create equal opportunities for people from low socio-economic backgrounds is even more difficult. The Bridge Group, though, has provided extremely useful guidance on both of these fronts. Their tools and documents can help you understand best practices for monitoring social mobility, analysing that data, and designing interventions that work.

One organization that works with the government and helps to enforce protections for equality in the UK is the Equality and Human Rights

Commission (EHRC). This body helps to enforce equal protection laws in the UK through litigation, but also acts as a resource to help organizations be more inclusive. Part of their work is in the social mobility space, despite the fact that this is not a protected characteristic under the UK's Equality Act. The UK government Social Mobility Commission (SMC) is an advisory body sponsored by the Department of Education that helps to increase social mobility in the UK. The SMC particularly helps by publishing research and by providing guidance to employers who seek to advance equality along social mobility lines.

DISABILITY

For working on issues of disability, guidance from the UK Civil Service is very useful and comprehensive. In particular, their page 'Becoming Disability Confident' has helpful tools and videos that make for good references when working specifically on disability inclusion. Furthermore, Remploy is another organization with extremely helpful cases and guidance to help your organization become more inclusive of those with disabilities. We suggest also using the Business Disability Forum to learn about best practices around workplace disability inclusion, as well as connecting with leaders in this field of work.

For more guidance on how to promote disability equality in the workplace, the Disability Rights Commission has resources for all sectors. As an independent body of the UK government, it helps to clarify the law on anti-discrimination for disabled persons, provide support and resources for disabled workers and students, and also helps employers become more accessible and inclusive of their disabled staff. While they are focused on the UK, their resources are helpful for anyone designing interventions for their organization to be more inclusive of disability.

Finally, for disabled workers seeking support, mentorship and networking with other disabled workers across the globe, Purple Space is a perfect platform. In addition to connecting disabled people with each other, it helps to connect employers with disabled talent and help employers with their inclusion agenda.

RELIGION

The Tanenbaum Center for Religious Understanding is a non-profit organization that has a plethora of useful resources around designing more religiously inclusive workplace policies and procedures. Some of their tools include etiquette guidelines, checklists, general policies, and many other helpful tips and guidance.

Similarly, the European Network Against Racism provides reports and toolkits on how to manage religious diversity in the workplace. This toolkit is useful for understanding the particular issues surrounding religious inclusion in Europe, as well as offering tips for creating more inclusive policies and cultures in the workplace around religion. The Society for Human Resource Management (SHRM) as well as the National Institutes of Health (NIH) also have similar toolkits available for US-based organizations, including legal advice and best practice toolkits.

AGE

The Age and Employment Network (TAEN) is a helpful place to go for information and guidance on creating workplaces that are more inclusive of multiple age groups. In particular, their guidance on managing multigenerational workforces and an ageing workforce can be particularly helpful both for companies struggling with large age gaps between management and entry-level employees, as well as organizations struggling to recruit a younger workforce.

Additionally, the EHRC (which we've discussed earlier in this chapter in relation to social mobility) has some of the best information for UK employers around preventing age discrimination. Their resources include explanations of employer requirements and responsibilities as well as best practice examples from other organizations.

For work particularly on the inclusion of older workers, Age Concern is a global network of charities, most significantly operating in New Zealand, Australia and the UK, that offer advice to employers and employees alike on ensuring age diversity at work. In particular, they offer guidance on appropriate accommodations that can be made to help older workers nearing retirement thrive.

PARENTING

The first organization we suggest going to for help as an employer seeking to be more inclusive of employees with children is Working Families. This organization not only helps with legal compliance, but also can help you design programmes that can both help parents balance work and family and also help them be more productive workers. They offer advice through their research and publications, best practice cases and consulting services.

Also, while it is primarily a forum for advice for parents, MumsNet also has a lot of useful information for workplaces too. In particular, they provide helpful ideas, suggestions and case studies around workplace flexibility for parents, returners programmes for those coming back from parental leave, and family-friendly policies such as daycare programmes or child-friendly social gatherings. She's Back is a fantastic organization that can also help in this space. They are a great resource both for people returning to work after a hiatus (whether from parental leave, a long-term illness, caring for a sick relative, or otherwise), as well as for organizations seeking to find ways to be more inclusive of returning workers.

We also suggest TheWorkingParent as a similar forum that, while useful for parents, can also be informative to employers. It particularly helps employers understand the needs of parents who work and gives suggestions on programming and best practices to be inclusive of those with caring responsibilities of all kinds. It is a particularly good resource for employers wanting to understand and accommodate the needs of parents with disabled children.

FLEXIBLE WORKING

When trying to develop a flexible working policy, we often advise clients to try to make flexible working the default rather than the exception. However, organizations often find this hard to do. Timewise is an organization that can help you design that policy, but can also help you create a more accommodating and adaptive culture where making use of flexible working policies won't be an inhibitor to progression as an employee.

If as an organization you are seeking to understand more about your role and responsibilities with regard to flexible working, Citizens Advice is the best source of information. This can be useful for any employer seeking to increase productivity and employee engagement and retention through work policies that actually work for employees. Moreover, they provide links to other organizations and resources that can help you design your flexible working scheme.

The Flex Agility Group is another organization similar to Timewise that can help you design your flexible working policy. Based in Australia, the organization offers services to help with the creation and implementation of your plan, but also provides a lot of other resources such as data analytics, research, governance, and health and wellness best practices around flexible working policies.

Finally, we suggest using the Flexible Working Day platform to help connect you to other organizations that are focused on making flexible working work. They provide research on the business and ethical cases for flexible work policies (which could help you get buy-in from others in your organization), examples of effective flexible working practices, as well as a network of people who have implemented flexible work schemes that can offer advice.

FURTHER READING

PSYCHOLOGICAL PROCESSES

The fundamental underpinning of diversity and inclusion work – how we develop biases in the first place, how we make judgments, why we think we're being objective even when we aren't, and other similar concepts we've covered throughout this book – is the psychology of decision making. There are a number of books, papers and articles by psychologists and experts in organizational behaviour that can help to explain these processes, but there are two sources in particular that we find to be the most comprehensive and useful.

The first, which we have alluded to in different parts of this book, is Daniel Kahneman's seminal work *Thinking, Fast and Slow* (Farrar, Straus and Giroux, 2011). It covers everything from his concept of System 1 and

System 2 thinking (which we describe throughout this book), heuristics and biases like anchoring effects (how hearing random numbers influences our numerical estimations), the difficulty of maintaining doubt and scepticism, differences in risk-taking behaviours, the psychology of optimism and pessimism, and the influence of emotions. This comprehensive work is essential to understanding basic decision psychology, and can be extremely helpful when trying to explain the concept of bias to those who are just starting their D&I journey.

The second work that is exceptionally useful when thinking about the psychology of D&I is Claude Steele's *Whistling Vivaldi* (WW Norton & Co, 2010). Using a combination of academic research and vignettes from his own life, Steele describes the way stereotypes play a powerful role in the way humans behave. This work is a fantastic follow-on from Kahneman as it takes concepts like heuristics that Kahneman describes and makes them more concrete. Steele is able to show in very compelling fashion how stereotypes are developed about others, but also how they are internalized by ourselves. He draws a clear and direct line between the development of these stereotypes through our experience of the world and results like higher incarceration rates of Black men than white men for the same crimes, and the Black-white achievement gap in the United States.

What is equally useful about *Whistling Vivaldi*, though, is that the second half of the book proposes potential interventions that could be made at various levels to mitigate the effects of stereotyping. These suggestions range from public policy interventions, to organizational programmes, to individual behaviours, to changes in the way we design physical spaces. This work not only helps to explain the psychology behind extremely powerful and influential processes, but also gives us evidence-based ideas of how to move forward and take steps to make our organizations better.

If you are more interested in listening to conversations about these topics, we recommend the podcasts The Hidden Brain, which explores the psychology of human behaviour, and Freakonomics Radio, which looks at the psychology of broader cultural ideas.

IMPLICIT BIAS

The idea of implicit or unconscious bias has been around for decades, but nobody has studied it more extensively than Mahzarin Banaji and Anthony Greenwald, founders of Harvard's Project Implicit. Their work has included analysis of data from more than 2 million individuals on a range of diversity characteristics that could trigger bias, from the classic examples like gender, race, disability and sexual orientation to identifiers less commonly thought of as potentially biasing, like accent.

They compile their findings from over a decade of research in their book *Blindspot: The hidden biases of good people* (Bantam, 2016). Their data has shown that having an automatic preference for white people based on their Implicit Association Test correlates with a host of real-world manifestations of that subconscious preference. For example, when seen in doctors, this preference is correlated with a suboptimal treatment of Black emergency room patients. When given to HR managers, this preference has been correlated with more negative judgments of Black job applicants than white applicants. And when given to random US citizens, this preference has even been correlated with voting behaviour – an automatic white preference was correlated with a vote for John McCain over Barack Obama.

While the test is by no means meant to be predictive of behaviour, it does help us understand what our default assumptions might be, particularly when we are more wont to use System 1 thinking making us more prone to bias. The biggest value of this book, though, is that it explains and provides evidence for the existence of implicit biases and helps us understand how to discover what our own biases are. This can be extremely valuable for those of us who are ready to confront our biases and start doing something about it. It is also a useful resource to fall back on when trying to convince those who are more sceptical about the existence of unconscious biases.

THE BUSINESS CASE FOR DIVERSITY

We discussed in Chapter 2 some of the evidence as to how diversity, when properly leveraged through inclusive cultures and behaviours, can provide incredible benefits to an organization or team. Two books that we have discussed throughout this book and found to be extremely effective at making the argument are Scott Page's *The Difference* (Princeton University Press, 2007) and James Surowiecki's *The Wisdom of Crowds* (Anchor, 2005).

The Difference is a particularly useful source when trying to convince the quantitatively minded sceptics about the business value of diversity. But more than that, it is a serious social science book written in a humorous, easy-to-read way that makes it accessible to everyone. *The Wisdom of Crowds* is a great alternative to *The Difference* for those who are less quantitatively inclined, both for those looking for a deeper understanding of the mechanisms behind the business case for diversity and those looking to arm themselves with evidence with which to convince others of its merits.

For more shorter, more practical how-tos for making the business case, we highly recommend CIPD's guidance called 'Diversity and Inclusion at Work: Facing up to the business case'. This gives a great summary of the arguments for the business case, and also a brief process you might follow in order to de-bias your HR policies.

NUDGES

In Chapter 8 we discussed how one effective method for counteracting our biases is through nudges. We briefly explained what nudges are and how they can be useful when designing interventions to help your organization be more inclusive. Nudges are an extremely powerful tool and have been used in a variety of contexts, from getting people to save more for retirement to increasing the number of organ donors. While Chapter 8 did go through a number of useful nudges to help your organization, there are many more potential nudges that one could use.

One extremely useful book is *What Works: Gender equality by design* by Iris Bohnet (Belknap Press of Harvard University Press, 2016). This book homes in on the nudges that could help to reduce gender inequality in the workplace and society. While the book almost entirely relies on academic papers as its sources, and is written by a Harvard economist, it is not a book that feels too much like an academic text. Bohnet weaves in useful stories to make the concepts vivid, but maintains a close relationship with the evidence and the data. She discusses somewhat smaller interventions like starting a meeting with a reminder not to use sexist language, as well as large-scale interventions like instituting a gender quota in elections and everything in between. And while Bohnet focuses on gender bias, many of the interventions can work for other marginalized groups as well.

Bohnet's work here is an essential guide when you're at the point of deciding what interventions to introduce for greatest effect. By providing detailed explanations of how each intervention works, how its effectiveness is measured, and the specific parameters that may influence whether it would work in other contexts, *What Works* lays out a menu of potential nudges you can implement in your workplace.

However, if your goal is to get a better understanding of nudges as a concept and gain deeper knowledge of how to leverage our predictably irrational behaviour in general, the foundational text to become familiar with is *Nudge* by Cass Sunstein and Richard Thaler (Yale University Press, 2008). This will give you a general overview of behavioural economics in a very non-academic way, and then describe various situations across many sectors where nudges (or what they call choice architecture) have been used to help people make better decisions. Sunstein and Thaler describe all kinds of useful nudges including framing effects, status quo biases and mental accounting. While some of these can more obviously be used in D&I initiatives, others are perhaps less useful in this context. However, the book will definitely provide helpful background when designing interventions, and could also help you come up with new interventions on your own that you can test in your organization.

PEOPLE STRATEGY AND TALENT MANAGEMENT

When it comes to designing more inclusive talent management processes, there are a few useful sources we often turn to. Of course, we turn to Stephen's other books (*The Inclusion Imperative* (Kogan Page, 2014) and *Inclusive Talent Management* (Kogan Page, 2016)) as they are a great source of information and techniques for being more inclusive in the way an organization hires, retains, promotes, and even dismisses employees. They use case studies ranging from the London 2012 Olympics to small charities and organizations in a variety of sectors. However, there are a multitude of other sources for specific tips and guidance on how to be more inclusive in your talent management.

One particularly useful book is *Work Rules!* by Google's former head of People Operations Laszlo Bock (Hachette UK, 2015). In this work, Bock describes a number of key factors he believes contributed to Google's success, and they effectively amount to inclusive people strategy practices. For example, Bock discusses how the culture of the organization was not just created by Google founders Sergey Brin and Larry Page, but by intentionally keeping Google's culture flexible and allowing it to change as the company changed. Emphasizing that everyone, not just those in power, has the right to critique or attempt to change culture is an inherently inclusive behaviour, and is one inclusive talent management strategy.

As another example, Bock also discusses the importance of transparency in decision making, both big and small. When a company is making a decision about a product launch, or when it is deciding whether or not to promote an employee, or any other decision situation, being completely transparent to everyone about the process that led to that decision is extremely important, Bock says. Without that transparency, he argues, you lose the trust of your employees. It's like a relationship of love; you have to be vulnerable and trusting with your employees for them to offer the same back. Transparency is a key tool we described as an inclusive management strategy in earlier chapters.

So while *Work Rules!* is not advertised specifically as a D&I people strategy book, it turns out that the interventions are essentially the same. It seems that an effective people strategy, then, is an inclusive one.

All of these resources have been extremely valuable to us in our work building inclusive organizations. While we outlined the ones we have found to be most effective and most relevant throughout this book, should you wish to delve deeper into the concepts we touch on, the resources above are a good supplement.

TAKEAWAYS

1 While technology isn't a cure-all, it can certainly support your D&I work. Consider using some of the apps we've suggested here to facilitate your organization's progress.

2 You are not alone in this work – make use of the forums, networks and platforms to communicate with other D&I practitioners around the globe. It can help you get support, be creative, and find new ideas.

3 Consider the underlying psychological processes of implicit bias for a deeper understanding and greater ability to explain concepts like bias, judgment, and objectivity.

4 Arm yourself with evidence and case studies about the business case for diversity so you can defend your strategy to potential detractors.

5 Have an array of options for interventions at your disposal when deciding what work can be done by familiarizing yourself with nudge theory and practice.

INDEX

NB: endnotes and 'takeaways' are indexed as such page numbers in *italic* indicate figures or tables